Measuring Service Performance

Measuring Service Performance

Practical Research for Better Quality

RALF LISCH

Routledge
Taylor & Francis Group

LONDON AND NEW YORK

First published in paperback 2024

First published 2014 by Gowar Publishing

Published 2016 by Routledge
4 Park Square, Milton Park, Abingdon, Oxon OX14 4RN

and by Routledge
605 Third Avenue, New York, NY 10158

Routledge is an imprint of the Taylor & Francis Group, an informa business

Gower Applied Business Research
Our programme provides leaders, practitioners, scholars and researchers with thought provoking, cutting edge books that combine conceptual insights, interdisciplinary rigour and practical relevance in key areas of business and management.

British Library Cataloguing in Publication Data
A catalogue record for this book is available from the British Library.

The Library of Congress has cataloged the printed edition as follows:
Lisch, Ralf.
  Measuring service performance : practical research for better quality / by Ralf Lisch.
    pages cm
  Includes bibliographical references and index.
  ISBN 978-1-4724-1191-4 (hardback) – ISBN 978-1-4724-1192-1 (ebook) – ISBN 978-1-4724-1193-8 (epub) 1. Service industries–Evaluation. 2. Quality control. 3. Performance technology. I. Title.

  HD9980.5.L57 2014
  658.4'013–dc23

                                                                        2013028767

ISBN: 978-1-4724-1191-4 (hbk)
ISBN: 978-1-03-283696-6 (pbk)
ISBN: 978-1-315-59441-5 (ebk)

DOI: 10.4324/9781315594415

Unless stated otherwise, all examples in this work are fictitious. Any similarity to any company or person living or dead is not intended and purely coincidental.

Contents

List of Figures

List of Tables

About the Author

Dr Ralf Lisch was born in 1951 in Bremen, Germany. He studied sociology with major focus on organizations and human resources as well as statistics and social research at universities in Germany and the USA. He completed his studies as Doctor of Philosophy.

After a decade in academic research and teaching at various universities, he joined Germany's leading consumer research organization where he was responsible for all comparative tests of the quality of services. Several of his research projects and related publications – like tests of panic safety of soccer stadiums, sponsorships for children, gambling, safety on board ferries and other services – were much acclaimed and gained high public attention.

Thereafter, he spent about two decades in leading management positions of the global logistics industry. He worked as senior director for sales and marketing as well as operational and administrative head office functions, established quality management and was managing director of several companies.

The author has dealt with services from multiple perspectives whereby his major focus was always on people – because in the service sector more than in other industries, people determine the business and decide on success and failure. It is the combination of the different views of the service sector that forms the backdrop to this book.

For the past 20 years, Ralf Lisch has been living in various countries in Asia. He is a permanent resident of Singapore where he works as a freelance writer and consultant.

Ralf Lisch has published numerous books and articles on scientific as well as popular topics. His most recent book was an analysis of Niccolò Machiavelli's *The Prince* from the management perspective under the title: *Ancient Wisdom for Modern Management – Machiavelli at 500*, which is also published by Gower Publishing.

Foreword: Service Performance and the Quality of Life

ANSGAR WEYMANN[1]

The importance of the service sector is immense, comprising maintenance and repair of housing facilities, cars and other durable consumer goods, Internet and telephone support, information, communication and the media, energy and water supply, legal advice and finance, trade, logistics, transport, tourism, hotels and restaurants, research and education, public health, medical treatment and psychotherapy, safety, security, insurance and welfare. The structure of the service economy is mixed – private, public as well as public–private partnership. The job markets range from poorly paid retail jobs to well-paid professionals, physicians, lawyers, scientists and engineers, to exorbitantly paid staff in investment banking.

The Rise of the Service Economy

Throughout history, agriculture and hunting, craft and local trade made up the subsistence economy of humankind. The productivity was hardly sufficient to survive. Then, in eighteenth-century England, the industrial age emerged and started accelerating its triumphal march through western Europe and all over the globe. However, after several decades of deindustrialization, the leading nations of the west, UK, France and the US, transformed into service societies. The once dominating industrial sector decreased and today contributes (on average) less than 25 per cent to the gross domestic product (GDP). Germany's stable industrial sector (29 per cent) is one of the exceptions in the western world. In contrast, the service sector contributes (on average) more than 70 per cent to the GDP. At the same time, newly ascending nations catch up in the race for economic leadership and global primacy. Within the last quarter of the twentieth century, in particular China and other Asian countries entered into the small group of leading nations in the global economy, whereas the G7 nations' joint GDP dropped from a two-thirds share of the world economy to only 50 per cent, falling further.

The catchwords for this transition from industrial to post-industrial society are 'service society' and 'knowledge society'. It is being debated whether the rise of the service sector is a blessing that gives hope of a better life to global humankind, or whether the service economy rather generates new problems in terms of prosperity, inequality and equity. However, the economic transition from the industrial to the expanding service sectors is unbroken. Because of that, it is an important question how to measure the contribution of service performance to the quality of a good life.

1   Ansgar Weymann is Professor Emeritus of sociology at the University of Bremen, Germany, at Bremen International Graduate School of Social Sciences and at the Special Research Centre Transition of the State. His fields of applied research focus on education, work and the labour market and on life course risks and transitions from birth to aging.

Gross Domestic Product, Organisation for Economic Co-operation and Development National Accounts, and the Quality of Life

The GDP is the standard measure for economic prosperity, and prosperity is seen as the fundament for a good quality of life. The GDP is defined as the total value of goods and services produced within a nation in one year. It is the prime measure of economic growth and distribution in total and per capita and therefore applied in international comparisons of prosperity among nations, cross-sectional as well as longitudinal. In the year 2011, the GDP ranking of the top ten nations was: United States, China, Japan, Germany, France, United Kingdom, Italy, Brazil, India and Canada.

However, the GDP just throws a spotlight on the quality and supply of goods and services. For this reason, the Organisation for Economic Co-operation and Development (OECD) provides enlarged and improved national accounts of the economy and living conditions. The indicators reflect the multifold prosperity inherent in the national accounts beyond the mere size of the GDP: production, consumption and expenditure, national and individual income, disposable income, structure and growth of capital and human capital in total and per capita, financial assets and liabilities, non-financial assets by households, net capital stock, household savings rate, net lending and borrowing, investment, exports and imports of goods and services, added value, total government expenditure and consumption, compensation of employees, expenditure by other functions, taxes, social contributions, social benefits, and so on (OECD 2013).

Compared to the GNP, the OECD national accounts include a wide range of goods, private and public services as well as multiple government functions. The accounts tell a lot about the quality and performance of private and public services over time and from an international comparative perspective. This can be further refined through Quality of Life Research, a worldwide network of research. Quality of Life Research investigates long-term social, economic and cultural trends in an international comparison based on continuous reporting and monitoring by means of numerous indicators for living conditions like: income and assets, housing, health, life expectancy, education, family and partnerships, demography, support networks, inequality, equity, participation, inclusion and exclusion, convergence and divergence, cultural change, integration and assimilation, transfer and redistribution, social and economic policies, personal attitudes and public opinion about happiness. Quality of Life Research strives to understand the living condition and happiness in welfare states and modern societies on a global scale (Weymann 2013).

As a consequence of the growth of the service economy, the contribution of services to the quality of life became increasingly important. Professional measurements of service performance turned into an indispensable tool of screening and evaluating service quality in order to inform customers, providers, the media and politics. Let's take a look at two prominent fields of applied practical research for a better quality of life in public–private service economies: studies on senior friendliness and education.

Aging and States' Senior Friendliness

In an aging world society, senior friendliness is an interesting case for studying quality and performance of private and public services. In an extraordinary and unconventional book, Charles Lockhart and Jean Giles-Sims (2010; Weymann 2012) analyze and evaluate statistical data on the conditions of aging across the US states and provide sophisticated rankings of what they call states' senior friendliness (SSF). The foremost intention of the research is to serve as a life guide on how to handle aging properly. The study encourages seniors to move from state to state to meet their changing needs as they grow older. 'For individuals, the information in this book illustrates the needs and the availability of opportunities and services as well as provides guidance for choosing where to live at various stages of aging. For relevant professionals and policy makers, the study shows the relative strengths of some states that may offer models for emulation.' (Lockhart and Giles-Sims 2010: 4) It is a captivating analysis of an increasingly important service sector that is relevant for the public – seniors and their children on one hand and service providers, professionals and politicians on the other.

There are five dimensions of SSF. The first dimension is 'Finding Fun and Companionship in a Warm Climate', measured by climate, companionship, active seniors and recreational facilities, net migration of younger and of older seniors, and senior suicide rate. The other four dimensions and their key indicators are: 'Making Meaningful Contributions and Finding Supportive Communities' with the indicators of social capital, voting, income inequality, percentage living above the federal poverty level, political culture and ideology, and electoral competition; 'Finding Affordability and Safety' with the indicators of non-metropolitan population, mortgage payment, medical assistance, household income, cost of living and safety; 'Sustaining Health and Obtaining High-quality Medical Care' with the indicators of support of healthy aging and Medicare quality, care near the end of life, population healthiness and physician availability; 'Finding Accessible and High-quality Long-term Care' with the indicators of long-term care venues and costs, number and quality of nursing facility beds, state Medicaid and home- and community-based service waiver expenditures, and quality-of-life outcomes. Figures present the rankings of all states on each dimension.

Seniors will have to choose different states to meet different priorities of their aging agenda. For example, a healthy young couple of retirees would look for the best recreational facilities, whereas an older couple with multiple maladies would look for optimal (long-term) medical care. In the process of aging, senior couples would have to move from state to state. Seniors have particular priorities in achieving a good life after retirement. They are aware of their priorities and consequently look for information on the opportunity structure of states. The two steps of rational decision-making are: first, getting good information about the senior friendliness of a state, and second, matching individual priorities against the quality and availability of opportunities in order to optimize the marginal utility of moving. The study aims to supply the necessary information and reduce the cost of information procurement. It is a good example of practical research for better quality of service and life.

Education as a Cure-all Service

It took half a millennium before literacy became a standard competence of the population. At the end of the fifteenth century, the European population was illiterate with the exception of the aristocracy, clergy and the small group of urban upper class males. Around 1800, still less than 50 per cent of the male population of the most progressive European countries was literate. It was only in the nineteenth century when a rapid acceleration of mandatory schooling and the breakthrough of universal literacy took place. In 1900, elementary school attendance exceeded 90 per cent in the advanced European countries, whereas Italy reached only 57 per cent, Russia only 29 per cent elementary school attendance, and the majority of the population of Spain and Portugal was unable to read. Even half a century later, in 1950, the illiteracy rates of Mediterranean countries were still high: Portugal at 44 per cent, Yugoslavia at 27 per cent, Greece at 26 per cent, Bulgaria at 24 per cent, Romania at 23 per cent, Spain at 18 per cent and Italy at 14 per cent (Weymann 2014). Finally, in the twentieth century, particularly in the second half of that century, mandatory schooling became the standard of life course conduct, exercising a strong impact on life opportunities and influencing the rationale of life decision-making for the young population all over the world. The years of life spent in education expanded rapidly and permanently. Kindergartens and preschools were widely introduced, attending secondary schools became the norm, and higher education attendance expanded rapidly. Whereas in 1900, only about 1 per cent of the 20 to 24-years-old population was enrolled in higher education, in 1995 their share was on average about 42 per cent.

In the course of modern history, education turned into a cure-all service, organized publicly, privately or in public–private partnerships. At the beginning of the twenty-first century, literacy is globally regarded as a birthright, while illiteracy is seen as a personal shame and national disgrace. Worldwide, education serves to achieve a good national and individual future and as a panacea against the multifaceted ills of modern society. Education is expected to improve the smooth exchange of goods and services and to facilitate the mobility of the work force in expanding markets. Education is seen as the key resource of nations to successfully compete for wealth and power in the context of growing global markets. In addition, education is perceived as the foundation of national achievements in science and technology. Furthermore, improving education is supposed to be an adequate policy to create better democratic participation. And last but not least, education legitimizes the unequal distribution of status among citizens by means of acquisition of standardized and publicly acknowledged credentials that govern life chances via allocation in the labour and marriage markets. In case of individual and mass unemployment, retraining and adult education are expected to provide new and more advanced skills, or at least to appease social unrest through inclusion in educational programmes. Lifelong learning or continuing education is expected to provide a stable equilibrium between the supply and demand of skills and the wider human capital of the workforce in the labour market. More generally, education is considered as a means to integrate society, as a key tool to improve economic growth, and as a social right.

Values of economic efficiency and the ideas of business management are applied to education institutions throughout the twentieth century (Donoghue 2008: 2). A good example for this development is higher education. Entrepreneurs join university boards of trustees. The entrepreneurial interest in higher education goes beyond generating profitability and includes educational governance, demanding a general accountability of higher education. The system provides a public or private service of delivering comprehensive and uniform credentials with the intention of thoroughly signalling to employers the grade of employability or non-employability of an individual higher education graduate. Current dynamics in the field of education are characterized by mixed private and public funding, the increased utilization of market mechanisms, a fierce and permanent competition of individuals, institutions and nations for comparative advantage, the promotion of screening, accounting and evaluation and the expansion of cross-border and for-profit education.

A prominent example for continuous worldwide comparative measurements of educational performance are academic rankings of world universities like the top world university rankings conducted by Shanghai Jiao Tong University and the *Times Higher Education* World University Rankings as well as rankings of the individual researcher like Google Scholars or the Hirsch-Index.

Measuring Service Performance and the Utilization of Information

Measuring service performance can improve the quality of life in the service society. But how is better knowledge applied? Often, better information is utilized and dispersed via the media by naming and labelling service problems in public (Wingens and Weymann 1988). Common examples are food scandals, deficiencies in medical treatment and pharmacology, the quality of nurseries and elderly care, IT support, transport bottlenecks and safety, shortcomings in tourism, hotels and restaurants, the performance of several sectors of the civil service, and the quality of schools and higher education.

Many private and public services are continuously evaluated. However, this does not necessarily mean that better information is actually applied to improve the standards of services because of high transformation and transaction costs of service improvement. Most crucial for the utilization of better knowledge is the public discourse preceding, paralleling and following decision-making in two respects. Firstly, it sets standards according to which the outcomes of services can be criticized. Secondly, it sets standards for the justification of further developments. The dissemination of findings helps the researcher to unfold their innovative knowledge which, often indirectly, exerts its influence on the decision-making processes in the service markets. Primarily, service measurement leaves marks on improved service performance if and as long as it plays an important role in public awareness.

Generally, service performance measurements provide criteria how to evaluate the abundance of services in terms of practical relevance for the consumers' quality of life. However, most media reports and public discussions deal with the scientific quality of service measurement in a rather non-professional way – which applies similarly to practical research in business. The producers of professional knowledge about service quality are not always mentioned explicitly in media discourses. Furthermore, participants in media discourses have their own favourite sources of scientific information to which they refer in discussions, and these sources, as a rule, are in line with the speakers' interest. Notably, pure research data is not the type of knowledge that prevails. There is no preference for brute facts in the public. On the contrary, scientific information is used as some kind of common sense, and in so doing, mass media strip off what makes the information scientific. Sciences are rather seen as a department store providing findings and arguments needed by the service providers, customers, consumer activists and media agents. Finally, the conclusions drawn from findings are often normative and prescriptive.

To sum up, the utilization of service measurement in the public sphere is a continual process in which scientific knowledge provides evidence for the conflicting views on service weaknesses or strengths that meet the service providers', the customers' and the media actors' specific interests, norms and wishes. Much like jurisprudence and the judicial system, science becomes a procedural technique for labelling dissent and processing conflict resolution whenever combatants' interests conflict with one another. Seen from this perspective, improvement and public dissemination of service performance data is part of the ongoing construction and reconstruction of social thought about what makes up a world of good services providing a good quality of life.

Measuring Service Performance is an extraordinary, useful, sophisticated and unconventional book on service quality and quality measurements, a very valuable contribution to achieve better practical research on service quality as well as to inform the recipients about the quality of findings available from service research.

1 *Introduction*

Much has been said about quality. Many authors have tried their hand at an understanding and definition of the nature of quality. Consultants never tire of promising guidance on the road to quality and books offer magic formulas on how to turn a lacklustre performance into quality service. Everybody has some ideas of what makes quality. Nevertheless, almost every day we experience disappointment when despite all promises the provided service quality does not meet our expectations. Even worse, quite often we cannot avoid the impression that the general service level is declining.

No doubt, the demand for quality studies is great. Bosses want to know how competitive the service is that their company provides. Customers look for quality information before they make a decision for one or the other service provider. Consumer organizations claim to safeguard the interests of customers and want to provide related advice. Journalists look for a good story and may jump on some service failure. They have all very different approaches to service quality. Bosses will refer to customers with whom they have talked. Consumers may have talked to their friends who have heard which service provider is good and which one is bad. Consumer organizations claim to know what consumers want and rate service performance like judges. And journalists pick up some service failure, dramatize it and do not hesitate to pillory a whole industry. They will all claim that they have collected sufficient information to make serious statements about service performance and how to improve quality. But sound research looks different.

To avoid possible misunderstandings right from the start, this book abstains from offering any panacea as a quick fix for all service shortcomings. Instead, it goes back to the original meaning of quality. Quality has its roots in Latin '*qualitas*', which again derives from '*qualis*' meaning 'of what kind'. Exactly that is the essential question: of what kind is a specific service performance? Does it meet expectations? Is it just so-so or does it have the certain something that turns an average performance into great service? Quality is the crucial question that determines customer satisfaction and decides on success or failure of service providers. Quality is a management task and a matter of attitude. At the same time, it requires a permanent follow-up by means of *Measuring Service Performance – Practical Research for Better Quality*.

Applied quality research and testing is a path to sustainable improvement and better service performance. This is not only required by quality management standards like ISO 9001 demanding 'measurement, analysis and improvement' but it is a naturally required feedback along the process of service performance. Of course, empirical research is not the only way to get such feedback. There may be gifted managers who have the gut feelings that provide the necessary feedback as well. But being dependent on gut feelings would not only be a rather unsystematic approach, it would also be risky because it lacks reliability and in many cases also validity – criteria that are essential elements of the methodology of empirical research. It makes sense to challenge what the boss presents as his ultimate knowledge about service quality and undertake systematic empirical research.

As a matter of fact, the world of the service provider and the world of the customer look rather different. Here, empirical research has an essential function as understandable and reproducible intercultural approach to a reconstruction of service reality.

Of course, quality research can fulfil this important function only when the research approach itself meets essential quality criteria. But exactly these are often – too often – not met. The reasons are manifold. Companies may approach such studies without a thorough understanding of the methodology of empirical research. Perhaps they approach social phenomena with a technical understanding of measurement or they miss the very point that questions in daily conversation are different from questions in a research interview. It may be a rather formal attempt to meet the requirements of the ISO standard without asking what measurement actually means. Or the research and development (R&D) budget is so tight that it does not allow for more than some trivial inquiry. And sometimes, service-related quality research serves more the purpose of an alibi than an epistemological approach to a better understanding of the market position and potentials for future developments. Epistemology from Greek 'episteme' and 'epistasthai' means to know how to gain knowledge. That is exactly what is needed – an understanding of how to arrive at a better knowledge of service quality.

Creative and methodologically sound empirical research is an essential basis for decision-making and an eye-opener for innovative potential. No doubt, practical research has to compromise sometimes – on budget restrictions or on feasibility. The real world is often not as ideal as described in the textbooks. Nevertheless, this is not an obstacle that prevents meaningful research. There is still enough room for creativity and a huge epistemological potential that just has to be exploited – in the interest of customer satisfaction and for the better of the service provider.

This book will assist practitioners in or related to the service industry to develop a more appropriate methodological understanding in the interest of meaningful quality research. It is about quality as success factor and intended as a critical contribution to a more creative and relevant analysis of the quality of services. The ultimate target is to develop the necessary knowledge that is required to improve service quality and stand out from the crowd – improving the market position as a result of better quality and higher customer satisfaction.

The target group of this book comprises quality managers and market researchers, MBA students and consumer organizations as well as journalists who deal with related studies. At the same time, it provides top managers in the service industry with a better understanding of what quality research can achieve. Furthermore, it offers a critical view of quality studies that time and again come along with the claim to the ultimate truth about service quality.

The text draws substantially on the author's experience from three sectors. Firstly is theoretical and practical experience from many years of academic research in methods and methodology of empirical research and statistics that resulted in several books and other publications. Secondly, are many years as head of department for the comparative testing of services at Stiftung Warentest (www.test.de), which is Germany's best-known consumer organization. During this time, a wide variety of service topics were analyzed in conjunction with the further development of the methodology and methods of comparative testing of service quality. The results of the research work were published in the consumer magazine *test*. Apart from the great public interest that these publications roused, several projects triggered significant changes to specific service segments.

Soccer stadiums were modified after a study about panic safety found substantial shortcomings. Charitable organizations changed their concept after a test of sponsorships for children raised serious doubts about this type of aid to developing countries. The quality of the after-sales service of household items improved substantially after a first test had shown disappointing results. Tests of the quality of advice in pharmacies triggered comprehensive discussions and resulted in changes to the service processes in pharmacies. Market shares changed after an analysis of games of chance. These are only some examples that show how powerful quality research can be. Last but not least, long-term practical management experience in the global service industry has contributed to this book. All three factors together provide the backdrop for the following discourse on practical quality research.

Writing a book about practical research is to some extent a balancing act. The academic world may miss some elaborated details and latest scientific knowledge while those who deal with practical research in the midst of all kind of constraints may deem some topics too demanding. After all, they have to deliver results that are comprehensible and relevant, find acceptance among their recipients and contribute to decision-making.

This book is written for practitioners. Intentionally, it abstains to a large extent from providing mathematical and statistical formulas. While formulas provide a precise, logical and highly efficient language for the description of facts and relations, they also have the potential to frighten readers who do not feel comfortable in the world of mathematics. Furthermore, computers make it largely unnecessary to deal with detailed formulas as long as the meaning and the crucial issues behind statistical models are understood. And this can also be imparted by means of common language.

To avoid misunderstandings and expectations that eventually cannot be met, it shall be highlighted that it is not the idea of this book to provide a handbook of empirical research and statistics. Above all, this book looks at practical research from a methodological perspective. It is about the meaning behind the actual research and the essential distinction between research results as facts and artefacts. This book understands research as a complex decision-making process that targets the reconstruction of social reality. The ultimately decisive factor is the practical relevance of the research results for entrepreneurial action on one hand and consumer behaviour on the other.

Measuring service performance is a complex topic with highly interdependent elements. In the interest of comprehensibility and readability, the structure of the book is to a large extent a reflection of the research process. But before we enter into the methodology and methods of quality research, the next chapter will first provide an introduction into the characteristics of service and the significance of the so-called tertiary sector – which is in developed economies actually the primary sector in terms of employment and GDP. We describe services as people business and look at service performance as a communication process. From there, we develop a distinctive approach to practical research and discuss the various perspectives of quality studies.

The following discussion of research methods will start where every research starts – with some thoughts about the research question and the research design. This makes it necessary to look at the various stakeholders in quality research and the impact of their specific perspective on the research design. Ultimately, it is about the essential question of what reality is. From there it is only a small step to the practical research process and how to manage it. This requires some thoughts on research economy and cost management and also a word on how to integrate research into the organization.

A major part of this book is dedicated to methodological questions. What may appear rather theoretical at the first glance is actually full of practical relevance. It describes research as a process and discusses what it means to 'measure'. Some common misunderstandings of empirical research as well as basic research requirements will be analyzed before common practical problems like reactivity, the non-response bias, missing data, outliers and their effects on research results are discussed. Furthermore, we deal with the concepts of operationalization, indicators and indexes before we move on to famous scales, rankings, trend analyses and intercultural comparisons as special approaches. Eventually, we are pretty well prepared to steer clear of some treacherous shoals of empirical research.

Of course, almost all research questions deal with a statistical population that is too large to include all its elements in the analysis. That's why we work with samples and try to generalize the results. This demands a discussion of representativeness, which is one of the most often misunderstood concepts in research. And just because representativeness has become something like the accolade of empirical studies, we remind of the benefits of case studies as an alternative to representative studies. We discuss also the question of how a sample can be drawn and how many cases are actually required in order to arrive at representative and valid research results.

After these methodological considerations, empirical research means data collection. And this comprises much more than the usual survey by means of interviews. We discuss a variety of empirical research methods – those that can be considered classical methods of social sciences as well as some that have been developed specifically for quality research. The crucial point is the understanding that every method constitutes a partly different reality, which makes the decision for an adequate method of empirical research so important.

Once data collection is completed, the researcher will sit before a bundle of interviews, protocols or other records and scratch his head. After all, it was not the intention to add to the complexity of the business situation and to multiply information but to reduce it to its essence. Research is about reducing information under consideration of relevance. We look at basic concepts of data analysis and some statistical models.

Highlighting the issue of relevance of research results, the question arises of how to transfer the findings of a quality study either to the management of a service provider or to consumers. After all, research results without related social action would be rather irrelevant. So the researcher has to consider how to present his research results. How to impart the findings best? How much statistics can the recipients take? And what reaction can one reasonably expect? Depending on the recipients of research results, we deal with different aspects of utilization. In any case, it is about changes to social behaviour.

As a conclusion, the last chapter is an appeal for quality research that meets quality criteria itself. It is a committed call for a reconsideration of quality research that is driven by a widespread but nevertheless inappropriate mechanistic understanding of the research process that focuses on methods instead of contents. It is an outlook on how to realize the knowledge of the book and add meaning to practical research work.

Throughout the book we'll work with a number of examples for illustrative purposes. They are not specific for a certain sector of the service industry but can easily be generalized and transferred to other sectors. At the same time, the book abstains from providing an 'ideal' or 'perfect' project. There is none. And reading the following chapters, it will quickly become clear why there cannot be any ultimate project. However, the following pages pave the way to a better understanding of quality research that will ultimately lead to better quality.

Critical readers may raise their eyebrows when they find that most of the examples in this book make use of the male gender – he instead of she. For the sake of political correctness, I would like to state that this is neither intended as an act of discrimination nor does it refer to any supposed gender roles. Instead, it is solely a contribution to better readability. It is at the discretion of the distinguished reader to replace he by she and vice versa.

Before we move on, I would like to express my sincere thanks to everybody who contributed one way or the other to this book. While not everybody can be named, I would like to emphasize at least a few names. A lot of my critical methodological understanding of empirical social research is owed to Jürgen Kriz[1] while I made once my first attempts to practical research under the guidance of Ansgar Weymann who has also kindly written the Foreword to this book. Over many years we have had numerous discussions and worked together in several empirical projects sharing especially the understanding that there is no contradiction between the requirements of practical research on one hand and a methodologically sound research design on the other.

Furthermore, I would like to mention Georg Sieber[2] with whom I cooperated in a number of projects and who was successful in finding in any research question the psychological component, which often added a captivating perspective to otherwise rather ordinary topics. These projects were the best proof that empirical social research is much more than sometimes rather boring surveys.

Here, also an encyclopedia on research methods and statistics shall be mentioned that I once published together with Jürgen Kriz (Kriz and Lisch 1988). Even 25 years after that book was written, it turned out to be surprisingly up to date and was of great help when preparing this manuscript. The fundamental chapters at the beginning of the encyclopedia, which were written by Jürgen, were especially of great help when writing some parts of this book. Furthermore, Jürgen had a critical look at several chapters of the manuscript despite his busy schedule. For all his support, I would like to express my sincere thanks.

I would also like to thank Martin West, Donna Shanks, Emily Pace, Kristina Abbotts, Christine Muddiman, Charlotte Parkins and the whole Gower team for their support and great cooperation that I enjoyed while working on this project.

Last but not least, I thank my wife, Ting Suk Yuan, for her great support and patience. She is always a curious and critical reader. Her remarks, questions, ideas and recommendations have substantially contributed to this text and helped to improve its readability. I am very grateful for her support.

---

1   Jürgen Kriz is Emeritus Professor of Psychotherapy and Clinical Psychology at the University of Osnabrück, Germany. Partly overlapping with his clinical chair, he held also chairs in research methods, statistics and philosophy of science at several universities and is still working as senior advisor for research methods in international university projects.

2   Georg M. Sieber is the founder of a psychological think tank under the name Intelligenz System Transfer, Munich, Germany.

CHAPTER 2
Services and Challenges

With all due respect to Mr Ford, his judgement was a bit too optimistic when he allegedly claimed that 'a business absolutely devoted to service will have only one worry about profits. They will be embarrassingly large.'[1] Also, Mr Shakespeare probably vastly exaggerated in his *Comedy of Errors* when he let Dromio of Ephesus wail about his fate as service provider: 'I am an ass indeed; you may prove it by my long ears. I have served him from the hour of my nativity to this instant, and have nothing at his hands for my service but blows. When I am cold he heats me with beating; when I am warm he cools me with beating' (Act IV, Scene 4). Well, being at others' service can be tough. Nevertheless, it is a matter of fact that no company will prosper long term without rendering good service. Providing great service is an art that requires an empathetic understanding of social behaviour as well as a permanent drive for improvement on one hand and deserves recognition and appreciation on the other.

Service quality is an essential element of business success. That applies to genuine service companies as well as to manufacturers. At the same time, complaints about poor service are nothing unusual and in some service sectors one cannot avoid the impression that companies try to substitute service quality for lower prices. Germans use the term *'Dienstleistungswüste'* [service desert], which describes an insufficient dedication to services and related customer requirements. Improved service quality is needed in order to stand out from the crowd of service providers and, in many cases, customers are even willing to pay for better service. Better service quality can pay off.

Service has many facets. Everybody has some experience with services – when going to the hairdresser, into a restaurant, to the doctor, to church, renting a car, moving house, going for vacation, you name it. We live in a service society. We provide services by doing work for someone, assisting or advising them. There are medical services, financial services, public services, transportation services, security services and many others. Serving food or drinks is a service and deserves a service charge. For your air conditioning or pest control at home you have a service contract. We expect service before and after buying a product and expect that it will last for years and provide good service. That is what you hope for when you put your car in for a service at a service station. So even after many years your car will still be serviceable. And when it breaks down eventually, although you got a service guarantee from your service assistant, it will be out of service and the end of the service life may have been reached.

---

1   Henry Ford (1863–1947), founder of the Ford Motor Company and the Henry Ford Company, which later became the Cadillac Automobile Company. Ford was a strong supporter of the development of the assembly line that made mass production possible.

An update to faulty or insecure software is nicely described as a service pack. Spacecrafts carry a service module with supplies. An apartment that provides not only space for living but comes along with domestic services is called a serviced apartment. For this extra service you may have to pay a service charge and goods and services tax on top – because when it comes to taxes, the supposed differences between goods and services that every textbook emphasizes are overcome.

Working for a company is deemed service and, showing enough staying power, you can expect a long service award. Putting yourself on the line for the security of your country is called national service, and the servicemen and servicewomen wear a service dress and a service cap and one day they may be honoured with a service star.

Services are a vast field where everybody can join in discussions. Every day we experience service and develop expectations and a latent idea of what is good service. The likelihood is high that someone has personal experience with a job in the service industry – thus knowing service also from the inside. Without arguing about the personal relevance that such knowledge has when it comes to the judgement of service performance and the decision pro or contra a specific service provider, the selective individual experience has limited relevance for other consumers who perhaps have different expectations. Service providers will also look at their customers as a much bigger group even if they claim that they provide individual service. So we have to look for a more appropriate understanding of service quality. This will require a methodological discourse and a deeper look into research methods that allow insight into relevant aspects of service quality as a basis for future decisions that target outstanding service performance. Indeed, it is worthwhile to go for it.

No doubt, service – and excellent service in particular – creates a vast potential for business development and improvement. But this raises some essential questions. What do customers actually expect? What is it that turns an ordinary performance into great service? How can it be determined if a service is just middling or good and perhaps even excellent? How can something as subjective and complex as service be measured? These are some of the questions this book will deal with.

As a starting point, this chapter will contemplate further on the nature of services and how this is related to customer expectations, customer satisfaction and ultimately service quality. Services are an increasingly important sector of the economy not only in terms of value added but also with regard to employment, which explains why service quality is not only nice to have but essential for every business. Depending on the stakeholders in the process of service performance, the perspective can be quite different, which has some impact on the approach to service quality. However, regardless from which position we look at services, service is a people business. People make the difference and that will explain why quality research in the field of services is actually applied sociology and psychology. We discuss what this means for the research approach. Furthermore, we deal with various perspectives of services and the related demand for information about quality. Some of these thoughts may appear a little theoretical. But they are necessary for a better understanding of how to approach service quality. After all, the world of services is more complex than some supposed panaceas want to make us believe. But this makes it even more interesting.

2.1 The Nature of Services

It is a word full of humbleness and devotion that describes the most important sector of the world's leading economies: service. Service goes back to the old Latin word '*servitium*', which means slavery. It was '*servus*' – the slave – who provided service. Similarly, old French '*servir*' had the meaning of serving at the table and in old English, service denoted religious devotion as well as the liturgy – service as religious devotion to serving people like slaves. The etymology of service describes pretty well how many people in the service industry may sometimes feel.

Of course, one can look at services also from a different and probably more appropriate angle – service as the unique chance to provide something that is non-material and volatile but nevertheless worth paying for because it makes you feel good. It is a difficult task that requires distinctive expertise, elaborate skills, experience, sensitivity and empathy. Everybody can put a plate with food on the table and may even learn to keep the thumb out of the soup but to make a dinner a delightful experience is the very art of service. Or look at container transport services. Every fly-by-night can do it but if the bill of lading is correct the first time, the box is delivered in time and in good condition, the transport can be tracked via the web and any irregularities are advised, the invoice is created in time and correct, and when you have a question you find a competent partner, then a simple transport can turn into a great service experience. It is people who make the difference – regardless if the service is related to people or to goods.

Economic statistics distinguish between services and products. Interestingly, it is difficult to find a meaningful self-sustained definition of services. Common definitions of services call in products and point at the differences between these two terms. So services are preferably defined in contrast to products. After all, everybody is familiar with products and the idea of an intangible product provides at least a vague idea of services that is good enough to develop a reasonable understanding of this important economic sector. A pragmatic approach to service quality does not require any desperate attempt to squeeze all specific characteristics into an academically acceptable definition that would ultimately be of little practical use. Nevertheless, it is worthwhile highlighting a few characteristics of services that will contribute to a better understanding of the following chapters.

No doubt, the most obvious characteristic of services is their intangibility. One cannot touch them but nevertheless they can be experienced. This service experience is usually very individual and – depending on the actually contracted service – determined by a number of variables like friendliness, timeliness, accessibility, readiness, degree of service fulfilment, price and others.

The intangibility of services makes them at the same time highly perishable. Services cannot be stored. And they cannot be exchanged or returned in case of dissatisfaction. Once they have been rendered they have been irreversibly consumed. Nevertheless, no ownership has been transferred. Services are volatile although their results and effects can be obvious and lasting.

Most services are performed in close interaction between service provider and service consumer. People-related services can only be performed if the consumer is present, which makes service provider and service consumer inseparable. Accordingly, for goods-related services, the goods must be present. In any case, the inseparability of service provider and service consumer is essential because services are rendered and consumed simultaneously.

These factors make services unique. At the same time, they make it difficult to standardize and reproduce a specific service performance. People change, mood changes, the environment changes, expectations change and what is good today may be criticized tomorrow – because experience impacts on expectations and expectations impact on perception.

Interestingly, the contrast to products that is preferably called in to define services is actually rather obsolete. There is no clear-cut line between products and services. Instead, there is a continuum from services to goods. As much as most goods have some kind of service aspect, services are more or less related to goods. While the service in a restaurant cannot be separated from the physical element of food, goods also have an inherent element of service, which becomes most obvious in conjunction with pre- and after-sales service.

In an environment where competing products of different brands become increasingly interchangeable and come often even from the same production line, differing in hardly anything but minor design elements and the label, the service promise that comes along with the product can make or break the deal. You cannot enter into a market with a new car brand that does not come along with a close service network. A cheap no-name washing machine may be good but will turn into a shelf-warmer as long as it is questionable if there will be someone who provides service in case of a breakdown. And what applies to after-sales service is also valid for pre-sales service whenever manufacturers run sales outlets under their own brand name. A positive purchasing experience can make a distinction. Luxury labels in particular have internalized this understanding as part of their brand philosophy by developing shopping into a lifestyle event.

The availability and quality of related services are important characteristics of a product. This may be just a pleasant experience when it comes to goods of basic demand. But it is essential in conjunction with more complex products or products that have a strong emotional or lifestyle dimension. In any case, it is value added that influences purchase decisions.

Services that are linked to goods are only one section of a much larger market segment that comprises also the classical services, which are related to people and usually provided by service companies or service people. It can be the business trainer who tries to prepare managers for the challenges of the world of management, the nurse providing hope for a speedy recovery or the financial consultant selling the promise of growing wealth, status and preparedness for the future. Furthermore, there are services that are contracted by people but performed on goods like the transportation of a container, gardening or a funeral that nevertheless will be assessed by people. Indeed, service is a generic term for a motley collection of a multitude of rather different performances, which makes an unambiguous classification almost impossible.

Instead of continuing our philosophical excursion into the nature of services, it is sufficient to work with this rather pragmatic understanding that has been developed so far. The much more decisive factor is its pertinence and quality. It is the unique nature of services that puts its quality above all. Providing high service quality is a never-ending task that requires dedication to quality and ongoing improvement as well as adaptation to changing expectations and requirements.

In contrast to goods, the quality of services cannot easily be standardized. Every service is unique. It is performed by people either on or in close relation to people. Even if one would be able to define every step of a service performance and train each staff member how to behave and what to say, customers with their specific expectations and experience cannot be standardized and may spoil the supposed standard situation. Furthermore, a well-trained 'Welcome to this wonderful company! How can I help you?' can sound rather different depending on the actual mood and other non-verbal expressions of the staff. After a while it may even get on the customers' nerves because they get tired of hearing the same dictum being reeled off time and again.

In this context it is crucial that what the customer expects is actually delivered. Theoretically, we can distinguish between expectations that serve as prediction and heightened expectations that define an ideal situation. Expectations as prediction are the maximum-likelihood scenario that defines a service standard as reasonable and realistic under consideration of all available information. This is the major reference point when judging service quality. On the other hand, developing expectations of an *ideal* service performance goes in many cases beyond realistic expectations and turns easily into wishful thinking. However, defining expectations as normative standard has the advantage of a fixed point of reference that makes quality assessments easier compared to expectations as predictions. On the other hand, a pragmatic understanding of service expectations as prediction is more relevant with regard to actual social behaviour but comes along with the methodological inconvenience of relative and context-related quality.

As said, this is a rather theoretical distinction. Real life is different. Nobody will expect white tablecloths and fine china in a fast-food restaurant. Service performance will always be judged in relation to what one can reasonably expect in a specific context and even perfect service in a fast-food restaurant will be judged differently in comparison to perfect service in a gourmet temple. So both aspects – expectations as prediction as well as expectations as normative standard – are usually on the mind when assessing service quality. Related research that wants to be relevant in the sense of actual behaviour would have to follow this pragmatic understanding. And coming to quality assessments, one would have to specify how quality in relation to expectations is actually defined.

As a basic approach to service quality and customer satisfaction, we look at the extent of congruency between customer expectations and actual service experience. The customer expects a certain service performance and compares his expectations with what he actually experiences as service performance. This can be quite sobering. Where you hoped for a smile, a grumpy waiter bangs the plate on the table. What was expected as nicely arranged delicacies turns out to be an overcooked mash covered under a thick layer of indefinable gravy. No doubt, the chef treats food as an enemy and cooks it to death and the waiter is of the same breed. Disappointment is guaranteed. Only the bill goes far beyond your expectations. The situation is obvious. What you expected to be fine dining will be a future no-go area. The gap between expectations and actual experience was too big. The bigger the gap the lower the customer satisfaction and perceived quality.

Of course, it could also have been the other way round. You enter the fast-food restaurant because you are famished and just need something to eat. You are then welcomed with a charming smile. The supposedly dirty place is neat and clean. The staff is friendly and makes some recommendations. And when you leave the place, you are not only full but have forgotten about too much fat, salt, cholesterol and simply feel good.

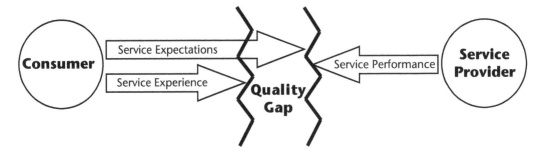

Figure 2.1   A (too) simple approach to service quality and customer satisfaction described as a gap between service expectations and perceived service experience

This time the experienced service performance was far beyond expectations. That is true customer satisfaction. One should remember that place. The service quality may make it worth another visit.

So far so good. But what looks rather simple and straightforward has various implications. First of all, it means that there is no absolute quality. Quality and customer satisfaction depend on individual service expectations and experience. This makes an important difference. It means that we do not talk about an absolute but a perceived quality, which can vary as much as the service performance. Obviously, a static model as shown in Figure 2.1 can only insufficiently explain the concept of customer satisfaction and service quality. In fact, the situation is much more complex.

For a more appropriate understanding of service performance and its perception, we transfer the classical concept of product utility[2] to services and distinguish between the basic or functional utility of a service and some added benefits. The basic utility is just a necessary but not at all sufficient condition of successful service that creates customer satisfaction. Going for a haircut and afterwards having shorter hair, the basic utility of a haircut cannot be disputed. But customers expect more. They look for a sense of well-being and a hairstyle that is stylish and fashionable. And it is here that it becomes difficult because the understanding of well-being and fashion varies. Hence, the hairdresser and the customer have to develop some common sense in order to meet mutual expectations. This will happen partly verbally – short enough or shall I cut a bit more? – and partly non-verbally when a relaxed smile approves the head massage and eventually the tip is generous.

This process of negotiating a common sense or joint understanding of the expected actual service performance is a process that is necessary to reduce the complexity of the service situation and to provide good service in the sense of customer expectations. It is a process that reduces the high number of options in a service situation. That makes it necessary to find out the expectations of the business partner and to develop expectations with regard to these expectations. Finding out what customers expect and developing expectations regarding their expectations is prerequisite for service fulfilment.

---

2   Wilhelm Vershofen (1868–1960) developed a utility scheme as a classification of the various utilities of consumer goods. See Vershofen 1940: 69–72.

Returning to the situation in the salon, the customer comes with certain expectations regarding the service performance and its result. The expectations may be latent because you just want to do something good to yourself or they can be manifest because you need a proper conservative haircut before you go for your job interview. Of course, the hairdresser also has some expectations. He will judge his customer and develop some presumptions of how to interpret his request for a haircut. Needless to say that the hairdresser's and the customer's expectations are not necessarily congruent. The definition of the service situation can be more or less precise and will leave ample room for interpretations. So both sides face a complex situation that can easily result in dissatisfaction. Something has to be done in order to reduce this complexity.

Here, like in any communication process, expectations of expectations come into play. The customer will make some assumptions about the expectations of the hairdresser. What information does he need in order to leave the salon with a haircut that does not have to be hidden under a cap? How will he interpret my request for a proper haircut? What can I expect and how will he deal with my expectations? What are his expectations of my expectations? Do I have to tell him that he must not cut too much? Accordingly, the hairstylist will develop expectations of the expectations of his customer. What does the customer expect when asking for a proper haircut? Such partly explicit and partly subconscious considerations determine the situation and help to reduce its complexity. One can even extend this reflexive process further because the assumed expectations of expectations will again be considered in one's own expectations. What will the other one assume regarding my expectations of his expectations? And so on.

Defining a service situation is a very normal multiple reflexive communication process. So what looks complicated at first glance is actually everyday and partly subconscious behaviour. The reflection of expectations reduces the complexity of a service situation. This is necessary and in the interest of the service provider as well as the customer because a clear and congruent definition of the service situation makes it possible to improve the service performance in accordance with customer expectations and thus creates customer satisfaction.

Of course, the expectations of both the customer and the service provider are not developed in a vacuum but related to a multitude of exogenous factors. Two of the most dominant factors are the competitive environment and the price. Every service performance takes place in a competitive environment that is an inherent element of service expectations and performance. It is the question of who is expected to meet these expectations best. This is of particular importance because it is the nature of many services that their intangibility makes it very simple to change the provider. Regardless who has shipped your container today, tomorrow you can book with another carrier. Airlines developed their bonus miles as a customer loyalty system and hotel chains, car rental agencies, credit card companies, restaurants and many others followed in a desperate attempt to make it more difficult for customers to change their service provider. Actually, these programmes link customer loyalty to – sometimes rather questionable – economic benefits instead of service quality. The problem is, however, that there is meanwhile such a multitude of point systems that customers get tired of them and recognize that these are in many cases rather additional costs than a loyalty discount. Administering your mileage and bonus points has become stressful. As a result, one may look for a lower price without gimmicks that have the sole purpose of discouraging the customer from choosing the service provider who is expected to meet their requirements best – provided somewhere out there is still a service provider relying on quality instead of a loyalty programme.

Information about competition provides the backdrop of service expectations and promises. This is information from the service providers themselves as well as from peers and the media. It can be information that hardly goes beyond an image or may be based on personal experience. Accordingly, the informational content can be rather different. It may just be based on hearsay and some general impression or it can be the result of comparative testing as provided by consumer organizations. In any case, it is an individual decision on how to judge the trustworthiness of the information and to what extent it will affect the choice of a service provider – who in turn has similar information and will react to it.

This information is put into relation to the price. Usually, service expectations are closely related to price. The higher the price the higher the expectations. Depending on the type of service, the price can be a crucial factor that largely overrules other information about a service offer. However, when it comes to the luxury segment, the price may rather be perceived as a quality criterion following the old marketing wisdom that what is not expensive cannot be good. Here, the prestige utility of services is brought into play. Look, I can afford it.

Some services are reduced to their basic utility and largely price-driven because their potential to differ from competition has fallen victim to austerity measures. Customer service functions are bundled in anonymous customer service centres that hardly deserve this name. Any attempt to find a competent partner has to overcome a long telephone menu – for English, please press '1' – just to be put on hold – sorry, all our customer service executives are busy, please hold the line – while being harassed with some nerve wracking commercials praising the outstanding service of this company. That is the very moment when you cannot avoid the impression that the Latin roots of service have been misunderstood and the customer has become the slave of the service provider.

The outlined model of service perception, customer satisfaction, service quality and price becomes even more complex because it changes in the course of time – as a result of experience as well as many other factors that may not even be directly related to the actual service situation. One may have been promoted to managing director and with the increased income the expectations also grow. Or one has read a book about body language and expects service staff to behave accordingly. Suddenly, you will not let them get away with their sluggishness. Indeed, there are many factors that impact on the assessment of service quality.

Of course, past experience also influences the perception of service. Expectations grow fast. What may be an overfulfilment of service expectations today will be the expected standard tomorrow. And if the perceived service falls short of expectations it may be tolerated once – but only once. After all, everybody can have a bad day. But it should not happen a second time. Everything will be carefully observed. Perhaps it is time to change to the competition.

Figure 2.2 describes customer satisfaction as an indicator of service quality and result of a dynamic multiple reflexive process that takes place between service provider and customer in an environment that is determined by a multitude of endogenous and exogenous factors whereby the actual effect of the various factors depends largely on the specific service situation. Actually, the figure very much resembles a typical communication model. This is no coincidence. Service means social interaction and the expectations that define the expectations and the perception and assessment are the result of a communication process.

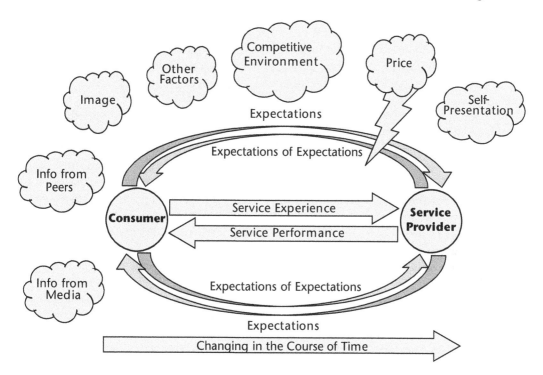

Figure 2.2   Factors of customer satisfaction and service quality

Good service pays off and provides a competitive edge. The figure highlights the complexity of the theoretical construct behind service quality. It is obvious that analyzing the factors that determine customer satisfaction and measuring service quality are essential steps on the road to an improved and competitive service performance. The simple question if a customer has been satisfied may meet the very point and is even a nice gesture when it comes from the service staff but it does not contribute much to a better understanding of the underlying factors of service performance. That requires more elaborated methods and a thorough understanding of the methodology, which will be the topic of the following chapters.

2.2 An Important Sector

The service sector owes its prominent recognition to a large extent to French economist Jean Fourastié (1907–1990) who once described services as 'the great hope of the twentieth century' (Fourastié 1963). Although his three-sector hypothesis was not really new but goes back to earlier publications from Allan G.B. Fisher (1935) and Colin G. Clark (1940) who in turn refers to Sir William Petty's (1623–1687) comparison of the economies of Great Britain, the Netherlands, France and others that was published already more than a quarter of a millennium earlier (Sir Petty 1690), it is usually Fourastié whose name is linked to the idea of splitting the economy into three sectors and the theory how these sectors will develop.

The primary or agricultural sector comprises the production of raw materials, which mostly includes farming, fishing and forestry. Manufacturing, energy production, construction and mining[3] are major activities of the secondary or industrial sector. And the tertiary or service sector includes all economic – government or private – activities that do not produce material goods.

Just for the sake of completeness it shall be mentioned that sometimes this three-sector classification is further extended to a quaternary and quinary sector although there is little consensus with regard to their definitions except that both sectors provide a further breakdown of the tertiary sector. The quaternary sector refers typically to knowledge-based services like advisory and information services, education, research and development but also other elements like the entertainment industry are sometimes subsumed under this category. The quinary sector, on the other hand, encompasses in some definitions categories like tourism, leisure, wellness and health whereas others use this term for the disposal and waste management industry. Obviously, these additional sectors pay tribute to the growing importance of the tertiary sector by emphasizing specific areas that have gained particular importance.

According to Fourastié and his intellectual predecessors, the focus of an economy shifts as part of its development from the primary via the secondary to the tertiary sector. In other words, what starts as an agrarian society will steadily develop into a service society whereby the industrial society marks an intermediate step. Fourastié describes this move as 'great hope' and foresees this development coming along with increasing prosperity and social welfare as well as more humane working conditions due to automation of the primary and secondary sector and eventually lower unemployment rates.

The three-sector hypothesis postulates that the tertiary sector will increasingly contribute to the gross national product and attract workers from the other sectors with the effect that the distribution of the workforce over the three sectors reverses from the first to the third phase. In fact, already Sir William Petty (1690: 12) had recognized that 'there is much more to be gained by Manufacture than Husbandry, and by Merchandize than Manufacture'.[4]

What Fourastié's three-sector hypothesis describes is the move from traditional civilizations of developing countries through a transitional period of industrialization, mechanization and automation towards the tertiary civilization of the post-industrial service society. Looking back, it was a rather euphoric view that predicted social security and social welfare, better education and higher qualification as well as a more humane working environment without unemployment because it was assumed that the tertiary sector could not be rationalized. From today's perspective, it looks like a wondrous promise of salvation that eventually faced a sobering reality. The technical development has outstripped imagination and proven several elements of the three-sector hypothesis rather questionable.

The 'great hope' that the tertiary sector would help to overcome unemployment has especially proven illusory. Many developed countries that make a high share of their GDP from services struggle with high and even growing unemployment rates.

---

3   It is sometimes disputed if mining belongs to the primary or secondary sector. As the statistical data that are used in this chapter classify mining as an industrial activity, we follow this categorization.

4   Petty's observation, which was also quoted by Clark, explains why the three-sector hypothesis is rightfully also called Petty's Law.

For example, Spain's service sector has an estimated 71 per cent share of the GDP but also almost 22 per cent unemployment. The situation in Greece is similar. Despite earning about 79 per cent of its GDP from services, the unemployment rate has reached more than 17 per cent – and the further outlook is gloomy.[5] Furthermore, employment in the service sector is to a large extent not linked to the supposed demand for higher levels of education. On the contrary, it comprises a significant share of jobs that require only a low education level. Accordingly, the gap in the distribution of income has not narrowed down but actually widened.

Nevertheless, a general trend to the tertiary sector is obvious even if a significant share derives from the information sector that some authors consider a separate sector. Within the European Union (EU), the tertiary sector contributes more than 73 per cent to the GDP and in the US it is almost 80 per cent. By contrast, industry contributes less than 25 per cent in Europe and hardly more than 19 per cent in the US. The agricultural sector manages to contribute a mere 1 to 2 per cent. In comparison, the figures for the whole world read 6 per cent, 31 per cent and 63 per cent for the primary, secondary and tertiary sector. These few examples prove that developed countries have transformed to service societies although countries like Germany with its strong export orientation or Norway with its oil industry still have a strong secondary sector.

This development is more than an academic perspective. It is an impressive and substantial economical, social and cultural challenge that proves the high importance of the service sector and turns into the imperative to deal with this development in a proactive manner. Service is much more than cutting hair and serving food and drinks in a restaurant. The traditional three sectors of an economy have become increasingly interrelated. The manufacturing and the service sector are particularly closely associated. Goods cannot be marketed without related services and services are in most cases accompanied by goods. So the traditional understanding of three largely distinct sectors has made way for a paradigm shift from a sectoral view to a more process-related view, which will eventually alter the major focus from manufactured goods to services as the driving force of developed economies.

Services make up a complex field that covers all segments of life and becomes increasingly global and is further driven by innovations that are, to a large extent, based on information technology (IT). This development is far from having reached its final stage and will continue and partly even accelerate. For traditional service providers as well as manufacturers, it is essential not to lose out on this development. But despite all technological developments that drive the service sector, its major focus is still on people and social behaviour and interaction – people as consumers as well as people providing services. People make the difference. They decide on success and failure.

Any research in the field of services has to consider and reflect this aspect in order to deliver reliable and valid but ultimately also relevant knowledge about services and service quality that can serve as sustainable basis for decisions on future developments and strategies in a highly competitive market on one hand and support purchase decisions on the other.

Assuming that the need for service improvement and innovations is well understood, many questions arise. What direction shall the future development take? What do customers expect? What is the potential for further service development? What is good –

---

5   The figures in this sub-chapter section refer to 2011 and are based on Central Intelligence Agency 2012.

or even great – service? And how to measure all this? After all, some gut feelings are not good enough for the development of concepts for a sustainable service improvement. The very point is that improved as well as new services not only have the potential to create new market opportunities but are accompanied by the inherent risk of blunder and undesirable developments. This demands a methodologically sound basis for management decisions if innovations are not to lead to a rude awakening.

The heterogeneity of the service sector, reaching from highly specialized and knowledge-based functions to basic services that require relatively little skills, makes it difficult to develop general models and approaches to these questions. So far, practical research in the service sector has been very much influenced by a technical understanding that derives from natural sciences. This book, however, deals with service as a people business. That makes a difference. It is an approach to quality that has substantial consequences for the methods and methodology of research in the field of services.

2.3 Applied Sociology and Psychology

Services have a rather strange character. They establish an economic sector that is usually not defined out of its own identity but in contrast to other sectors. So instead of saying what services are, most definitions start highlighting what they are *not*. In the end, services establish some residual category – whatever does not belong to the agricultural or industrial sector is considered service.

That description makes services part of the total production process of an economy. Since the small agricultural sector can almost be neglected, developed economies are characterized as a dichotomy of manufacturing and services whereby services have to a large extent the function of adding value to manufactured goods. This is apparent in after-sales service that adds the value of reliability and peace of mind to manufactured goods and reduces insecurity from the possibility of product failure. And it is also the case when, for example, food is served in style or flowers are bound into a nice bouquet. All these examples represent an understanding of service as an add-on to manufactured goods.

It is an economic perspective that is to some extent historically justified. After all, it took some time until manufacturers realized how important it is to add service functions to their manufactured goods. Furthermore, one could argue that usually the product comes first and creates opportunities for services. On the other hand, looking at the value added that services generate, one could question why services should be an add-on to goods instead of looking at it from the opposite direction. Considering the transformation to a service society and in view of a share of more than 70 per cent that services contribute to the GDP of developed economies, wouldn't it be more appropriate to describe goods as an add-on to service?

It depends, one may say, and refer to a services–goods continuum as described earlier. From that perspective, the weighting of the two factors could decide the issue. Or one looks at the logical sequence whereby the car has to be manufactured before it can go for regular servicing whereas one would first have to visit the doctor before medicine is prescribed. But as usual, the more appropriate answer will not be found somewhere between the two perspectives but at a different level.

Services are a people business. Regardless of if and how they are related to goods, services are negotiated – partly silently and partly expressively – between service provider and customer. People constitute services. And that means that the mechanisms of services follow the principles of social behaviour and social interaction.

Accordingly, dealing with service performance as well as service quality and customer satisfaction is not so much an issue of economics but makes service a subject of sociology and psychology. After all, these are the sciences that deal with social behaviour. And exactly here lies the key to a better understanding of services.

During history, sociology has been defined in different ways. French philosopher Auguste Comte (1798–1857), as one of the founding fathers of sociology, defined the term 'sociology' as a new way to look at society after he and others had referred to 'social physics' before. The coinage of 'sociology' is a combination of the Latin word *'socius'* for an associate or companion and Greek *'logia'*, which refers to a science. For Comte, sociology was the ultimate and most complex science that one day would comprise all other sciences and develop their knowledge into an interdependent holistic understanding of society.

Well, sociology is not only far away from fulfilling such claim, there is also no serious sociologist who would still subscribe to Comte's approach. Although there is no common definition of sociology, German sociologist Max Weber's (1864–1920) understanding of sociology as science that deals with the course and effects of social action is deemed more appropriate and is widely accepted. According to Weber, sociology develops an interpretive understanding of social action and thus explains the cause of its development and effects. Weber refers to social action, which he distinguishes from action. Action is human behaviour that is subjectively meaningful. Sociology, however, deals with social action, which he defines as action that in its meaning and course is oriented according to the behaviour of others (Weber 1922: § 1). And that is exactly what we are dealing with when analyzing services. It is all about social behaviour in social interaction.[6]

This approach is closely related to psychology and social psychology in particular. Psychology as a combination of the Greek words for the soul and the mind on one hand and science on the other refers to the study of the mind and shall provide an understanding of intellectual functions and behaviour.

Sociology as well as psychology are empirical sciences by nature. The term 'empirical' – from Greek *'empeirikos'* – relates to experience and skills and refers back to the understanding that knowledge is generally based on experience rather than doctrines.[7] Empirical sciences put theory and empirical data into relation and try to derive an understanding of their observations with the target to find explanations in the sense of general rules. It is common to distinguish between pure and applied sociology.[8] In this context, pure sociology defines the terminology and the interrelations of theoretical constructs. Applied sociology, on the other hand, analyzes social processes and applies theoretical constructs to empirical observation. In short, it is the distinction between

---

6   We abstain here from the discussion of services in the context of other sociological theories because this would develop expectations that are intentionally not met in the following chapters. At this point, it is sufficient to introduce Max Weber's understanding of sociology as illustration that sociological theory and methods provide an appropriate context for the analysis of services.

7   Empiricism as an epistemological approach developed in the seventeenth century and was strongly influenced by English philosophers Francis Bacon (1561–1626) and John Locke (1632–1704) as well as Scottish philosopher David Hume (1711–1776).

8   German sociologist Ferdinand Tönnies (1855–1936) introduced this distinction in Tönnies 1887.

sociological – or psychological – theory and its application to the real world by means of practical research.

This distinction is relevant because the theoretical and the empirical world look to some extent different. In this context, service is a theoretical construct that in its pure form will hardly be found in the empirical world. This has to be kept in mind when dealing with the empirical world. At the same time, it makes the life of the researcher more interesting but also more troublesome.

Describing services as a sociological – and partly also psychological – phenomenon suggests an empirical approach to their observation, analysis and understanding. Results and related theories are empirical when they are based on observations and can be examined by means of sensory perceptions rather than pure theory or logic. Accordingly, empirical social research describes the systematic collection of data related to social action and its analysis and interpretation with regard to the underlying research question.

The term 'empirical social research' is a generic term for a bundle of rather heterogeneous approaches to reality. In addition to interviews as the most popular and best-known method, there are observations, content analyses, experiments, group discussions and focus groups as well as a number of less prominent approaches. And each of these methods describes again a variety of different approaches, like for example in the case of interviews, which can be standardized or non-standardized, structured or unstructured, face-to-face, via telephone, mail or Internet, written or oral, it may deal with individuals or groups, and so on. Some of these categories describe even a continuum, which increases the complexity further. However, the very point is that the various methods do not deliver a picture of 'the reality' but reconstruct *different* aspects of social reality. So empirical research is not about finding the best technique or method to picture 'the' reality as objective and factual as possible. There is no objective reality. Instead, it is about the question 'Which approach is most adequate with regard to the research question to reconstruct the relevant aspects of potential reality?' In fact, it makes a distinction as to how the potential reality is approached.[9]

This book will deal with services in the sense of applied sociology and psychology and focus on the methods and methodology of empirical research. It is the aim to develop a more appropriate understanding of practical research in the field of services. The result will prove that methodologically meaningful research is no contradiction to the pragmatic requirements of research in the real business world but provides a more reliable and valid approach to a better understanding of services and their quality.

2.4 Where Service Begins

Services are a vast field. There is hardly any area of life that is not one way or the other related to services. We have mentioned that every product has some service component and services come along with a product component. So much complexity demands structure.

There are many attempts to categorize the service sector. Long lists try to bring some structure into this hotchpotch of performances that cover all areas of life and are

---

9   This important aspect is discussed in more detail in Chapters 4 and 6.

so manifold that it is hard to nail down their specific characteristics. Accordingly, the epistemological value of such compilations is somewhat limited. Usually they are made from an economical perspective and result in categories of typical industries and some examples like the following:

- Tourism and leisure: Air travel, hotel services, casinos and so on.
- Transport and traffic: Public transportation, container transportation, courier services and so on.
- Entertainment: Philharmonic concerts, cinema, fireworks and so on.
- Health care and wellness: Medical services, hairdressing, spa services and so on.
- Pre-sales and after-sales service: Sales advice, maintenance, repair and so on.
- Financial services: Banking, insurances, investment and so on.
- Education and training: Schools and universities, tuition, professional training and so on.
- Governmental or public services: Military services, registrar of marriages, environmental protection and so on.
- Consultancy and advice: Management consultancy, headhunters, tax advisory and so on.
- Legal services: Lawyers, arbitration, notaries and so on.
- Waste disposal: Garbage collection, incineration, recycling and so on.
- Information and communication: Broadcasting, telecommunications, libraries and so on.

It is a chequered list that contributes little to a better understanding of services apart from demonstrating how manifold the service sector is. The categories are not distinct and the list is not exhaustive. Adding a category 'others' would not make it much better. It is obvious that this attempt is not very helpful as classification because many services belong to more than one category. For example, a travel portal on the web belongs not only to tourism but can also be considered under transport, consultancy or information. Is air travel tourism or transport? Is investment banking a financial service or consultancy? Does a government hospital belong to health care or government services? Would it perhaps help to understand the tertiary sector better when it is further broken down into a quaternary and even quinary sector? It depends, one could always say. Apparently, such categorization does not contribute much to an attempt to structure the service sector.

Alternatively, one can distinguish between services that are related to persons and to objects. In that context, the transportation of passengers would be different from container transportation. But also that distinction is not particularly enlightening because the customer of container transport services is of course a person even if this person represents something as anonymous as a company. And if a person is travelling, this person may bring a suitcase along. So what value can such differentiation have?

Other categorizations distinguish between original services like a haircut on one hand and services that come along with a product as value added on the other. But what about the fantastic shampoo against hair loss that the hairdresser tries to sell you after the haircut? Also attempts to distinguish between largely standardized services like the service of a fast-food chain on one hand and individualized services like a good massage on the other are not of particular help. Of course, an individualized service also has standardized elements and a standardized service comes along with some individual elements. So what does it really say about service quality?

Obviously, all these categories highlight some aspects of services but do not really get to the point. They just emphasize the vast diversity of the service sector that reaches from rather simple support functions to highly elaborated professional services. Also the market structures of the various service sectors are extremely different. They reach from monopolies to atomized markets. These aspects indeed become relevant when developing a research design. A highly fragmented business sector requires a different approach compared to a monopolistic or quasi-monopolistic market. A standardized service can be measured against the standard whereas an individualized service can only be measured against customer experience and expectations.

An adequate research design for quality studies must not only reflect the research question but also the context in which a specific service is performed. At the same time it must not get lost in insignificance but must strive for relevance in terms of management and consumer decisions. Already at this point it should be obvious that there cannot be any magic formula for quality research. The crucial question is, 'What actually are the relevant categories when it comes to service quality?' And this is apparently not about theoretical economical classifications but about very practical sociological and psychological categories.

We have said repeatedly that service is a people business. Services do not create tangibles but change existence and consciousness, cognition and feelings. From this perspective, one arrives at very different categories that could look, for example, as follows:

- Social relations and communication: Living in the information age and having more communication channels than ever before does not mean having stronger social relations. Social networks offer to develop social relations, flower services help to stay in touch and information services promise to stay on top of the news.
- Health, wellbeing, recreation and relaxation: Health and related services promise fitness and efficiency, which allows one to control one's own life.
- Clear conscience and harmony: Like the medieval selling of indulgences, charitable organizations offer a clear conscience against a small donation.
- Peace of mind: Companies offering maintenance contracts promise to take the risk of failure off the shoulders of their customers and provide calmness and peace of mind.
- Experience and adventure: Most people live a rather ordinary and monotonous life. Tour operators promise to spice up the daily boredom with some extraordinary days or weeks even if their package tour is as standardized as the rest of the life of their customers.
- Reliability and order: Government services focus on bringing order into an otherwise unreliable world. The same applies to consumer organizations when testing services and providing guidance in a market that is difficult to overlook. Also customer service signals reliability – we are here to help if something goes wrong.
- Safety and security: When browsing a newspaper, crime, accidents and disasters are looming and provide the market for safety and security providers. Safety and security are also inherent elements of many other services like insurances or transport.
- Happiness and luck: No new year greetings are without good wishes for luck and happiness. And even if everybody has a different understanding, there is a never-ending quest for this ultimate meaning of life. Dating agencies promise happiness and also financial institutions try to sell happiness – despite the good old saying that money doesn't buy happiness.

- Hope: Hope is always the hope for the better. Religions offer hope but psychological and medical services also sell hope.
- Future: The uncertainty of future developments makes it necessary to be prepared for whatever may come. Insurances and all kind of advisers offer their services.
- Prestige and status: Prestige and status determine the perceived social position that someone assumes in society. Credit cards or loyalty programmes offer the possibility to buy status. A platinum card beats the gold card and a frequent traveller boards the aircraft before the ordinary passenger.
- Advice and knowledge: Education, knowledge and experience are linked to power and influence. Schools and universities promise to pave the way to the top. Consultants and other advisors offer their supposed expert knowledge.

The list could be continued and refined further. Of course, also these categories are not distinct. But the purpose is not to create a new distinct and comprehensive but eventually still theoretical system of categories. Instead, it shall prove that relevant criteria of service quality are actually very different from common economical categories.

Service quality follows the principles of sociology and psychology. Accordingly, the measurement of service quality is applied sociology and psychology. This is also reflected in the variables that make up customer satisfaction and quality. It is a perspective of services that is often better understood by public relations strategists than by market researchers who are still in search of 'objective' quality criteria. The above variables are examples for characteristics that make the distinction. Every airline can fly from A to B. But it is a different experience if you clutch the armrest nervously during the whole flight and read the safety instructions repeatedly or if you lean back, relax and look forward to your next flight.

It is obvious that most services are related to more than one of the above categories. Take for example a cruise. It is about experience and adventure, social relations and communication, prestige and status, happiness, wellbeing, recreation and relaxation, safety and security and perhaps also some other aspects. There are many highly complex constructs that are actually hidden behind a supposedly simple question like: How satisfied were you with your cruise? Even if customer satisfaction is the ultimate criterion of service quality, it requires more than a casual question to understand the dimensions of service quality and to arrive at insight and conclusions that are relevant for management decisions.

Take (legal) gambling as another example. One could assess the quality of games simply by means of statistical probability. The expected value of a game is the product of the likelihood of winning and the value of the prize. So the higher the expected value the better the quality of the game? That sounds logical but gamblers will judge it differently. There is not only a major difference between mathematical and subjective likelihood,[10] which results in misjudgements of chances even if the mathematical parameters are known. There is also the question if a high likelihood of a small prize is as good as a small likelihood of a big prize. Both may have the same objective expected value but gamblers

---

10   Subjective likelihood deals with the subjective assessment of likelihood, which is based on personal experience and learning. By contrast, the mathematical likelihood of a specific outcome of an experiment is derived from the number of favourable results in relation to the number of all cases (assuming that infinite repetitions of the experiment are possible and all events have the same likelihood). This allows the determination of likelihood logically without empirical examination.

will come to very different conclusions. And then there is of course the question of what a gambler is willing to pay for the experience of hope, luck and the social situation that many games provide. Some lotteries are even linked to charity and offer not only the chance to win but at the same time a clear conscience. These are aspects of gambling that have little to do with an objective measurement of chances but, nevertheless, they are essential factors of customer satisfaction (Lisch 1984). Asking gamblers if they would recommend a specific lottery or casino to a friend would hardly contribute to a better understanding. Deeper insight is required.

Obviously, the 'technical data' of services are not sufficient for the description of service quality. They describe the necessary but not at all sufficient criteria of good service. Excellent service goes far beyond such minimum requirements. Service quality begins where the mechanical service performance ends.

2.5 Distinctive Perspectives

Service-related quality research deals with a number of stakeholders who are for various reasons interested in this topic but have a gradually different underlying interest. First of all, there is the group of those stakeholders who are directly involved in a service performance. These are the service provider and the private or commercial customer. But there are more parties who have an interest in a better understanding of customer satisfaction and the quality of services. Consumer organizations that claim to be legitimate representatives of consumer interests have a sound interest in a comparison of the quality of service offers. The media claim a similar role although their methodical approach is usually rather plain in comparison to what well-established consumer organizations deliver. Also, consultants romp around in this field and are sometimes more interested in the client's budget than scientific standards. Furthermore, academic research deals with services and seeks a better understanding of this important sector of economies. Last but not least, there is an ISO 9001 standard[11] under the title 'Quality Management Systems – Requirements' that more than a million enterprises worldwide have subscribed to and which demands in section 8 'measurement, analysis and improvement'. It is worthwhile having a closer look at these different perspectives of service quality.

Most areas of the service sector are marked by strong competition. At the same time, consumers can change their service providers easily. This calls for a clear positioning in the market and a thorough understanding of customer expectations on one hand and experience on the other. Only when these factors are sufficiently congruent is success likely. But things change and that means that research into customer expectations and satisfaction is not accomplished with a static snapshot but has to become an ongoing process. The target is not necessarily to provide the *best* service but to render the *most successful* service in terms of long-term profit and lasting customer satisfaction.

Earlier, we have described customer satisfaction as the gap between customer expectations and perceived service performance whereby the comparison between expectations and experience is a reflexive process in a complex environment. An adequate operationalization of this theoretical construct depends on the type of service.

---

11   The International Organization for Standardization (ISO) is the international union of national standard-setting organizations.

Examples for common indicators are the willingness to contract a certain service again, to recommend it to peers, to accept other services from the same provider, to enter into a long-term contract or to accept price increases. The advanced level of customer satisfaction is customer loyalty.

Customer satisfaction as an indicator of service quality does not blossom in a vacuum but has to consider competition offers and other influencing factors as intervening variables. Accordingly, competitive intelligence has to supplement all research into quality in order to position a specific service offer. Competitive intelligence demands not only the collection of information about competitors but also about further stakeholders as well as the entire business environment.

This business intelligence comprising information about the business environment on one hand and customer satisfaction on the other follows Niccolò Machiavelli's (1469–1527) proven imperative to know the business environment because 'if he who rules a principality cannot recognize evils until they are upon him, he is not truly wise' (Machiavelli 1532: Chapter XIII). Chinese military strategist and philosopher Sun Tzu (about 544–496 BC) also highlights the importance of business intelligence when he explains the 'Art of War': 'Hence it is only the enlightened ruler and the wise general who will use the highest intelligence of the army for purposes of spying and thereby they achieve great results' (Sun Tzu: Chapter XIII, 27). Well, this is not a call for illegal corporate espionage but highlights the importance of a comprehensive understanding of the environment in which a service provider operates.

The collection and analysis of information about service quality in the context of the business environment is an imperative of successful management that has meanwhile even been constitutionalized as part of the ISO 9001 standard that defines the requirements of quality management systems. Since its first internationally accepted version in 1987, it has been slightly revised several times and is now available in its fourth version as ISO 9001:2008. As part of a bundle of standards that belong to the ISO 9000 family dealing with quality management systems, ISO 9001 is another good reason for service providers to look into the quality of their services.

Service providers can undergo a process of certification that eventually confirms that they have a quality management system in place that meets the requirements of the standard. This certification is not done by the International Organization for Standardization (ISO) itself but by independent third-party bodies. In 2011, more than 1.1 million companies had been certified according to this standard. European companies account for almost 44 per cent and more than 42 per cent are from East Asia and Pacific (ISO 2012). The high number of certified companies does not necessarily reflect a wholehearted dedication to the principles of quality. Often a certification is hardly more than a necessary evil because commercial customers especially demand ISO certificates from their service providers.[12] So they undergo the lengthy process of certification, nominate a quality manager, hire consultants who write a quality manual, put a big 'Q' on the wall and add some slogans like 'Quality Forever' or 'Forward through Quality', compile a few non-conformance reports, teach the staff how to pass an audit and if everything goes well, they put a nice certificate on the wall and issue a press release – before everything turns back to normal and they continue their work as before. Only when the certificate has to be renewed will the organization fall again into

---

12   In that respect, it is no surprise that the vast majority (about 30 per cent) of certified companies are from China.

hectic activities and prepare for the quality audit. This is of course not the idea behind the quality standard.

As a matter of fact, an ISO certificate is no guarantee for a change of mind. Even worse, the ISO standard says little about the quality of the services that a company renders. Assuming that an ISO 9001 certified company delivers better service than other companies can be a misconception. In fact, the certificate asserts only that a company has a compliant quality management system with related procedures in place. It does not say much about the level of quality.

Nevertheless, the standard forces certified companies to deal with 'measurement, analysis and improvement' of the service performance and the auditors may ask for proof when the certificate is due for renewal. As one of the critical issues, the standard mentions the measurement of customer satisfaction and the conformance of the service to customer requirements. Also, other data related to process and service characteristics as well as subcontractor performance have to be analyzed as part of quality management and are supposed to be used for continual improvement of the service performance.

What could be a meaningful requirement often turns in reality into a rather doubtful procedure. Quality managers who have never before dealt with empirical social research develop questionnaires, sales people ask their customers how satisfied they are with the services, supposed results are interpreted according to the liking of the bosses and when the next audit is scheduled, frantic activities break out in order to make up for all the shortcomings of the past. This may be sufficient for the renewal of the certificate but it has little to do with serious quality studies. Even worse, it misses the chance to develop a better understanding of the service performance and potentials for improvement. A methodologically sound approach to the analysis of customer satisfaction and service quality would not only be more adequate in view of the underlying philosophy of ISO 9001 but has also the potential to contribute to a strengthened market position.

Consumers have a rather straightforward interest in services that complements the view of the service providers. Consumers just want to know where one can get the best service at the most reasonable price. It is as simple as that. But the definition of 'best service' will vary. And so will be the perception of a specific service performance. Service expectations and service experience are not static but undergo a permanent process of change and adaption. At the same time, consumers have limited sources of information about service quality. Where commercial customers may sign detailed contracts, agree upon penalties for non-performance, develop performance indicators or score cards and do everything to ensure that specified service requirements are met, private consumers are rather helpless in the face of a multitude of service offers. Apart from their own experience, they depend on hearsay among their peers, the image of service providers as well as information provided by the media. Unfortunately, these sources are usually not particularly reliable and the validity of the available information is often rather doubtful.

In most cases, the judgement of service quality that peers can contribute to a decision-making process will hardly be better than one's own assessment. But personal esteem may lend weight to it. On the other hand, such advice will not necessarily correspond to the answer to what is often considered the mother of all questions about customer satisfaction: would you recommend this service to a friend? The answer to such hypothetical question may be rather different from actual behaviour. Indeed, the world is more complex than a one-dimensional question. So one may look for better sources of information. The image of a service provider as a result of advertising and other image campaigns as well as further information from the media will have an impact on consumer decisions. Also the price and perhaps other easily available data will be considered and interpreted in terms of reasonable quality expectation. Yet it is a rather weak foundation for decision-making and disappointment is looming. Here, consumer organizations step in with their expertise and try to provide relevant information about the quality of services. The demand is high. And so can be their impact on consumer behaviour.

While leading consumer organizations like Which? in the UK, Stiftung Warentest in Germany, Consumentenbond in the Netherlands, Consumers Union in the US and others have originally started with the idea of comparative testing of consumer goods, they have soon discovered the demand for information about service quality and provide related tests. The name of German Stiftung Warentest particularly – which means literally: foundation for the test of goods – makes obvious that services were originally not on the mind of the founding fathers. This organization is a good example of the specific role and power of quality research that established consumer institutions can deliver.

It took ten years after its foundation in 1964 until Stiftung Warentest – describing itself as 'the strong partner of critical consumers' – established a department for the comparative testing of services. This step followed the understanding that in view of an increasingly similar quality level of consumer goods, the focus will shift more towards related services. In addition, the testers faced a growing interest in information about financial services and other service sectors like tourism as well as public and health-related services. This was a rather natural development in line with the move of the economy into the direction of a more service-oriented society. While the traditionally strong focus on comparative tests of consumer products was maintained, the public interest in the quality of services developed quickly and the originally limited scope was extended to further areas of the service sector including remote topics like astrologists, non-medical practitioners or undertakers. There was hardly any service sector that was not made accessible to quality research.

According to its constitution, Stiftung Warentest is committed to applying scientific methods to its – usually comparative – projects in order to arrive at an appropriate judgement of the quality of services and to inform the public about the test results. For this purpose, they publish research results in their consumer magazines that provide related information allowing the recipients to become familiar with the market in general as well as the particular services of selected providers. It is a twofold approach that combines individual research results with general information – enabling the consumer not only to better understand a specific segment of the service sector but to develop the necessary skills to judge service offers also beyond those that were the subjects of the comparative test. This is practical consumer education in the interest of better consumer protection. And it is a practical reflection of often atomized markets in the service sector that make it impossible to include all service providers in a test. Where such a situation prevails such as, for example, when testing car repair shops, a consumer organization can only deal with small samples of service providers and try to derive general issues that a consumer should consider when deciding where to have his car serviced. Eventually, the available information will be a combination of specific but exemplary results of quality assessments on one hand and general consumer information on the other.

No doubt, consumer organizations like Stiftung Warentest have substantial market power. Their judgement can change markets and turn customers away from service providers that receive a negative verdict from the testers. On the other hand, a good test result can propel the business of a service provider and is often used for advertising purposes. For example, a comparison of the odds of legal gambling had a clear impact on the market shares of some games. Similar effects could be observed after a field experiment that dealt with donations for charitable organizations that are active in developing countries. Donators reacted in a very sensitive manner to information about administrative overheads and the way that donations were actually used. In any case, published test results have an impact on consumer behaviour. That makes it so important that they follow scientific standards and approach the topics in a way that is practically relevant for consumer behaviour and consumer decisions. Meeting these ultimate criteria is the linchpin of the power of consumer organizations.

Considering their market power, consumer organizations are under an obligation to service providers and consumers that makes high scientific standards a condicio sine qua non. Research designs that provide results that hardly go beyond vague impressions and gut feelings would be torn to pieces once a service provider challenges them in court. This would not only affect the service provider but also spoil the reputation of the consumer organization. Scientific uprightness is a major asset that must be maintained. At the same time, this makes it more difficult to communicate research results.

It is an essential part of the role of consumer organizations to inform the public about the results of their research activities. But where newspapers write a more or less enjoyable and preferably non-committal story adding some personal impressions and opinions, a consumer organization is expected to deliver scientific and 'objective' results. This is supposed to meet the informational demand of the readers and provide reliable and valid research results in conjunction with practical guidance. At the same time, the information should be entertaining and easy to digest – in other words, just the opposite of common research reports. These requirements usually result in two reports – a rather sober scientific report of the research results that is subsequently translated into a story that highlights the crucial issues and is supplemented by tables showing relevant factors and related results. It is the art of consumer information to translate a scientific report into readable, easy to digest and at the same time relevant information. As part of this conversion, it is important to deliver the fundamentals of the research design determining the context in which the results can claim relevance. As a matter of fact, scientific standards and general comprehensibility are no contradiction. Scientific research can be made understandable. Not only in consumer research but also in business.

Compared to consumer organizations and their publications, newspapers and magazines have a much simpler role. It is not their primary interest to provide a scientifically sound comparison of service providers. Instead, their focus is mainly on a story that catches the interest of the reader. And perhaps they have some lucrative advertisements in mind. This does not demand scientific research but takes just the necessary journalistic care that requires to bend the facts not too much and stay within the bounds of the freedom of the press.

Contrary to consumer magazines, newspapers, journals and other media are usually not focusing on the 'normal' but make their stories from the extraordinary. The service of safety onboard cruise vessels becomes a topic only when a disaster has happened. And such a topic disappears from public interest as fast as it has emerged. Nothing is as old as yesterday's newspaper. Similarly, the service of a car rental company is only an issue when something goes completely wrong. And the service of ticket vending machines will only make the headlines when the journey ends hundreds of kilometres away from the intended destination. Such journalistic approach paints a rather distorted picture of customer satisfaction and the quality of services. It deals with service performance based on news value. It is not primarily an attempt to reflect something like reality but constitutes a journalistic world that follows its own rules. There, negative news usually sells better than good news and the unexpected catches more interest than the ordinary. If such news can be personalized, it is even more newsworthy. Accordingly, the daily experience of hundreds of thousands of people enjoying reliable public transport services has hardly any news value. However, when a train breaks down and hundreds are stranded, it becomes a topic. And it becomes even more interesting when the mishap can be personalized. If a highly pregnant passenger goes prematurely into labour because of such an incident, she can be sure to make the headlines. Wow! That is the stuff that makes the circulation leapfrog.

The impact of news value on the selection and publication of information results in a very specific reality, which makes the media a rather biased source of information about the quality of services. On the consumer side, the journalistic selection of news is complemented by a typically subjective selection of information. News about well-known companies or services that are of supposed personal interest attract more attention than others, which increases their effect when it comes to public opinion and social action. It is difficult and can be a lengthy process to readjust the message that such news transfers. Something will always stick to the recipient's mind. The best way to avoid such unwanted news is to maintain a high quality standard.

Last but not least, academic research is also dealing with services. Academia as well as politics have identified services as an important sector with substantial growth potential. This assigns a fundamental role to academic research in the service sector. It is not so much about analyzing the quality of individual service providers but looking at the challenges ahead of the service sector. There is still a lot of potential that can be exploited in cooperation between theory and practice.[13]

The opportunities that the service sector provides are in many areas contrasted with insufficient awareness of its importance. As mentioned before, services are often seen as a supplement to manufactured goods. But in view of their contribution to an economy and the important role that they play in everyday life, service work deserves more recognition and appreciation. At the same time, many areas of the service sector show significant room for improvement. Training concepts are required.

This goes hand in hand with concepts for an improvement of the efficiency of services. However, higher efficiency must not result in a deterioration of the service performance. This speaks against an increasing trend towards something that could be labelled as modern Taylorism,[14] which effectively results in growing anonymity of the service performance. It is a trend that largely ignores the nature of services as a people business.

Data centres, bundling of functions and outsourcing are some keywords that dominate the discussions about higher efficiency of services – and result often not so much in reduced costs but eventually in a deterioration of the service quality.

---

13   For an overview on research perspectives, see also Ganz 2005.

14   Taylorism describes a management approach that breaks down working processes into standardized elements with the target of increased efficiency. It is also known as Scientific Management. The term Taylorism refers to US-American Engineer Frederick Taylor (1856–1915). Charles Chaplin (1889–1977) dealt with Taylorism in his 1936 movie *Modern Times*.

This applies to some purchasing, documentation and customer service processes in particular. Where customers were once facing competent partners who were familiar with complex business processes and – even more important – were easily accessible, they deal now with badly paid back room staff who are only responsible for a limited segment of the service process and hardly familiar with the business. If you want to complain and ask for the manager, you can be sure that he is in a meeting – so sorry, Sir. It is the preliminary stage of automation. As a result of such soulless service processes, the staff turnover is high, the motivation is low and considering all related troubles, the actual savings are rather doubtful. There should be better approaches to increase the efficiency of services without compromising the quality as well as the working conditions.

No doubt, the service industry still has great potential for innovations and improvements. While some branches of the service industry have gone through a number of innovations especially when exploiting the potential of IT, other parts of the service sector show only gradual developments. Here, academia as well as politics can contribute to greater awareness for service innovations and provide guidance.

Take for example the container transport business. Since the invention and – despite all initial scepticism of supposed experts – highly successful introduction of the standard box,[15] the shipping industry is lacking substantial innovations. The standardization and interchangeability of transportation equipment leaves little opportunity to stand out from the crowd. Ships have become bigger making use of the economies of scale and they steam at slower speed in order to save bunkers[16] and to cope with overcapacity. Every carrier does it. If one carrier has the idea, the others will follow suit. The market situation demands for such measures. So where are the real service innovations?

Ideas to develop additional market potential through new container types have long been given up after such alleged innovations had turned into a burden because they had a negative impact on the equipment imbalances resulting in higher costs. Efforts to keep the transport prices high failed although liner shipping was for decades one of very few industries with legal cartels. Looking back, this protection appears to be rather a curse than a blessing because it safeguarded the industry far too long against natural economic mechanisms. Nowadays, container shipping faces the fact that with negligible differences between operators, prices simply follow supply and demand and are the very criterion when choosing a carrier. Container shipping finds itself in a dilemma between high investment, heavy dependence on the price of oil as one of the most speculative commodities and a strong influence by national interests that sometimes overrule economically necessary decisions on one hand and lacking innovative potential on the other. The outlook is rather gloomy.

Austrian–American economist Joseph Schumpeter (1883–1950) described entrepreneurship as a permanent striving for innovations in order to improve the competitive position – until the innovation is imitated by competition and the process starts anew. It is not the size of a company that determines success but its innovative potential. Schumpeter describes innovations as 'the Process of Creative Destruction' (Schumpeter 1942: Part II, Chapter VII). Only as long as a company stays ahead of competition in this race of innovation and imitation is there a competitive edge.

---

15   Malcolm McLean (1913–2001) is considered the inventor of the intermodal container that revolutionized worldwide cargo transportation since its beginning in 1956.

16   Bunker is the fuel that ships use.

Where this lead is lost, competition is reduced to the price. This applies not only to manufacturing but to services as well. In analogy to a well-known slogan of a German carmaker, one could call it 'Vorsprung durch Innovation' [Leading by innovation].

Apple created one of the best examples for the potential of innovations in the service sector when they linked their iPod to the services of the iTunes Store. The idea of a portable music player, that Sony once made popular with its Walkman but that was limited to the hardware, entered new dimensions when Apple developed a revolutionary service component and combined its lifestyle hardware with the iTunes software.

It is easy to predict that most future innovations in the service sector will be related to IT. But this should not distract from the fact that also in future, customer satisfaction and service quality as the ultimate criteria of success and failure will be related to people. Even if service providers fully automated their services, it is still people who judge the service performance and assign the responsibility for its quality to the people behind the scenes.

The following chapters will cover service quality from the perspectives of service providers as well as consumers. While private consumers will not be in a position to perform comprehensive research projects, their interest is well represented by consumer organizations and their comparative approach, which can also be an appropriate method for commercial customers. Service providers, on the other hand, will always look at the market from the perspective of their own service offer. But regardless of the particular perspective, quality research is about empirical social research and the reconstruction of a specific reality.

3 *Framework and Design*

Once a manager thinks a little longer than usual and possibly even looks into a book or searches the web, he will describe it as research. A knowing look and a casual statement like 'I have done some research' puts weight to otherwise rather plain thoughts. Who would dare to contradict? When these thoughts are eventually turned into a well-animated PowerPoint presentation, the manager will not hesitate calling it a study. The business world is full of research and studies. Studies are the heightening of research. Both come along with associations of science, integrity, truth, objectivity and wisdom – and provide, in many cases, nothing but everyday experience and gut feelings where a solid basis for management decisions is required.

In fact, practical research is often marked (and marred) by an amazing discrepancy between a claim for ultimate truth and a thorough ignorance of the basics of empirical research. What is supposed to deliver facts creates eventually nothing but artefacts – invalid research results that are caused by flaws in the research process and lead to fallacies and misinterpretations. The consequences are not only a waste of resources but also a high risk of making wrong decisions.

Newspapers are full of reports about the latest studies of often dubious researchers and even more dubious topics. Only when research and studies have the certain 'wow!' effect will they hit the headlines. Everything else is 'academic' at best and hardly worth a story. The simple presentation of some doubtful conclusions as a 'study' puts aside all questions about further details. The word 'study' speaks for itself. Studies promise investigations and analyses and come along with decent connotations to science and ultimate truth. So much alleged objectivity prevents from further inquiries. No wonder that the supposed results will quickly develop some momentum of their own. But what is nonchalantly labelled as a study does not always contain serious research.

Take for example the results of a ranking of the world's 'Top 10 Most Beautiful Air Hostess Airlines', which was supposedly performed by the 'World Air Hostesses Association'. Journalists jumped on it and the readers liked it. After all, the smile of a stewardess is part of the service of an airline. No wonder that such groundbreaking study was followed by lengthy debates on several news portals. It was a good opportunity to contribute own impressions and prejudgements. Even better, this study had some sex appeal. The winning airline did not want to hold back and quickly published a press release highlighting that, according to the ranking, they have the most beautiful stewardesses caring for the well-being of their passengers – because it is not only about safety and security but also about an attractive smile of the crew when choosing an airline. Well, that's true.

On second thoughts, however, one could have asked how beauty was defined in this study. Everybody knows that beauty is in the eye of the beholder. So it would be interesting to know how and by whom the ranking was done and what criteria had actually been chosen. But that remains a secret. Also, a search for the World Air Hostesses

Association turns out to be futile. Obviously, this association does not exist. A search for any further explanations of the empirical approach is in vain as well. So where does the supposed study with its beauty ranking actually come from? Was it a hoax? Perhaps some kind of viral marketing? Or even the smart idea of a researcher who wanted to prove how uncritically research results are received by the public just because they are labelled as a study?[1]

Perhaps one has to go back to the original meaning of a study, which has its roots in old French. Study is a short form of '*estudie*', which is related to the Latin word '*studium*' denoting zeal and a meticulous exercise. Research has similar roots that also go back to old French. It is the word '*recerchier*' that is made from '*cerchier*' meaning to search, which is reinforced by the prefix '*re*'. Accordingly, research can be described as a powerful search for knowledge – which in real life often suffers from weak methodology. Unfortunately, many studies lack the necessary meticulousness and are rather superficial or do not deserve the labels 'study' or 'research' at all.

Research about quality and customer satisfaction touches the nerve of a business. Quality decides over success and failure. Where so much is at stake, vague and unsystematic impressions can only provide a weak basis for management decisions. Many so-called studies hardly deserve such designation. As a matter of fact, practical research is not exempted from scientific principles. So it is worthwhile having a closer look at how knowledge is actually gained and accumulated as a basis for decisions.

To start with, one has to realize that scientific experience is rather different from everyday experience. And that distinguishes research and studies from general impressions and gut feelings. Scientific experience is a systematic interaction with the world, which demands a common understanding of some basics of the underlying epistemological process. It is the crucial insight into the processes behind the development of knowledge that is necessary for a better understanding of research methods.

In this chapter we take a look at the complexity that researchers have to tackle when dealing with quality and ask why personal impressions and gut feelings cannot substitute practical research. Furthermore, we discuss the basic research process and describe how practical research can become integral part of working processes.

3.1 Complexity

Quality research takes place somewhere between likely incongruent specifications, expectations and perceptions of a number of stakeholders. The management of a service provider defines the specifications of a service offer. This definition reflects previous service experience as well as the expectations and expected expectations of the potential customers, which may be appropriate or not. Broadcasting the definition will somehow create related expectations on the side of the customers, which may be appropriate or not. In any case, they will be relevant for the decision if the service offer is to be taken up or not. These expectations on one hand and previous service experience on the other will influence the perception of the actual service performance. It becomes more complicated because the actual service performance is not necessarily identical to the original service

---

1   See also Welt Online 2012. The 'winning' airline has meanwhile removed the respective press release from its website.

definition. After all, the service is usually not delivered by those who defined it but by service staff who may have developed their own interpretation of the service performance because the original definition was insufficiently communicated or simply not accepted by the frontline staff. And of course, the stakeholder groups of management, staff and customers are unlikely to be homogeneous with regard to their experience, expectations, expectations of expectations and perceptions. Quality is a concept that is exposed to all kind of broken promises, disappointed expectations and other misunderstandings. That makes customer satisfaction and the quality of services much more volatile than the quality of manufactured goods.

This does not only apply to the general concept of quality but also to dimensions like reliability, status, friendliness, competence, credibility and other characteristics of service quality. Depending on the type of service and the specific service situation, the relevant characteristics of service quality and their particular importance can be rather different.[2] Furthermore, the interrelations between the various characteristics depend largely on the specific service situation. All this contributes to the complexity of the situation.

Eventually, there are numerous interfaces between original specifications, actual performance, experience, expectations, expectations of expectations and perception as well as the interrelations between the various dimensions of quality on one hand and heterogeneous groups of management, staff and customers on the other. Every interface bears the risk of incongruence, misunderstandings and ultimately lacking compatibility. And then a researcher comes and wants to sort things out.

Obviously, it is not an easy task that a researcher takes on. Above all, a call for objectivity rings out. While it is accepted that every stakeholder of a service situation has his own view and interests, the researcher is assigned a neutral role and faces the expectation to deliver 'objective' data and 'true' results.[3] It is almost a mission impossible.

In such environment, it is no wonder that so much complexity awakes a natural desire for a simple answer to all the struggles for a better understanding of service quality that gives researchers no rest. Smart alecks make use of this situation and do not hesitate to present their panaceas that do away with all complexity and reduce it to a simple question – one-dimensional, all-embracing, omnipotent. If the world would only be that simple.

In fact, there is nothing like an objective quality because there is also nothing like an objective reality so the search for a magic formula will be futile. Service is generated in the course of social interaction. Social situations and social action constitute social reality. At the end of the day, it is the perception of a service performance that decides over success and failure. Research that deals with quality must reconstruct this situation and face the complexity if it wants to be relevant.

Accordingly, there is no absolute service quality. Measuring service quality is largely different from measuring fever or the distance between two points. Quality like other latent variables is a theoretical construct that can be operationalized in different ways.

---

2   For this reason, we abstain from a detailed definition of the elements of quality. There are several attempts to find the ultimate dimensions of quality and their contribution to a theoretical understanding shall not be disputed. For the purpose of practical research, however, it is necessary to define one's own concept of quality as an adequate reflection of the research question. Most important, this concept together with its operationalization has to be made explicit and understandable.

3   See section 4.2 on the actual meaning of objectivity in social research, which is different from its common understanding.

Depending on the context, the same service performance can be perceived differently. The situation becomes even more complicated because the actual service performance can fluctuate over time due to its dependency on insufficiently standardized human behaviour. Despite extensive training, only robots would provide a consistent but at the same time also rather questionable service quality. After all, it is the human touch that ultimately determines service quality.

As much as a specific service performance at a certain time and in a particular environment will affect a consumer and make him happy or unhappy, satisfied or frustrated, from a statistical research perspective, this is not particularly relevant for a judgement of the overall quality of a service provider. While every case – and critical cases in particular[4] – can help to find weaknesses and inconsistencies in processes, these individual cases say little about general service quality. Descriptive case studies on one hand and hypotheses testing representative studies on the other are substantially different approaches. Depending on the research question, both are legitimate approaches that can supplement one another and thus provide a more comprehensive understanding.

Analyzing quality focuses eventually on the questions of who is best and where does a service provider stand in relation to the competition. It is about customer satisfaction and perhaps even customer loyalty on one hand and the balance sheet on the other. The question deals with many unknowns and no objective solution. Instead, the answer is based on the specific perspective of the stakeholders and their perception.

From the perspective of a service provider, the focus must be on meeting the customers' demand. Unless one wants to get lost in expensive and potentially hazardous trials and errors, the essential question is what potential customers actually expect and how these expectations can best be met. Theoretical models about elements of service quality can provide guidance but cannot substitute an empirical analysis. The subsequent step must be to analyze to what extent the actual service offer matches customer demand. Focusing on the future, this leads to the question of how the business can be shaped in the sense of service innovations that create demand and offer a competitive edge.

Consumer organizations usually go a different way when they follow the concept of the homo economicus[5] and define the weights of the quality criteria based on supposed expert knowledge. They assume to some extent the role of a nanny of consumers – instead of trying to find out what consumers expect, they presume to know well what is best for consumers and define what they should expect. This is a major difference between the perspectives of service providers and consumer organizations.

The categories of service quality that consumer organizations choose and the weights that eventually affect an overall rating or quality index – like very good, good, satisfactory or poor – may well be different from the evaluative system that underlies the much less formalized but ultimately decisive judgements of consumers. Some rigid readers of consumer magazines like to interpret such discrepancies as proof that a consumer organization has actually no clue of what they talk about and what is 'really' important. But in fact, the discrepancies are nothing but the result of a different perspective of the potential reality, which is absolutely justified provided – and this is the crucial point –

---

4   See also section 6.6 on critical incident technique.

5   The homo economicus or economic human is a theoretical concept of humans as rational actors who have sufficient information and clearly defined targets to make rational decisions that maximize benefits, which can be either utility or profit – depending on perspective.

the approach is made intersubjectively understandable. As long as the readers of the results are in a position to understand how the testers arrived at their findings, it is at the discretion of the readers to decide if they want to accept them or not.

This explication of decisions along the research process is essential and good scientific research practice. It does not only apply to research undertaken by consumer organizations who are always at risk of being challenged in court over their methods and results but to *all* research. It is the only way to deal with the complexity of this world in general and quality in particular.

3.2 Experience and Reality

Facing so much complexity and missing the ultimate authority that defines something like an 'objective' reality, one may be tempted to give up. Seasoned bosses may even claim that their entrepreneurial instinct and their gut feelings are a better approach than any expensive research. But as much as personal experience determines social behaviour and expectations, this experience is rather unsuitable to scrutinize reality. Personal experience deals with potential reality in a very subjective manner. So what is perceived as 'reality' is not the result of 'neutral' perception but a very personal aspect of reality that creates experience. That means that the world as people perceive it is not homogeneous. Depending on the personal context, the perception of the world establishes specific areas of meaning that are shared with others only partially.

Obviously, we are not dealing with an 'objective' world but experience the world in a very subjective manner. Subjective experience constitutes this specific reality and determines the framework for its perception. Nevertheless, we are able to communicate and understand one another to a large extent because everybody is borne into a society that has already established some meaning and common sense. Furthermore, as part of communication we negotiate a shared social reality. Yet, some misunderstandings will occur and prove that there is still latitude for subjective interpretations. And the more we leave this area of common sense and enter into specialized – for example professional or scientific – areas the more difficult the mutual understanding will become.

In everyday life, such misunderstandings do not cause major problems. However, research has to go a step further. Research accumulates knowledge that is accepted as valid and makes sound prognoses and decisions possible. Business decisions do not allow for a mumbled apology – so sorry, I misunderstood – when thousands or millions of dollars are at stake. Practical research is much more than a non-committal talk with some vague understanding of quality as something that can be good or bad. Practical research that deals with quality demands for quality itself if it wants to provide a reliable and valid base for management decisions.

Research focuses on very specific and necessarily clearly defined questions. Dealing with these questions will constitute a particular reality that can best be experienced using specific receptors. Since services are the result of social interaction, the methods of empirical social research are the obvious choice when tackling questions related to the quality of services. Tackling social behaviour and social interaction, methods like interviews, observations, content analyses and the like reflect the human senses. Nevertheless, the research questions as well as the way that these senses are utilized are not the same as in day-to-day life.

Putting questions, observing behaviour, interpreting spoken or written words are common everyday activities when trying to develop understanding and gaining experience but this is substantially different from scientific perception, understanding and experience. Scientific interviews have little in common with casual talks. Reading the newspaper is different from scientific content analysis. Looking at people in whatever situation is no scientific observation. Scientific research follows specific patterns that are not derived from everyday behaviour but agreed by the scientific community because they have proven to be successful in the scientific discourse.

Considering that scientific experience is different from day-to-day experience, it is obvious that both use a different language. An interview in social research means something different from a journalistic or job interview. And a question as part of a social scientific interview is different from a question in daily life. This distinction between scientific and everyday perception (and the language that represents it) is so important because it is a common pest in practical social research that someone who is able to use his senses in everyday interaction is quickly inclined to be convinced of his expertise in empirical research.

Science as a paradigm provides a system of methodological rules that determines the research process and defines what meets scientific standards. Nevertheless, these processes will neither target at nor result in an ultimate reality. On the contrary, scientific paradigms leave room for different perspectives and even encourage them because different perspectives that follow the same paradigm constitute a broader view of reality that becomes more independent from a specific approach and hence more relevant for decision-making. Providing a relevant basis for management decisions – that is exactly what practical research is all about.

3.3 Process and Decisions

It is essential to understand research as a complex and interrelated process comprising several steps and many explicit and implicit decisions that have a substantial impact on its outcome. Unfortunately, the reality of practical research looks often different. Many studies start with some diffuse idea to do something about customer satisfaction. Perhaps there is a dip in the turnover and the boss has asked for a 'study'. The quality manager will understand immediately – and jumps without any further consideration on the decision to do some interviews. The questions are already on the manager's mind: how satisfied are you with our service? Please tick on a scale from 1 = unsatisfied to 7 = very satisfied. Once he has piled up a number of interviews that he deems representative, he will calculate an arithmetic mean and if the result confirms what was anyway expected, everybody will be satisfied. You see, the boss will say and his words will serve as ultimate proof of validity. Everybody will be happy but in fact, the better conclusion would have been the decision to scrap this so-called study. This kind of layman research is nothing but a waste of resources, which becomes even more critical if it results in management decisions.

The implicit understanding behind such a naive approach to research is the usually subconscious assumption that it would be possible to render reality completely, realistically and unbiased. It is the idea of an universal empiricism that makes it possible to optimize this epistemological process. One would just have to use the best method in order to get something like a perfect reflection of a complex reality. This sounds enticing but unfortunately, such approach quickly reaches its limits. In fact, things are more difficult.

The shortcomings of this cognitive approach can best be explained when thinking of the question of how one's hometown can be described in the most complete and most detailed manner. One may consider a map, a video, aerial photography, statistical data, a list of all inhabitants, the yellow pages, a history of the town, answers from tourists to the question what they like most and recommend to other visitors or perhaps something else. In any case, the answer to the question what would best describe the town is always the same: it depends. And the same applies to a study that shall deal with, let's say, the quality of a company's after-sales service. What provides the best answer? Is it the availability of the customer service in terms of opening hours or the number of staff or rather the waiting time? Perhaps the customers' responses to a question about their satisfaction with the service? The share of customers who would recommend this service provider to their friends? Or is it the number of times that customers have to call until their problems are fixed at last? Once again: it depends.

Obviously, different approaches deliver different answers, which would be better described as different aspects of reality. There is no 'best' answer. The search for 'the' reality is futile. Reality is a matter of perspective and research interest. Accordingly, the very point is not which research approach is best but which one is adequate and most appropriate in the context of the research interest. Ideally, various approaches are combined in order to cope with the complexity of the underlying research question.

One must realize that contrary to the ideal world of mathematics, empirical assertions are always related to a specific experience of reality. As a consequence, what is usually described as research methods are actually no methods in the sense of tools that deliver results that are free of any value judgement. Instead, the so-called methods can better be described as models – images that reflect a certain epistemological interest and can be more or less appropriate in this respect. Models do not only arrange a complex world more clearly, they also reduce the informational content, which is not a question of right or wrong but can only be judged in terms of appropriateness in relation to the research interest. So the choice of a certain approach to empirical research must be a conscious decision as part of the research process. One must be aware of the practical and epistemological strengths and weaknesses of that specific model. Nevertheless, it is common to use the term 'method' instead of 'model'. However, we use both terms synonymously while being well aware of the methodological implications.[6]

The epistemological process that research represents can be split into three phases: (1) the context of discovery; (2) the context of justification, which is also called context of analysis; and (3) the context of utilization and effects.[7] This is not only a theoretical distinction but has concrete consequences for the practical research process.

The initial context of discovery provides the background of a project in terms of the research question and the underlying economical, social or political problem. This is the groundwork of any study. Usually, some literature studies will be required, checking for example how others have defined the concept of quality or to see if there are perhaps relevant studies that can serve as a template for this project and eventually allow a

---

6   See also section 4.1 for further discussions of the difference between methods and models.

7   This distinction of different contexts of research goes back to physicist and philosopher Hans Reichenbach (1891–1953). The following description of the research process assumes a hypothesis testing approach. It will be slightly different in case of a purely descriptive study.

comparison of the results. Breaking new ground may even make it necessary to first engage in some pilot studies in order to have sufficient background knowledge to deal with a certain research question.

In the course of this initial phase of a study, the problem that was the starting point of the project will be specified further and converted into a clearly defined research question. This defines the environment and framework of the research project.

So far, it is no issue what methods will later be used for data collection and analysis. It is solely about a research question and its theoretical and practical context. 'Doing interviews with customers' does not constitute a research question. However, 'analyzing determining factors of customer satisfaction of clients of the inland revenue authority of Singapore and exploring potentials for improvement' establishes a research question that will be specified further in the course of the study.

In fact, many research projects fail at this early stage. The consultant is told to do some research and nonchalantly delivers his standard concept that hardly provides answers to the problems the client is facing. That proves why it is so important to clearly define the research question and choose advisers carefully. Good consultants and considerate researchers will always sit together with their clients and jointly develop a clear and comprehensive research question. This is an essential part of any project. A clear understanding and definition of the research question is prerequisite for the following stages of the research process.

The second phase is the context of justification that deals with the underlying methodological assumptions and requires decisions on methods and procedures that eventually define the context in which the results can claim validity. As a first step, the research question is specified by means of hypotheses. Furthermore, the statistical population to which the results can later be related will be defined.

The researcher will then decide which method of data collection is deemed appropriate. This decision has to consider not only the research question but also practical feasibility as well as available resources. Is a one-time study or a trend analysis over a certain period more appropriate? Should the project be designed as a representative study or as a case study? This is closely linked to the question of how many cases should make up the sample and how should they be selected. Which empirical research method is deemed most appropriate? Interviews, observations, experiments, content analysis, what else? Or maybe a combination of various methods? It is important to be aware that the decision to use a specific method of data collection specifies a certain sector of potential reality. Interviews constitute a different aspect of reality compared to a content analysis or observations and often it is only the combination of various approaches that may appropriately reconstruct a sufficiently complete part of the potential reality. The world is complex and so are the empirical research methods.

Depending on the decision on the methods of data collection, the research instruments have to be developed – which may be questionnaires, observation records, a system of content analytic categories or other instruments – and their practicability has to be tested. Such pretests with a limited number of cases preceding the actual data collection can provide important information about the practicality, comprehensibility and logic of the research instruments and help to improve the reliability and validity of the data. The more complex a study is the more important it is that the research instruments undergo a pretest that helps to avoid expensive flaws.

A crucial part of the construction of the research instruments is the operationalization of the theoretical concept. Since most variables like customer satisfaction, friendliness or competence are latent variables that cannot be measured directly, one or several empirically observable manifest variables and their interrelations have to be identified as indicators of the theoretical constructs. For example, the number of customer service contacts until a problem is finally resolved could be used as operationalization of competence. But it would be a rather simple understanding that may not explain the more complex theoretical construct of competence sufficiently. Obviously, an adequate operationalization is a crucial step in the research process because it establishes the link between the theoretical concept and the empirical world.[8]

In most cases it will not be possible to analyze the complete statistical population. It is not only for practical reasons but also a matter of research economy that speaks against an analysis of the total population. Instead, one will select a representative sample from which the information about the statistical population is inferred.[9] For this purpose the sampling procedure has to be defined. This is an important step of the research process that impacts on the reliability and validity of the data and subsequently the research results. Nevertheless, the reality of practical research often looks different when the basics of random sampling are simply ignored and nobody cares what rationale – if any at all – is underlying the selection of the participants in a study. It is easily forgotten that it is not the number of cases that decides the validity of generalizations of sample data but the randomness of their selection in conjunction with the number of cases. A biased sample – regardless of how large it is – will not deliver valid results.

Once the framework is defined, the research instruments are developed and tested and the sample is drawn, the fieldwork begins with the actual data collection. The data that have been recorded as answers to questions, entries into an observation protocol or by any other means will then be processed for further analyses. They will be checked with regard to obvious mistakes and contradictions and create the basis for the statistical analysis. Depending on the research question as well as the level of measurement, appropriate statistical models will be chosen for the test of the hypotheses that were developed as further specifications of the research question. At the end of this phase stand the statistical results and their interpretation in the context of the research question and design. But the research process is not yet at its end.

As nice as it is to have some research results at last, they will only become relevant when they are transferred to the real world where they have an impact on actual decisions and can contribute to the solution of the problems that marked the start of the research project. This is meant with the context of utilization and effects. It is an important aspect of relevance that is usually realized through a presentation or publication that may have a direct impact on management decisions and consumer behaviour or could be the basis for further studies. Depending on the respective target audience, different methods of publication will be required in order to ensure relevance of the study and its results.

In view of this complex process, every study demands an elaborated research design as adequate realization of the research question within a defined theoretical framework and under consideration of limited resources. Research costs time and money. It is the objective of an elaborated research design to optimize the research approach with regard to its adequacy on one hand and limited resources on the other.

---

8   See section 4.1 on the logic of measurement and 4.7 on indicators.

9   See Chapter 5 on samples and representativeness.

Another important aspect of the context of utilization and effects must be considered. Research aims at a *reduction* of complexity. Nobody is interested in the detailed information that is collected in the course of a study. Even for the researcher these individual data are just a means to an end. The ultimate objective of research is to reduce the vast complexity to substantial (and substantiated) conclusions. For this purpose, the comprehensive individual data or 'facts' and their interrelations that are recorded in the course of the data collection phase have to be structured and reduced to knowledge and rules that are to the point and – this is particularly important in applied research – relevant for future behaviour and decisions. Studies that do not provoke more than making the readers shrug their shoulders and coax a disinterested 'so what?' out of them are not worth the time and money that was spent.

In any case, it is obvious that the dependence of research results on the underlying research design makes it absolutely essential that the theoretical and methodical framework of a study is disclosed. Without providing information about this context, the recipients of research results would not be in a position to develop an adequate understanding and to judge their relevance. Nevertheless, business presentations usually abstain from providing such information when reporting the results of the latest study. The management does not want to waste time on that kind of information. Please get to the point. And it does not look better when newspapers or magazines report on the results of the latest trailblazing studies. Perhaps the journalists have some subtle feeling that adding this essential context information would immediately disqualify many supposed studies. Hence, most newspaper articles provide at best the number of cases that were analyzed. The more the better. Because with the number of cases the trust in the representativeness of the study will grow – who cares that this is a misconception? After all, even the weirdest studies find their audience as long as they meet demand.

A well thought-out methodology in conjunction with an elaborated research design is not academic luxury but a matter of research economy. It ensures a deliberate and appropriate use of the limited resources and makes it possible to discuss the results and their relevance for future decisions and action.

One more important point. Whatever the decisions are and regardless of how the research design will eventually look, the basics of research ethics have to be considered because service and related research deal with people. Social research does not take place in a vacuum but affects the social environment. It goes without saying that testing the service of safety and security must not put people at risk. Testing medical services must not expose people to health risks. And especially in social research, confidentiality and data protection are essential. Researchers assume responsibility for the participants in their research work. Responding to a questionnaire means trust in the researcher that the information including personal details will not be abused. The customary promise that all information will be kept strictly confidential and will only be used for scientific research purposes must not be an empty phrase but must be a commitment that guides the research process. The researcher cannot escape this responsibility. After all, any abuse of the trust that respondents put into a research project as well as the researcher will spoil future research.

It is not simply chance or fate that more and more people refuse to participate in empirical research projects. It is rather the result of studies that do not deserve this name. Nobody wants the mailbox flooded with spam after having replied innocently to a questionnaire. Research ethics demand honesty and integrity of the researcher.

3.4 Research Management

Research is an inherent part of service. It is indispensable for the understanding and assessment of service performance. As much as a personal impression can be important and helpful in a specific case, it cannot substitute empirical research. Only a systematic analysis of service performance and customer feedback will ensure that customer expectations are met and a high service standard is maintained. This requires a management approach that understands and appreciates research as a driving force of the business.

Research is not a one-time affair but a continuous process that can only claim relevance if essential standards are met. Amateurish surveys that are performed hectically at the eleventh hour just in order to meet ISO requirements before an audit for the renewal of a quality management certificate takes place fulfil an alibi function at best. Also so-called ad hoc projects that are quickly initiated whenever the management stumbles across a problem but neither coordinated nor communicated will result in little but inefficiency and confusion. Successful organizations will quickly develop a healthy natural immunity against such uncoordinated research activities and will simply not accept the results while others may be led astray by research results that hardly deserve this term.

The situation does not become better if research is done individually in specific departments or subsidiaries and perhaps even in competition to one another. Such scattered research activities without a company-wide coordination will almost inevitably reduce the epistemological value of quality research. It will not only result in an inconsistent methodology with limited comparability of data but also in higher research costs because of avoidable double work. Since most departments will not have qualified researchers with the necessary know-how, this kind of research will be done on the side and come along with all kind of methodological and methodical dubiousness. It is an expensive approach to the measurement of quality with limited practical value.

Research management is required. Research management understands quality research not as an occasional addendum to service performance but as a continuous and structured process that covers all elements of the business. It is a centralized function that requires a thorough understanding of the methodology and methods of empirical research on one hand and comprehensive knowledge of the business processes on the other. Neither the scientist in the ivory tower nor the practitioners with rolled-up sleeves will handle this task successfully. Instead, a scientifically sound approach in conjunction with an elementary understanding of the business is vital for quality research that is eventually relevant to management decisions and consumer behaviour.

An established research management understands quality research not as selective measure but as a continuous and comprehensive approach that is an integral part of the business processes. This requires a systematic review of the demand for analyses that goes beyond the measurement of quality and customer satisfaction and covers – based on the chosen theoretical model of service quality – also related areas like business-to-business relations as well as the competitive environment. Research management is a proactive approach to quality research that provides information in anticipation of management requirements.

Quality research does not only deal with data that are collected through surveys. In fact, companies usually sit on a wealth of information about their service performance that could be used for related analyses. Many important data are by-products of the business processes and thus directly or indirectly available in the systems. They can be made accessible through interfaces, which means that the business systems must consider research aspects in order to avoid double work and inconsistencies. Professional business software is usually prepared for this requirement but many – especially smaller – businesses operate with homespun IT solutions that lack the necessary access to relevant data for research purposes.

Regardless of the source of data, the crucial criterion of practical research is relevance. After all, practical research is not done in an ivory tower but deals with a very concrete situation. Relevant research results affect social action like management decisions or consumer behaviour. This requires a research design that is considered adequate in the context of the research question as well as the theoretical approach and delivers reliable and valid results. Moreover, it is vital to communicate the research results in order to achieve relevance. Top secret research results or results that lack contact to the 'real world' cannot develop the necessary impact on social action and remain largely irrelevant.

Communicating research results and their methodological context is prerequisite for the acceptance of related management decisions and contributes to the development of a research culture that provides the basis for business intelligence as well as competitive intelligence as tools to recognize threats and opportunities at an early stage.[10] Where practical quality research follows this understanding of relevance it is not only essential for marketing strategies and general management decisions but contributes also to risk management. It follows Machiavelli's basic approach to risk management highlighting that 'when the evils that arise have been foreseen (which it is only given to a wise man to see), they can be quickly redressed, but when, through not having been foreseen, they have been permitted to grow in a way that every one can see them, there is no longer a remedy' (Machiavelli 1532: Chapter III). An organization that is guided by an effective research management and inspired with a research culture is likely to develop the necessary intelligence that provides a market advantage.

Nevertheless, a well-established research management will also have to cope with limited resources. Hence it is one of its essential functions to ensure an effective cost management and ultimately cost efficiency. Substantial costs for research are only justified if the results contribute to an improvement of the company result by means of better service. Spending money on alibi research or methodologically inadequate and thus meaningless results would be a waste of resources. Only research that meets essential methodological standards has the power to contribute to a better understanding of a company's service performance showing opportunities for a strengthening of the market position. In view of the costs, research has to prove its relevance for the future of a business.

This puts professional quality research in a pivotal position. Not every business will be able to hire a researcher and the idea of just compiling some questions into a questionnaire may be enticing – after all, what is so special about surveys? One can find the result of such a naive approach to quality research on many websites. These so-called surveys are not only a nuisance for every consumer, they also spoil the field for those studies that meet scientific standards. So wherever the necessary understanding of empirical research is lacking, it is the better approach to gain it through cooperation with research institutes,

---

10   Business and competitive intelligence are complementary approaches to a better understanding of the situation of a company. While business intelligence follows more an introspective view of the business, competitive analysis focuses on external observation.

reputable consultants or universities. This may look expensive at the first glance but it is well-invested money. Besides, not all questions require comprehensive studies.

Instead of an encyclopedic questionnaire it may be sufficient to add a few questions to an omnibus survey of a reputable professional research institute that provides the necessary advice. An omnibus survey can reduce costs because it comprises a wide variety of subjects from various participants. The answers to the specific questions are proprietary content whereas common demographic data are shared. The costs of participation depend usually on the number and complexity of the questions that are added to the omnibus. Eventually, there may not be so many questions once the ballast of all the nice-to-have topics is thrown overboard.

An omnibus survey is just one possibility to control the costs of quality research. There are many others. The very point is, however, that while the available resources set limits, the final decision on the research approach must be guided by the research question and the underlying theoretical concept.

Going through a critical evaluation of costs and benefits at the end of every research project will contribute to the cost efficiency of future projects. It is a learning process that deals with the methodology and methods of research in the context of related published research. It does not only contribute to an efficient utilization of resources. Such open discourse will also create a research culture that surely benefits future projects.

In any case, a research management that links up practical research and business processes and meets vital research criteria can add substantial value to a business and strengthens its market position. Best of all, it creates an environment that is supportive to service quality.

4 *Methodology*

When a manager presents his bosses the latest quality study, he will not miss the opportunity to brag a little. Our methodology was a questionnaire, he says and nods with an important look because methodology sounds so much better than method. He can almost be sure that his bosses will be impressed. A good man, they will say and keep it in mind for the next salary review – until someone speaks up timidly and spoils the show: no, interviews or other approaches to empirical research are methods – or to be even more precise, models. Methodology, on the other hand, is the systematic study and analysis of the theory behind methods.

It is a bit like the common mess-up of technique and technology. Unfortunately, the words technique or method lack all glamour. They sound like recipes of the latest how-to guide. Techniques and methods are craft whereas technology and methodology stand for art. The word 'method' refers back to Greek '*methodos*', which is a combination of '*meta*' meaning 'higher' or 'beyond' and '*hodos*' denoting 'way'. Hence, '*methodos*' is the 'pursuit of knowledge'. In Middle English this turned into a rather profane 'prescribed medical treatment for a disease'. But the simple suffix '*ology*' can lift the word to higher spheres. An '*ology*' describes a branch of science. That sounds more impressive – and denotes the reflection on the theory behind the methods.

Methodology is an essential part of the philosophy of science, which deals with the framework, conditions, rules, methods and targets of gaining knowledge. In particular, methodology deals with the development of theories and hypotheses as well as their examination with special focus on the collection of empirical data and their processing. The target is to reduce the complex information and find answers to the research question. In a nutshell, methodology can be described as meta-science of empirical research methods. It scrutinizes their framework and the assumptions behind the methods dealing with their principles and rationale. This rather philosophical discourse is indeed essential for empirical research because it establishes the necessary background for the application of the methods. Without a sound methodological understanding, research methods would actually be reduced to simple recipes – with a stale aftertaste.

This chapter will deal with several essential facets of methodology. A description of the epistemological concept of measurement will be the starting point. Before we move on from there, we'll discuss some common methodological misunderstandings that can easily spoil an appropriate research approach. Then we look at essential quality criteria of research and discuss the issue of reactivity, which refers to the manifold effects of the research situation on the results.

Anyone who has done practical research will know how difficult it can be to find people who are prepared to join a study. Sometimes some decent coaxing may be required. And if that is not successful, we have to deal with the problem of missing data.

It is the crux of social research that quality, customer satisfaction and other essential topics are theoretical constructs that cannot be observed directly. So in order to get to the heart of an issue, the researcher has to identify manifest variables that can serve as an indicator for these latent concepts. This leads further to the construction of indexes and key figures.

The very question of quality research is where do I stand in comparison to the competition? Rankings that compare with others may provide an answer. The ultimate target is to stay on top. And this not only at a certain point in time but for a long time. Longitudinal studies can analyze the development. Furthermore, international business deals with different cultures, which affects the comparability of research results. The focus is on the reconstruction of meaning.

A vast variety of topics will be discussed in this chapter but it is crucial to develop critical awareness for these basic research issues because they have an impact on every study. Even if methodology has been described as the science behind the methods, these topics are no dull theory but an indispensable and crucial element of empirical research. What may sound like dry stuff is actually closely related to real life.

4.1 Measurement

Empirical research aims at a reduction of complexity. It is an attempt to structure the complex empirical world from a specific perspective with the aim of finding answers to questions and eventually making the right decisions. So we take off for the fountain of knowledge and harass hundreds or even thousands of people with questionnaires, record our observations, analyze all kind of documents or develop highly elaborated experimental designs. And when the data collection is completed at last we find ourselves with a huge amount of information. 'Oops!' one may be inclined to say and rubs one's eyes. Because what has started as an attempt to *reduce* complexity has actually *multiplied* the available information.

Fortunately, our researcher is a dedicated quality manager and will not give up. So he starts reading hundreds of questionnaires in an attempt to understand all the information. It does not take long until his head is spinning. He has read dozens of questionnaires but instead of knowing more he cannot even answer simple questions like what impact age has on the judgement of customer service performance or how the educational level is related to the capability of handling the service of a ticket vending machine.

Apparently, there is an intellectual barrier when dealing with the high complexity of research data. The human brain is not made to digest and structure a huge amount of data in a systematic way. Reading and digesting questionnaires or other research documents does not really help to draw reliable and valid conclusions. One may develop some ideas but these will be rather biased and somebody else who reads the same questionnaires would probably come to different conclusions. Such results would be very unreliable and could hardly claim validity. So we better forget about trying to understand the complex world directly and look for other means that help to reduce the complexity of the pictured segment of the real world.

One possible way out of this dilemma is an epistemological detour through the numerical world where mathematics provides algorithms that help to structure and reduce complex information. For this purpose, it is prerequisite to translate our empirical observations into the numerical world. This process is known as measurement. In empirical research, measurement is the allocation of figures or symbols to empirical objects and their characteristics and relations according to specific rules. In other words: the process of measurement transforms observed parts of the empirical world into the numerical world. As a result, every element of the empirical world shall correspond to a figure in the numerical world. Provided it is possible to transform the elements of the observed empirical world appropriately into the numerical world, it is possible to reduce its complexity using mathematical algorithms, which are usually known as statistical methods – or better: statistical models.

We touched already earlier on the different functions and meaning of models and methods. While it is common in practical research to talk about statistical methods, one has to understand the different concepts behind these two terms. A method is something that is used to get from a defined starting point to a defined end. Regardless which method is used, the result will always be the same. The result is independent from the method that was applied. If the end is reached, it was the right method. Otherwise it was the wrong method.

Models are different from methods. A model is a picture of a clearly defined structure from a specific point of view. Depending on the underlying question one arrives at different pictures or models, which cannot be assessed as right or wrong but can only be judged according to their adequacy. At the same time, the specific perspective that has resulted in a certain model defines its limitations because models are limited to information that is relevant in the context of a specific research question. Accordingly, the use of a model is restricted to the information that it reflects. Trying to derive knowledge from a model that was made for different purposes will fail and result in artefacts. This is obvious when looking for example at a tourist map of a historic town, which provides a model for the sole purpose of guiding visitors to the places of interest. That's why it is normally not to scale and some roads may have been left out in the interest of keeping things simple. Trying to get information about exact distances from such map would most likely fail.

In analogy, this applies also to empirical research. Empirical research deals with information structures from a certain perspective. Data collection delivers a specific reality that is determined by the research interest and depending on the data collection process and subsequent statistical analysis. So it is more appropriate to refer to models instead of methods when talking about data collection and statistics. At this point, one may argue that mathematical statistics are a collection of methods. This is true as long as one stays in the world of mathematics. However, once mathematical methods are applied in empirical research their meaning is limited to the corresponding empirical world and they serve as models.

Of course, one can say that it doesn't matter if one talks about methods or models because it is common practice to refer to methods of empirical research as well as statistical methods. There is no objection – provided the methodological implications are understood and considered. However, looking at common practical research there is serious doubt if this is really the case because, too often, the terminology is not just some sloppiness but an expression of a lack of understanding of the nature of empirical research work. Instead of reflecting relevant decisions in the research process, it is not unusual to rely on mathematical algorithms without questioning their meaning or recognizing obvious nonsense and contradictions.

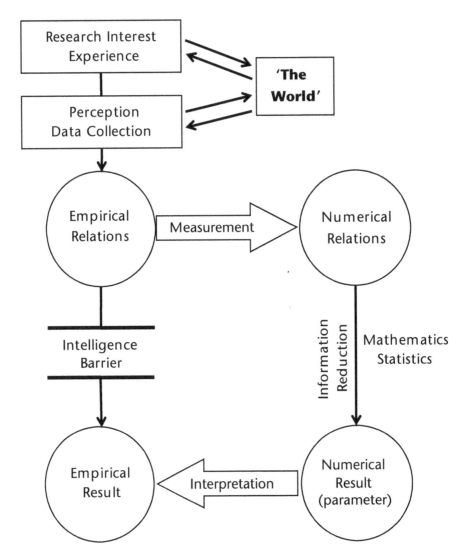

Figure 4.1   The process of measurement

Note: This figure is based on Kriz 1988: 56.

Ludwig Wittgenstein put it simply when he stated in his *Tractatus Logico-Philosophicus* (1922: propositions 6.2331–2): 'Calculation is not an experiment. Mathematics is a method of logic.' That is the very point. Only as much as mathematical operations correspond to reality, the mathematical logic provides an efficient way to deal with empirical observations. Figures as such have no meaning and no relevance. Accordingly, at the end of the statistical analysis the statistical parameters of the numerical world have to be translated back into assertions in the empirical world. This step is known as interpretation. Figure 4.1 summarizes the whole process from measurement to interpretation.

A genuine transformation of the empirical observations is an essential condition for the detour through the numerical world. That means that assertions in the numerical world are only valid if they are also valid in the empirical world. Such relation between related objects in the empirical and numerical world is the result of a homomorphic transformation. For example, every person has a certain age. But knowing the age, one cannot refer back to this specific person because several persons may have the same age.[1]

Provided the condition of homomorphism is fulfilled, we can resort to the numerical world of mathematics and statistics. The advantages of dealing with figures instead of the actual observations are obvious. The world of figures is unmistakable because the mathematical language and their symbols are clearly defined. Mathematical operations are explicit and objective and they can be reproduced. So contrary to normal language, mathematical symbols are not exposed to cultural influences. Furthermore, formal operations can be optimized with regard to certain criteria.

Of course, only those mathematical operations that correspond meaningfully to the empirical world are valid. It depends on the quality or scale type of the empirical information which numerical operations and statistical models are permissible. This is described as level of measurement whereby four types of scales are usually distinguished.

Nominal scales have the purpose of distinguishing between objects in the sense of equal or unequal. This applies for example to telephone numbers. Whether a telephone number is higher or lower does not provide any relevant information and the numerical difference between such numbers has no empirical meaning. The same applies to sex or religion. The only purpose of allocating a number to a certain faith in the course of statistical analysis is to distinguish it from other beliefs. Whether this number is higher or lower does not provide any meaningful information.

Only data that have ordinal scale level can be interpreted in the sense of better or worse, greater or smaller, higher or lower or in a similar manner. A typical example is the favourite Likert items that are hardly missing in any questionnaire: how would you rate your overall experience with our customer service? Please tick on a scale from 1 = very bad to 7 = very good. This reminds us of grades in the old school days and, indeed, the problems are the same. While it has become almost common practice to calculate an arithmetic mean, it still does not make much sense because the assumption of equal distances between the different scores is obviously questionable. However, this condition would have to be met in order to calculate an arithmetic mean.

Nominal and ordinal scales are also described as topological or qualitative scales. Metric or quantitative scales, on the other hand, comprise interval and ratio scales. Only at interval scale level can we also interpret sums and differences, which would be required in order to calculate the arithmetic mean. Temperature in degrees centigrade (°C) is a classical example for interval data. The distance between 0 and 10 degrees is the same as between 20 and 30 degrees. But 20 degrees is not twice as warm as 10 degrees. Such interpretation would only be permissible at ratio scale level. Age, distance or percentage are typical variables at ratio scale level. It makes sense to describe someone as twice as old as somebody else. And of course, one can rightfully ascertain if someone is of the same age or not, younger or older and how many years the difference in age is. In any case, the information that lower scale types provide is also covered at a higher level. Table 4.1 presents an overview of the different scale types as well as the

---

1   Relations that apply also the other way round are called isomorphic. For example, a passport number establishes an isomorphic relation. It is a unique number that applies only to one person. So a passport number is allocated to a certain person and knowing the passport number, one can determine the person. In social research there are hardly any isomorphic relations between empirical and numerical world.

defined relations, permissible transformations and interpretations together with some empirical and statistical examples.

What looks pretty much straightforward can actually be a little tricky. Because it is not always obvious at first glance which level of measurement can rightfully be assumed. Take for example the blood pressure that may go up when dealing with the customer service of some companies. Of course, blood pressure can be measured at ratio scale level. However, only medical experts will be interested in the blood pressure as such whereas in social or market research it could, for example, be an indicator of stress. Suddenly the level of measurement looks different. Now the blood pressure can only be interpreted at ordinal level – the higher the blood pressure the higher the stress level.

Or take another example. No doubt, income can be measured at ratio level and a statement such as person A earns twice as much as person B makes sense as long as it is about nothing but money. Understandably, most respondents to questionnaires are not willing to provide the exact amount of their income. And in most cases, such detailed answers would not even be required. That's why questionnaires usually provide income groups that offer some anonymity and help to overcome the natural reluctance to provide such personal and confidential data.[2] The grouping has, however, an impact on the level of measurement. Now, what could be the ideal of ratio scaled data meets only ordinal level. However, what looks like a downgrading does actually not much harm because contrary to the inland revenue authority, the social researcher is usually not interested in the exact amount but uses income as an indicator of, for example, social status – which would be measured at ordinal level anyway.

Table 4.1   Levels of measurement

Scale Types	Nominal Scale	Ordinal Scale	Interval Scale	Ratio Scale
Other descriptions	topological scales 'qualitative'		metric scales 'quantitative'	
Defined relations	$= \neq$	$= \neq$ $< >$	$= \neq$ $< >$ $+ -$	$= \neq$ $< >$ $+ -$ $\times \div$
Admissible transformations	one to one	monotonic	positive linear $x' = bx + a$ (with $b \neq 0$)	$x' = bx$ (with $b \neq 0$)
Admissible interpretations	equal – unequal	smaller – bigger	differences (intervals) have an empirical meaning	fractions (ratios) have an empirical meaning
Examples	Sex, religion, citizenship; Mode	Rankings (e.g. Likert scales), marks (school); Median	Temperature in °C; Arithmetic Mean	Age, distance, percentage; Geometric Mean

---

2   Nevertheless, personal or family income is probably one of the most biased items in a questionnaire.

As a matter of fact, social research hardly produces any data that goes beyond topological scales – and quality research in the service sector is no exception. The very point is that the level of measurement decides on the statistical models that can be used meaningfully. Table 4.1 shows the effect of the level of measurement with regard to parameters of central tendency. While a simple arithmetic mean requires at least data at interval scale level, at ordinal level only the median – the value that separates the higher half of a sample or population from the lower half – can be interpreted in a meaningful way. At nominal scale, however, the only meaningful parameter of central tendency is the mode denoting the value(s) that appear most frequently. We'll see in the following chapters that, in social research, the limited level of measurement of empirical data restricts the statistical analysis quite substantially because most complex statistical models require metric data.

Many researchers misunderstand this situation as an invitation to a very generous interpretation of the level of measurement of their data and simply do away with all scruples. The common but nevertheless inappropriate practice of interpreting ordinal measurements as interval data has already been mentioned. Equal distances between the items on the ordinal scale are simply assumed whereby it remains in the dark which empirical meaning the interim values between the items actually have. Who will really question the meaning of the results? After all, the mathematical algorithms will produce some figures that always allow a generous interpretation. Every weird result will find its believers as long as it meets the demand of its recipients. But that is not exactly the idea of empirical research. Measurement and research results that are based on inappropriate assumptions will lead to invalid interpretations and conclusions. In other words: GIGO – garbage in, garbage out.

No wonder that such inappropriate use of statistical models often goes hand in hand with a lack of transparency in the research process. As a result, recipients have no chance to take a deeper look into the genesis of the results. Instead of facing the scientific discourse and making relevant decisions in the process of measurement and statistical analysis understandable, the recipients of the results are deprived of background information and have only the choice to believe the results – or not. This assigns another meaning to GIGO: garbage in, gospel out.

Research is a process and the outcome depends on assumptions and decisions along this process. That makes it so essential that recipients of research results can understand the context from which the results have developed. Measurement is not an end in itself. Only when basic requirements are met does the knowledge at the end of the research process become meaningful and claim relevance for decision-making. That should be kept in mind when reading the dictum at the facade of the Social Research Building of the honourable University of Chicago: 'If you cannot measure, your knowledge is meagre and unsatisfactory'.[3] Perhaps, one should have added that while no measurement may be meagre and unsatisfactory, meaningless measurement is useless.

---

3   This is an abridged version of a statement by Irish-born British physicist William Thomson, First Baron Kelvin (1824–1907) in his lecture on 'Electrical Units of Measurement' (3 May 1883): 'I often say that when you can measure what you are speaking about, and express it in numbers, you know something about it; but when you cannot express it in numbers, your knowledge is of a meagre and unsatisfactory kind; it may be the beginning of knowledge, but you have scarcely, in your thoughts, advanced to the stage of science, whatever the matter may be.' See Sir Thomson 1889–91: Vol. I, 73.

4.2 Quality and Quantity

The collection and analysis of data in empirical research projects is often marred by a peculiar polarity of quality and quantity. There is the category of qualitative methods on one hand and quantitative methods on the other. Quality and quantity – that is a dichotomy that runs through literature as well as the common methodological and epistemological understanding of market and social research and causes confusion time and again. If these were just two names that described different methodological concepts, one could simply take it as slightly misleading labels. But unfortunately, this contrast obstructs the view of the essential.

'Quality' derives from Latin '*qualitas*' meaning 'of what kind' something is in the sense of its characteristics and condition. 'Quantity' has its origin in Latin '*quantitas*', which means 'how much' or 'how great' and refers to the greatness or extent of something. It is common to use quantity and quality in close analogy with objectivity and subjectivity. Accordingly, quantitative methods claim objectivity whereas qualitative methods come along with the stigma of subjectivity. It is the latent idea that objective and quantitative methods present the world as it is whereas subjective and qualitative methods are influenced by emotions, feelings, culture, experience, expectations and similar supposed misperceptions. Furthermore, quantity is usually related to figures that open the door to the precise and unerring world of mathematics whereas qualitative methods lack this supposed accuracy. Instead, they come along with the rather doubtful reputation of purely personal impressions.

The contrast between quantity and quality is great enough to invite a number of more or less helpful aphorisms. A German proverb claims that 'Quantität ist nicht gleich Qualität' [quantity is never the same as quality] and Seneca highlights that 'it is quality, rather than quantity, that matters'[4] although others will claim that size doesn't matter. And then there are some smart people who put on a knowing look and point at Friedrich Engels' *Dialectics of Nature* (1925) and 'the law of the transformation of quantity into quality and vice versa'. Eventually, everybody is puzzled and wondering what is behind. Indeed, the relation between quantity and quality is somehow irritating and what looks so simple and logical at first glance turns out to be rather misleading when scrutinized. So it is worthwhile having a closer look.

Qualitative research is often described as the collection and analysis of non-standardized data. In other words, the researcher abstains from formalizing the observed structures. In the terminology of the process of measurement, this means that the researcher abstains from converting the observed empirical relations into numerical relations that will eventually be analyzed further by means of statistics. Following this understanding, the encoding of answers to open questions in an interview or the categorization of unstructured observations of social behaviour and their subsequent statistical analysis and interpretation of the parameters would be examples for quantitative research. In contrast, abstaining from 'quantification' and assessing the answers or observations in an intuitive or hermeneutic manner would be understood as qualitative research. So quantitative and qualitative methods are two different epistemological roads to knowledge that differ in their degree of formalization and standardization.

---

4   Lucius Annaeus Seneca (about 4 BC–65 AD) was a Roman philosopher, statesman and one of the most read writers of his time. The quote is part of his Moral Epistles.

One may ask, which road is the right one or at least superior to the other one. It is a question that has sparked off complex debates about the relation between qualitative and quantitative methods. Advocates of quantitative methods like to accuse qualitative methods of being unscientific, subjective and arbitrary because of their lack of standardization. Furthermore, they claim that the necessary efforts of qualitative research will hardly allow representativeness. On the other hand, proponents of qualitative research highlight the particular contribution of hermeneutics to a better understanding of social behaviour.[5]

Qualitative – and that often means casuistic[6] – methods extend the perspective to areas that are hardly accessible with standardized research methods. In fact, there are a number of partly new and successful approaches under names like narrative interview, qualitative content analysis, method of thinking aloud and others that have proven their potential in some research areas where classical methods would hardly arrive at such deep insight. Contrary to the nomothetic approach of quantitative research that targets 'ordinary' or average situations and tries to develop general laws, qualitative research follows an idiographic approach that focuses at specific – possibly unique or extreme – situations in an interpretative and reconstructing manner.

One may be wondering why some dispute could develop around the question if quantitative or qualitative methods are 'better' or contribute more to the understanding of social phenomena. There is no doubt that both approaches complement one another very well. So both proponents have a valid point and, nevertheless, the answer to this dilemma can once again not be found somewhere in the middle but only at a different level. The very point is neither quality nor quantity but relevance. The crucial question is what the relevant dimensions of the research subject are. The number of variables and parameters that can describe a research subject is actually infinite. At the same time, the theory that is underlying a research project will deal with a limited number of variables, which are deemed pertinent and claim relevance. Without a thorough discussion of the aspect of relevance in the context of the research question, it will be impossible to develop a meaningful research design that would allow a decision on whether a formalized quantitative or a more hermeneutic qualitative approach or perhaps a combination of both is most appropriate.

In this context, it is important to realize the role of mathematics and statistics, which have the function of an intersubjectively understandable language for the description and processing of complex structures. It says, however, nothing about relevance. Instead, it is a mostly theoretical decision which elements of that structure are relevant. It is exactly this decision that will allow conclusions on which approach to the research topic is most appropriate.

It is also worthwhile to look at the supposed analogy of quantitative and qualitative with objective and subjective because this polarity is also not tenable. Instead of dealing with objectivity and subjectivity as a contrast, Niklas Luhmann's social systems theory links these labels to relevance and describes them as similar terms in different systems. Whatever is proven successful in the interactive system of the society is deemed objective

---

5   Hermeneutics is the science and art of interpretation and refers to an understanding of meaning out of itself. The term derives from the Greek word *'hermeneutikos'* meaning to interpret. It has its likely roots in Hermes, the Greek messenger of the gods.

6   Casuistry deals with case studies in an idiographic manner, which means looking at what is special and unique in an individual case instead of dealing with the 'ordinary' as a nomothetic approach would do.

because it is accepted and shared within the community. Accordingly, whatever is not in line with this objective system of the community but has proven successful only as part of the individual realization of reality is subjective (Luhmann 2002). Although working with different theoretical concepts, this view is very much in line with 'The Social Construction of Reality' as described by Peter Berger and Thomas Luckmann (1966). They highlight in their classic of sociology that social reality is constructed through subjective perception and cannot exist as objective reality independent from subjectivity. In other words, social reality – or what could also be described as objectivity – is a product of social perception and interaction that results in the social construction of reality. So the search for something like 'the reality' will be futile.

This leads straight to the supposed polarity of hard and soft data, which is another famous analogy to quantitative and qualitative. Instead of going through the hassle of social scientific research, which always leaves some imponderables behind, consumer organizations as well as market researchers like to resort to comparisons of supposed hard data that are easily available or can at least be measured in terms of natural sciences. When it comes to service quality, many studies do not go beyond variables like number of outlets, number of staff, the price tag for certain services, waiting time in the customer service hotline, distance between the rows of seats onboard a plane, the angle of the maximum decline of the backrest, number of cabins onboard a cruise vessel, the guaranteed delivery time of a pizza service, the availability of certain equipment in a hospital – you name it. These are all data that are either proudly presented on the website of a service provider or can easily be measured. They can be counted, checked with the tape measure or timed with the stopwatch. It cannot be denied that so much supposed accuracy has its charm.

No wonder that the analysis of these data is accompanied by an image of accuracy, reliability and objectivity – in one word: facts. Hard data are deemed secure knowledge. It is easy to decide if they are right or wrong. Beside hard data, soft data turn pale. They have a hard time standing on the shaky ground of opinions, assumptions, expectations, interpretations or other allegedly insecure information. But things are not that easy. In fact, the distinction between hard and soft data is rather artificial and misleading.

Many so-called hard data are not at all as hard as it may appear at first glance. Take for example the number of staff. That looks like really hard data. Indeed, it looks so easy to count heads. But then you start counting and wondering why everybody arrives at different figures. Should one count heads or man-days? What about those on maternity or sick leave? Being on the payroll without working? There are also those who have joined to replace someone but their predecessor has not yet left because the new staff member has to be trained. How to count temporary staff? Furthermore, do you want the headcount as an average or based on a cut-off date? So how accurate and hard are these data?

Even more important, the very question is what these hard data actually stand for. After all, we want to know more about service quality. Interpreting the headcount as an indicator for the service level appears to be rather obvious since we have stressed that service is a people business. So the straightforward interpretation that more people mean better service appears to be evident. However, if that is the case, we would not only have to exclude all staff who are on leave for whatever reason but also those who are not directly involved in providing the service. So what about the manager who is only indirectly involved in the actual service performance – and may in some cases even have a negative impact on the service level. The performance may be worse or better without having the manager in the background. And adding a second manager would probably not improve the service quality although using the supposedly hard data of the head count as an indicator of quality would result in exactly that conclusion.

Or take for example the distance between two rows of seats on an aircraft and the maximum angle that the backrest can be declined as a measurement of comfort and service quality. At first glance, things are very straightforward. The bigger the gap between two rows and the further the backrest can be declined the higher the comfort, which can be considered an element of service quality. After all, in first class you can stretch your legs without reaching the seat in front and put the backrest down until it is a flat bed, whereas in economy class you feel more like chickens in battery cages. Unfortunately, economy class is not that spacious. So things become more difficult. What may be reasonably comfortable[7] for small people can make giants feel like they are being caged. And while a large angle makes it more comfortable for a passenger when putting down the backrest as far as possible, this can easily trigger an outcry in the row behind because that passenger will define comfort differently once your backrest ends up in his face. So in the row behind, the comfort is higher if the backrests can be declined less – until these passengers also want to rest.

There are many examples of the weakness of hard data. Let's take the critical aspect of safety onboard aircrafts, which is an essential aspect of the service quality of airlines. The obvious idea would be to compare the safety records of these airlines. Nobody wants to board a never-come-back airline so why not have a look at the crash records? In the airline industry, such statistics are easily available[8] and newspapers are happy to turn them into headlines: how safe is my airline? Or: these are the safest airlines of the world. And to make it even more eye-catching: the most unsafe airlines of the world. That's the stuff that makes a true must-read.

Everybody who has ever flown and gone through turbulence can probably contribute his own nerve-wracking stories. And then you take a closer look at the rankings or indexes with several digits behind the decimal point and ask what incidents are actually relevant when it comes to safety? Of course, one can count how many planes of a particular airline have crashed and how many people have lost their lives in a defined period of time. But does it make a difference if the airline was at fault or not? For sure not for the victims. On the other hand, for the judgement of an airline's safety record it cannot completely be ignored. What about a near miss? And how to deal with incidents without casualties? Furthermore, does it make a difference if casualties happened many years ago or only recently? Can one hold an airline responsible for people who do not buckle up despite repeated reminders and hence suffer injuries from unexpected turbulence? What about people who are rescued in critical situations due to the pilot's and crew's excellence? Does this give some bonus to an airline's safety records? And last but not least, what is the normal risk of life?

Obviously, hard data are not that hard once they are confronted with the concept of relevance. Nevertheless, newspapers and magazines like to provide matrixes with comparisons of 'technical data' of service providers. Each column represents a service provider and the rows show supposedly hard data – metered, counted, measured and

---

7   One may forgive me for using this word in conjunction with economy class.

8   For example, the German Jet Airliner Crash Data Evaluation Centre JACDEC (www.jacdec.de) publishes these statistics on an annual basis.

weighed. That looks like indisputable and verifiable objective information. Only critical readers may be wondering what practical use such information can offer apart from a compilation of technical data that leave the underlying meaning to speculation. Once again, relevance is the crucial point. Only when the manifest data are used as indicators of latent variables like service quality, can they claim relevance. The isolated presentation of some measurements, however, has hardly any practical relevance. Nevertheless, these data will usually come along with some subtle valuation that is never explicated and hence subject to everybody's free interpretations. Some readers may be satisfied with such presentations and pick from the data whatever they deem a confirmation of what they believe anyway. These data are flexible and always welcome as pseudo-scientific proof of one's own conviction – you see? I knew it! – until the first 'but' shakes up the ground and weakens the supposedly hard data.

Only when the underlying variables become part of a theoretical construct like 'service quality' and related hypotheses about their effects and interactions, can they help to reconstruct social reality and claim relevance. No doubt, the idea of a quantitative world of objective reality is quite enticing because it would offer researchers a lot of convenience and make the search for truth much easier. But the world is not that simple. Once again, the very point is relevance – relevance for social behaviour and related decisions in the context of the research question.

4.3 Basic Demands

Research is something like the search for a specific reality. The results have to be reliable and valid. They must not change every time measurements are repeated and they should reflect something like what is commonly considered truth. That's the least one would expect. After all, research is supposed to help with making better decisions.

Reliability and validity are essential criteria of research. Reliable and valid research results provide a basis for successful prognoses and decision-making. That's what is required when it comes to quality. Of course, everybody has some gut feelings, assumptions, opinions, impressions and experience, one comes to conclusions, develops ideas about connections and interrelations and one may even arrive at something like ad hoc theories from which decisions are eventually derived. But this very individual road to knowledge is neither reproducible nor fully understandable to others and thus cannot claim validity. Such a highly personal and intuitive approach would not result in a comprehensible process that leads to better knowledge but would turn discovery into a power game. But you can see, people will argue and fight for the prerogative of interpretation – until their supposed knowledge fails because it is neither reliable nor valid.

Reliability describes to what extent it is possible to reproduce measurements under the same intersubjective conditions. It is the straightforward question if research results are reproducible and comprehensible: would other researchers working with the same measurement tools and dealing with the same research topic arrive at the same results?

In this context, intersubjectivity assumes that some common sense exists among researchers of how things are perceived, classified and interpreted. Hence, the perception and understanding of complex structures is not limited to unique receptors but can be shared and reproduced among researchers. While subjective experience is only accessible to an individual person and cannot claim generalization, intersubjective experience can be exchanged. This is though different from an understanding of objectivity as facts that can be deduced by means of mathematical or logical proof. The very point is that intersubjectivity requires a defined methodological and epistemological context.

So intersubjectivity and reliability have a very pragmatic function. It is the condition that allows sufficiently equal experience with regard to specific research areas. Without this condition, it would be impossible to communicate research results and come to meaningful conclusions with regard to future decisions and actions. Contrary to the individual and singular experience that is used preferably in discussions that do not focus on the best solution of a problem but are rather a power game laying down the battle-lines, high reliability allows intersubjective experience in the interest of epistemological progress. Only research that meets high reliability and hence can be understood intersubjectively allows a better understanding of a research topic. Where this reliability and intersubjectivity is lacking, research results are not necessarily wrong but cannot claim relevance because they are not reproducible. Unreliable research results do neither allow prognoses nor are they a good basis for decisions.

However reliability is not everything. Even inadequate measurements may well be reproducible and highly reliable without resulting in knowledge that fits into the theoretical framework of the study and allows prognoses that come true. This refers directly to the second crucial criterion of good research: validity.

The concept of validity relates to the correspondence between research results and the theoretical framework of a study. An important aspect of this criterion deals with the operationalization of theoretical constructs. After all, the researcher is not interested in the simple figure that describes how many people complain about a company's customer service. Instead, he will be interested in the quality of the customer service, which is a theoretical construct that is measured through various manifest variables as indicators. For example, the number of complaints may be used as an indicator of service quality that can be measured with high reliability and is understood and accepted in the relevant community as valid. So validity refers to the question to what extent a research instrument actually measures what it is supposed to measure. Furthermore, it deals with the question of whether the research results and related prognoses prove successful when it comes to prognoses and decision-making.

High reliability is prerequisite for high validity. It is obvious that what cannot be reproduced cannot claim validity. Reality that is only accessible through individual ability and not reproducible can neither claim validity nor relevance for future action. Nevertheless, high reliability is no guarantee for high validity.

At the same time, high reliability and validity do not coincide with high relevance. This becomes obvious when comparing laboratory experiments with practical field research. The laboratory experiment creates an artificial environment that allows control of a number of variables and guarantees high reliability of the measurement. Furthermore, the results can claim high validity under the conditions of the laboratory. However, life does not take place in the artificial environment of a laboratory but in the real world where all the variables that were well controlled in an experimental design may look rather different. As a result, the perfectly reliable and valid results of the laboratory experiment may be hardly relevant for real life. Actually, this applies also to natural science although natural sciences are often perceived as being superior to social sciences in the sense of accuracy. The very point is, however, that natural sciences deal mostly with artificial situations and under well-controlled and constant conditions. In such an environment, natural sciences are indeed more successful with regard to reliability and validity. However, the situation looks very different once the natural sciences leave the controlled environment of the laboratory and suddenly face natural phenomena. Then it is over with alleged superiority. Just look at the weather forecast, which deals as much with uncertainties as social research.

Apart from reliability and validity, objectivity is often mentioned as a criterion of good research. At first glance, that makes a lot of sense. Objectivity in the sense of an exclusion of all latent and subjective factors would be a step towards the ultimate truth. After all, one does not want to spend money on research that hardly delivers more than the personal opinion of the researcher. Unbiased results of objective research are wanted. Nothing but the black marks on white.[9] But this idea of objectivity misses the very point that meaning and understanding do not come with the black marks on white but depend on conventions and interpretations in the sense of intersubjectivity and social relevance. Without conventions that define something like common sense, there is no meaningful communication about supposed reality. This applies to all forms of communication and their perception. Already the decision to read a text in a certain direction does not come with the printer's ink but is based on conventions. That's why, from an epistemological perspective, the demand for objectivity is actually not tenable. Accordingly, objectivity must not be understood as the elimination of personal decisions that result in specific perceptions and interpretations. Instead, objectivity demands the explication of the decisions that underlie the research process. It is this explication that allows the community to discuss the appropriateness in the sense of intersubjective knowledge. That is exactly why this book stresses time and again the importance of the explication of decisions along the research process.

Returning to the concept of reliability, the question arises of what this means for practical research. After all, the research situation is determined by an infinite number of conditions, which cannot all be reproduced. And this is not at all required. The crucial question is, which variables are actually *relevant* with regard to the research question? The researcher has to make this decision and he has to explicate it in accordance with the theoretical background of the study. This is the basis for any further examination into the reliability of the research instrument.

There are a few common approaches to reliability. A rather simple concept is the split-half. As the name suggests, all research material – interviews, observation records, content analytic coding sheets or similar – are split at random into two halves. Then the measurements of both groups are compared by means of correlation coefficients – the higher the correlation the higher the reliability of the measurement.

Another approach is known as retest whereby a measurement is repeated on identical subjects and with the same research method. Retest reliability is defined as correlation between the two measurements. Ideally, a repeated measurement should result in the same findings. However, the obvious problem of this concept of reliability is the effect of the learning curve. Retesting the service orientation of staff will probably have to take some learning effect from previous measurements into consideration. As a result, it is not clear if deviations between both measurements are attributed to the research instrument

---

9   To limit the analysis of texts to the black marks on white was once a central thesis of Bernard Berelson's understanding of content analysis, which predominated the discussion for a long time. See: Berelson 1952.

or to the participants in the study because they have learned from the first measurement. That means that the second measurement may rather reflect something like learning capacity or adaptability than the degree of service orientation.

So instead of testing the same subject with the same method twice, one could do a parallel test, which means that the same person is tested with two different methods whereby it is assumed that both methods measure the same phenomenon. Once again, the correlation between both measurements determines the reliability of the data. The parallel test avoids the learning effect – and comes with just another problem. How appropriate is the hypothesis that both tests do really measure the same? Some uncertainty remains.

A special case is the categorization of open-ended questions in interviews, texts in content analyses or observations of specific behaviour. In all these cases, the great variety of data has to be structured according to their assumed meaning in the context of the research question. This demands concurrence of the coding decisions that can only be achieved through comprehensive training. The research results would be useless if every encoder interpreted the same observation differently. Only far-reaching agreement between observers will result in high reliability of the data.

It is noteworthy that all discussed reliability measures refer to the interaction between participant and research instrument or between research instrument and researcher. But this is actually not the major concern in a research study and just a necessary condition on the way to results. So the question arises for what purpose the research results shall be reproducible – which refers directly to the issue of validity.

There are several concepts of validity reflecting different aspects that are partly overlapping. The simplest and most common approach is known as face validity. It could also be described as a plausibility check. Face validity deals with the rather general question of whether research results are in line with the current state of research and knowledge. It is an essential although rather weak approach. But there are more specific concepts of validity.

Construct validity deals with the question of to what extent chosen operationalizations are adequate in the sense of measuring what they are supposed to measure. Take for example the complex theoretical construct of customer satisfaction, which could be operationalized through a number of questions in a questionnaire. Construct validity queries to what extent these questions actually measure what is defined as customer satisfaction. Only when the methodical approach reflects the complex theoretical construct comprehensively can construct validity be assumed. Furthermore, different methodical approaches to the same theoretical construct should show a high correlation. This requires a thorough definition of the theoretical construct and a methodical approach that covers all its aspects.

Alternatively, one could compare measurements of different operationalizations of the same or related theoretical constructs whereby one operationalization has previously proven successful and is hence deemed valid. The correlation between the measurements of different operationalizations describes the concurrent validity of a theoretical construct.

Compared to the rather static comparison of two different approaches to the same theoretical construct, the concept of predictive validity provides a more future-oriented perspective. After all, practical research focuses usually on future experience and behaviour and should make it predictable. Accordingly, the concept of predictive validity deals with measurements that are taken at different times. For this purpose, prognoses are derived from research results and tested at a later stage based on the same group of individuals. A high correlation between the first and the later measurement can be interpreted as high predictive validity of the underlying construct. For example, the predictive validity of a recruitment test that focuses on service orientation could be validated by testing after some time how well the selected people are actually doing in the service sector. A high success rate would indicate high predictive validity. The problem is, however, that it is usually unknown if there is a direct relation between the earlier measurement and the later findings or if the relation is affected by some other sources of interference instead.

Another important aspect is the internal or content validity, which refers to the unambiguity of measurements in a way that they are not affected by uncontrolled variables. High internal validity excludes alternative explanations for observed effects through the control of confounding variables[10] such as, for example, learning effects or reactivity. This is also described as *ceteris paribus* validity because in an experimental design, apart from the independent variable and the related dependent variable, all other factors are held constant.[11] Of course, a laboratory experiment creates the best environment to keep confounding variables under control but, unfortunately, it is also a very artificial environment that easily lacks relevance.

Nevertheless, internal validity is a necessary condition for external validity,[12] which is the crucial question of to what extent research results can be generalized. Of course, this refers directly to the representativeness of the underlying sample. But reactivity and other unwanted effects may have an impact on the external validity. On the other hand, repeating the study with different participants or under different conditions and arriving at corresponding results will increase the external validity.

It is obvious that the concepts of internal and external validity are to some extent contradicting. On one hand, internal validity is a prerequisite for external validity. On the other hand, we have seen that internal validity is easier to achieve in an artificial research situation whereas a more realistic environment bears the risk of uncontrolled interference, which would have a negative impact on external validity. But what appears to be a contradiction looks different from the perspective of research logic. Research does not target the verification of a theory but instead its falsification. This is because, logically, universal statements cannot be verified but only falsified. As long as a theory is not falsified it will last – subject to further research.[13] Only when it has been exploded will it be rejected. In that respect, reality is the best proof of external validity while any criticism of the validity of research results actually deals with internal validity.

The above list of concepts of validity deals only with the most prominent concepts. But it makes obvious that there are many and partly overlapping aspects of validity, which eventually are important for the relevance of research results. And that is the crucial point. Without relevant results, research would not be worth the effort. Nevertheless, discussions of practical research hardly go beyond a quick look at face validity. And should there still be any doubt, it will be brushed away with a short remark: but you can

---

10   Confounders are uncontrolled factors that interfere with an observed exposition. One of the most famous confounding effects is the Hawthorne effect. See section 4.4.

11   The Latin phrase '*ceteris paribus*' can be translated as 'all other things being equal'.

12   This is also called criterion validity.

13   This is an important point when it comes to statistical hypothesis testing. See also section 7.2.

see. Unfortunately, it is not that simple. The concept of validity is much more complex than a quick look at the research approach can reveal. Validity is an essential criterion of research. And the same applies to reliability as a condition of validity.

Validity and reliability are not some abstract methodological concepts but have practical relevance in the research process. They make it possible to share experience and to enter into a meaningful discourse of research results. It is this intersubjective comprehensibility that adds practical relevance for decision-making and future action to empirical research results. This should be kept in mind when discussing further aspects of the practical research process in the course of the following chapter.

4.4 Reactions

It is always the same. You watch a soccer match on TV and because nothing much happens on the pitch the camera is wandering around and eyes some spectators. They look rather normal, just like spectators look during a hardly exciting match – until a sudden metamorphosis happens. They jump up from their seats, hop like mad and wave frantically. Has one missed some action on the pitch, has anybody shot a goal? No, nothing happened – except that these people have recognized that a camera is pointing at them. Only those who observe this transmutation in the stadium will see its second act. The camera turns away and those who just appeared like notorious cases of ADHD sit down again as if nothing had happened.

Researchers are well aware of this phenomenon but instead of describing it as some hyperactivity disorder, they talk about reactivity. It is a common experience in social research where it describes changes in the performance and behaviour of the participants in a study due to the awareness of being observed. As a consequence, the study may produce artefacts instead of facts.

Since it is usually not the target of a study to learn how people behave in a test situation but to understand their attitudes and behaviour under 'normal' circumstances, reactivity can seriously spoil the validity of a study. Accordingly, empirical social research distinguishes between reactive and non-reactive methods of data collection. Whenever someone is aware of the research situation, one has to expect some hardly controllable reactions to these extraordinary circumstances. Typical reactive research methods are, for example, interviews, group discussions, non-covert observations and laboratory experiments. In all these research situations the participants are aware that their responses and behaviour are recorded. They are on stage and will do everything to deliver a good – but likely atypical – performance.

Non-reactive methods on the other hand deal with data that are not initiated by the researcher but derive from material that has been produced independent of a particular research interest. Non-participant covert observations or content analyses of available material like newspapers or documents are good examples for such non-reactive research methods that shall be discussed in more detail at a later stage.

Without any doubt, reactivity can have a serious impact on empirical research results whereby the sources of such effects can be manifold. They can be found in the behaviour of the researcher, interviewer or observer as well as in the behaviour of the participants in a survey. Also the research material itself – the questionnaire, checklist or other records – can be a source of reactivity that eventually leads to biased results.

One of the major causes of reactivity can be summarized as social desirability. Interviewees especially show a tendency to adapt their answers to patterns that are deemed socially desirable. Take for example the question: how important are sustainability and environmental protection when you choose a service provider? Unimportant, somewhat important, important or very important? Who would dare to say 'unimportant' outing yourself as environmental polluter? It is understandable and simply adequate to adapt to social norms because deviations are usually sanctioned. This adaption to social desirability is not necessarily a conscious decision but, to some extent, it may simply be a subconscious process – socially desirable but unwanted in the research situation.

While honesty as such reflects of course a virtue, everybody is well aware that this virtue would not prevent from sanctions if one would frankly declare that one does not abide by ethical, environmental or other social norms. So most interviewees will probably think twice before they answer a questionnaire. Of course, they will present themselves as nice guys. The effect is obvious. So pretended adherence to social norms and political correctness will affect the research results. And the impact on the validity of a study will be the greater the more the questionnaire is related to social norms and values.

Also interviewers and observers cannot free themselves of the effects of reactivity. They perceive and interpret answers and observations not only according to their perception of the respondents but also through the filter of their own attitude and opinion. If a company sends their sales people with a questionnaire to their customers in an effort to better understand how the customers rate their service, one should not be surprised if the look through rose-tinted glasses results in a biased view of the world. This should not be misunderstood as fake interviews but stresses only the influence of individual perception in an interview situation. At the same time, the respondent will answer a questionnaire according to his perception of the interviewer and his assumed expectations and interpretations of the interviewer. In other words, the respondent will adjust his answers according to his interpretation of the situation. One may argue that this is a normal process in all communication. This is of course true but an interview situation where answers are recorded will amplify the effect.[14]

It is a complex, reflexive process of perceptions, expectations and expected expectations that does not become much simpler in written interviews or interviews via a website. Even if no researcher is present, the respondent will develop related assumptions and an image of the people behind the project and will behave and respond accordingly. It is an effect that is not limited to interviews but can be observed in all reactive research approaches.

Expectations as well as expected expectations determine the research situation. The Hawthorne effect is the classical example for this guinea pig effect that describes behavioural changes due to the awareness of being in an experimental situation. It owes its name to experiments in the Hawthorne Works that were operated by Western Electric, which was an electrical engineering company.[15] From 1924 until 1932, a number of studies were performed with the target of improving working performance. These experiments dealt with the question of to what extent the performance of the workers will improve if

---

14   One of the best descriptions of the mechanisms of social interaction is provided by Erving Goffman (1959). His description of social interaction as role play in theatre can also be applied to reactive research situations.

15   Western Electric Co., Inc. was founded 1872 and operated the Hawthorne Works from 1905 until 1983 with up to 45,000 workers in Cicero, Illinois.

certain working conditions are changed. In one of the experiments, the lighting in the factory halls had been improved and indeed, the performance increased. But the assumed causal relation between lighting and output appeared in a different light after a look at the control group. Surprisingly, the performance had similarly improved in the control group where no changes to the lighting had been made. Even more surprisingly, the higher performance was still maintained after the lighting was readjusted to its original level. Apparently, it was not the lighting that had an impact on the performance but probably the simple but confounding fact that the workers recognized an interest in their working conditions as well as feedback by their management and the researchers, which was a new and encouraging experience for the workers.

Another classical reaction to a test situation is the John Henry effect. John Henry is a legendary American folk hero who worked at the end of the nineteenth century as a steel driver.[16] When he was told that his performance would be measured against a steam-powered hammer he worked harder and harder to outperform the machine. The legend has a tragic end. John Henry dies – living on in many ballades. This tragedy is used as an allegory of the common effect that people who are aware of being a member of a control group try to overcome that alleged disadvantage through higher performance. Such efforts 'against the odds' can easily spoil a research design.

Researchers are not immune to effects that lead to biased results. The Pygmalion effect[17] is a classical case of the effects of expectations. It owes its name to Roman poet Ovid (43 BC–17 AD) whose protagonist *Pygmalion* fell deeply in love with the statue of a woman that he himself had carved from ivory. He made offerings to Venus and wished that his future wife should be like the statue. When he returns home he kisses the statue and her lips feel warm and the statue comes to life – his wish was granted (*The Metamorphoses*, Ovid, Book X, Fable VII). Research is less romantic but the effect is similar. Regardless if stereotypes that a researcher associates with his counterparts are true or false, they will have an impact on the research results and turn out to be true.

This is the classical case of the self-fulfilling prophecy – a term that was coined by American sociologist Robert K. Merton (1949) and refers back to the Thomas theorem (Thomas and Thomas 1928) stating that 'if men define situations as real, they are real in their consequences'. A self-fulfilling prophecy will make an originally false definition of a situation come true because it causes behavioural changes, which are used retroactively as a confirmation of the prophecy. In other words, when researchers have already developed certain expectations, attitudes or prejudices, it is likely that they find them confirmed in the sense of a self-fulfilling prophecy. Accordingly, a self-destroying prophecy is a prophecy that will not prove true because it has become known.

The very point of all these concepts is the fact that human behaviour adapts to the definition of the situation. Applied to a specific research situation, it becomes obvious that the data collection and research results will very much depend on how the situation is defined by those who are involved in the research process and data collection. Insufficient congruence of these definitions will affect the validity of the study.

---

16   Steel drivers were the men who forced with their hammer and chisel holes into the rocks that were then filled with explosives to clear the way and build the tunnels that were needed for new railroad tracks. The working conditions of the steel drivers were extremely hard and dangerous.

17   The Pygmalion effect is also known as Rosenthal effect referring to an experiment by Robert Rosenthal and Leonore Jacobson in 1965 that dealt with interactions between teachers and students.

While these classical examples refer mostly to experimental situations, analogous effects can be observed in conjunction with all reactive methods. Whenever participants in a study are aware of the specific test situation and regardless of if they know the research targets or have only developed some assumptions, they will react to the situation and adjust their behaviour. This is most obvious when it comes to the placebo effect. It describes the phenomenon that patients who are given a placebo – look-alike medicine that does not contain active substances – often show measurable reactions in the sense of the expected drug. It proves how much expectations can change reality.

The test material itself can also be a source of artefacts. In interviews, for example, the sequence of questions can make a difference because questions together with their answers have an impact on the responses to the following questions. The answers are likely to be different if a questionnaire about one's recent cruise experience deals first with a shipping disaster and asks only then how safe one has felt onboard or if the question about safety is nicely wrapped somewhere between questions about entertainment, food, drinks and service quality during the cruise. This halo effect, which describes the 'radiation' of preceding topics on the answers to subsequent questions, cannot be completely avoided but it has to be considered when questionnaires are designed. And it can be controlled to some extent if the sequence of questions in a questionnaire is varied and the answers to these different versions are compared.

Sometimes the answers to questionnaires do not even depend primarily on content but just follow an acquiescent response set – agreeing to every statement in a questionnaire regardless of its actual content. Even if the statements are worded the other way round, which should logically trigger the opposite response, these yeasayers will still agree. A similar effect is the consistency bias that describes the tendency to respond to related questions in an attempt to establish a consistent response pattern even if this does not reflect the real situation. Eventually, respondents develop a fictitious story of their life just to ensure that it appears conclusive. Similarly, it is not unusual that respondents develop a central tendency to choose preferably the middle categories as their answers. This becomes particularly obvious when judgements are based on scales from something like agree to disagree and a respondent chooses more or less consistently the undecided categories in the middle – neither agree nor disagree. Working with an even number of categories, which forces the respondent at least a little into a decision for one direction, would hardly be a convincing cure.

Obviously, there are quite a number of unwanted response sets that affect the validity of a study and the above mentioned issues are not at all exhaustive. But they make clear how far the research situation can affect the results in a reactive research design. The less the context and meaning of the research material is defined the more it will be exposed to inadequate response patterns. Such response sets will provide an expression of the personality of the respondents at best but this will hardly be the topic of the actual study. Awareness is important and some thorough control is required because these effects have the potential to impact on the research results, spoil their validity and turn facts into artefacts.

The best way to overcome the problems of reactivity is to resort to non-reactive methods. Far too often and usually with too little reflection, research is translated into interviews, which are necessarily reactive. Accordingly, the term 'survey' is used synonymously with interviews and questionnaires although its original meaning is related to Latin *'supervidere'* meaning supervision – without referring to the method of supervision. Instead of defining a clear research question *before* discussing what methodical approach may be the most appropriate way of data collection, quality managers or other practical researchers state that they want to do interviews with their customers or other stakeholders. They talk about methods before the content and research interest are defined. One may deem this pragmatic but it puts the whole research process upside down.[18]

Only when the research question is clearly defined and translated into indicators and variables that shall be measured is it time to consider what approach to data collection is most appropriate. Suddenly, one may recognize that there are alternatives to the tiring flood of questionnaires. In fact, the world is full of data that have been created independently from a specific research situation. They are open to non-reactive approaches that do away with the artefacts of a reactive research situation.

When it comes to public and semi-public sectors like infrastructure, education, social welfare, public health, medical services, care of the elderly, information, communication, media, transport, safety and security, energy, sustainability and ecology, complex data are usually available that just have to be accessed. Many data are accessible through data banks, others are generated as a result of institutionalized processes such as, for example, administrative or customer service acts. All these data are a great source for secondary analyses. It just requires a bit of fantasy to explore these sources.

A lot of information can be collected using a non-reactive approach. Content analyses of web pages, newspapers, magazines, documents, letters and other written material are a fruitful source. Non-participant covert observations can be a key to social behaviour in specific situations. For example, think of a study with the target of improving the check-in procedures at an airport. There is no need to ask the passengers how satisfied they are with the service. The answers would probably deceive. Instead, one can watch the scene and record the observations. Furthermore, social behaviour usually leaves traces behind that can be a great source of knowledge for many research questions. There is no need to ask museum visitors how they enjoyed an exhibition and what they liked most. The better approach would probably be to just follow their movements and see how long they dwell in front of certain exhibits. Perhaps it turns out that the exhibition setup is not optimal.

Non-reactive approaches can offer deep and comprehensive insights that practical research makes so far too little use of. It is an approach that – more than standard interviews – requires some fantasy and creativity. In practical research especially, the potential is by far not exhausted. At the same time, it must not be withheld that non-reactive approaches are not free of problems and some unresolved issues. Their weakest points are insufficient information about their reliability and validity as well as limited control over the sample. That can make it difficult to realize representative samples when working with non-reactive methods.

Therefore, the ultimate question is not if in a specific research setting one should make use of a reactive or non-reactive approach. This is not a matter of mutually exclusive alternatives. In many cases, non-reactive approaches cannot fully substitute reactive methods. At the same time, they can provide information that one would hardly get through reactive methods. The answer may be a combination of various approaches resulting in a multi-method study that eventually reflects a wider scope of reality, provides deeper insight and helps to overcome misleading reactions to the research situation.[19]

---

18   For a discussion of the steps of the research process, see section 3.3.

19   For a more comprehensive discussion of multi-model approaches, see section 6.7.

4.5 Convincing

Everybody has gone through this nuisance experience. You want to leave the website of a big company and, instead, a window pops up asking you with sugar-coated words to please take a few minutes of your precious time and 'help us improve by taking our survey'. Or your bank informs you that they have contracted a market research company that will contact you within the next few days for an interview that will help to improve their service and products. Kindly assist. And when you have returned from vacation, your tour operator will send you a friendly 'Welcome home!' before they come straight to the point: 'In an effort to continually improve our service, please take a moment to share your thoughts on your recent vacation with us. To complete the questionnaire, please click here.'

It is not much better the other way round. In some companies one could easily employ dedicated staff to do nothing but fill in questionnaires. Everybody wants to hear your opinion. Customers, subcontractors, associations, authorities, students, research institutes – please tick as appropriate. It will take only a few minutes and of course, everything will be absolutely confidential and anonymous – scout's honour!

Then you face the crucial point: to answer or not to answer – that is the question. It is not only a crucial question for the people who should be interviewed but also for the researcher because the decision of the members of his sample will have an impact on the research results and ultimately decide over success and failure of the study. So it is worthwhile having a closer look at possible reactions to an invitation to participate in a quality study. It is all about convincing those who make up the sample.

Apart from some notorious naysayers, the first reaction of people who are chosen for a study will probably be positive and driven by curiosity and cooperativeness. After all, it is a chance to point out one's own opinion that so far nobody was really interested in. But then you think of your workload and your limited time. Too often you have had the experience that the promised ten minutes that the survey would take becomes 20 minutes and more. Or perhaps the answers that you are supposed to tick do not reflect your thoughts. And whenever you have highlighted some room for improvement it was in vain. Regardless of how many studies you have supported, the service quality has never improved. So why should one answer these questionnaires or join in some discussions?

You may start a simple cost–benefit analysis and wonder if the efforts will really pay off. In business-to-business (B2B) commerce, the decision is simple whenever the questionnaire comes from a customer. Of course, it is a pleasure to answer – regardless of how meaningless the questions are. The customer is always right. Also government agencies will receive an answer. Reluctantly. And being a member of an association, there is no doubt that one feels obligated to respond. But what about all the others who bother you with questionnaires and claim to be interested in your opinion?

No doubt, performing a study and sending out questionnaires, one faces immense reluctance that can easily spoil the response rate and – even worse – the validity of the study. Usually, those who deal with questionnaires are well aware of this phenomenon and make an effort to convince the members of their selected target group to reply. One way or the other, they try hard to convince them of the great advantages of a participation in the study. The scale of friendly arguments and decent bribes reaches from some nice words to tangible rewards. The end justifies the means.

Nice, friendly words that appeal to the good heart of a candidate for an interview are the classical approach to overcome the reluctance to accept an invitation for participation

– hoping to convince people that answering the questionnaire is in their own best interest. But that may not be sufficient in times of an ever-increasing number of surveys. Stronger medicine could be required. So one could flatter the candidates, telling them that this questionnaire is only sent to a selected group of customers. Wow! The chosen few may be overwhelmed with so much honour and reply quickly. Crossed fingers. To have an even stronger case, one can tell them that their answers are decisive when it comes to product developments. Your answers count, one will promise – and hope that they are grateful enough to believe it and feel pleased.

Unfortunately, as necessary as such honeyed words are, in many cases they will not be sufficient. At times of high sensitivity towards data protection, it is essential to convince participants in a study that their data are anonymized and handled in strict confidentiality. A statement like, 'the information that you provide will be combined with others who have recently done business with us and will be used in the strictest of confidence' may help to overcome their concerns. As a precaution, a reminder to tell the truth may be added: 'Thank you for sharing your honest opinions with us.' It is give and take – the researcher guarantees the confidentiality of all data so the interviewee should kindly provide the truth.

That sounds only reasonable, but as much as confidentiality may be promised as part of a cover letter or invitation for an interview, the following questionnaire can easily spoil these efforts. One can be rather sure that, for example, airline passengers who are asked to provide their departure date and flight number together with the seat number will develop some serious doubt to what extent the study really is anonymous. It is even worse if questionnaires carry a number that apparently has the purpose of identifying the respondent. Also email reminders – we have unfortunately not yet received your completed questionnaire – are rather counterproductive and will quickly ruin all promises of anonymity.

It is these little things that can spoil the success of a survey based on interviews – despite all prudent efforts. It is not sufficient to take holy oaths that all data are protected if the questionnaire points in the opposite direction. And even if someone would trust the researcher, it may still not be sufficient to convince hardcore ignoramuses to respond to a questionnaire. Stronger arguments are required. Convincing benefits.

What does a researcher have to offer? Some come up with the promise of sending a summary of the results of the study. But the interest is probably limited. Who wants to read the results of a study that one would never have initiated? Others promise to raffle off some fancy items. Unfortunately, that creates new problems. Linking a questionnaire to a lucky draw makes it necessary that the respondent provides his name and address, which could have just the opposite effect. Is it a dirty trick to get hold of personal data? Is the data collection perhaps not as anonymous as they claim? Suddenly, everything is back to square one.

Another question is what value the items in the lucky draw should have. If they are too petty and lack attractiveness they will not have the hoped-for effect. The same will apply even if an attractive item is up for grabs but it is too unlikely to win because there will be only one winner or the prize will be given only to the first few respondents. So in order to have the necessary persuasiveness, not only the rewards offered but also the chance to win should be inviting. Furthermore, the lucky draw should be attractive to everybody who is asked to participate in the study. It would be difficult to attract men to participate in a study about the customer service of a golf club manufacturer when it is linked to a lucky draw of a set of lady's golf clubs. As a result, the intention of increasing the response rate may result in a biased sample.

Some studies go a third way and promise to donate a certain amount to charity for every questionnaire that is completed. Such reward does not even make it necessary to provide a name and address. It is a rather subtle approach because it requires some hard-heartedness to reject such offer. Do you really want to be responsible when a dollar less goes into the protection of the rain forest? Can you imagine the faces of the children in the orphanage who do not receive a donation just because you refused to fill in a simple questionnaire? But then you remember that you recently donated a much bigger amount to charity and, anyway, who knows how trustworthy the promise to donate for every questionnaire actually is? And some people may even be annoyed about so much subtlety and refuse to reply just because of this.

It is a real dilemma that researchers face when they look for respondents. What may have been established as a representative sample suffers from all kinds of effects beyond the researcher's control. The situation has not become any better since most interviews are no longer conducted personally but through the Internet. Where one could once try to judge the trustworthiness of an interviewer one is now confronted with a machine. Some question marks remain. So who will actually answer? And what is the impact on the representativeness of the sample?

Considering all the pros and cons, offering some reward is in many cases the easiest way to improve the willingness to answer a questionnaire. But it comes at a price. As a result, the effect of social desirability will become stronger. We have already described the phenomenon that people respond to interview questions preferably in a way that reflects socially desirable values, attitudes and behaviour. This is a normal and understandable reaction because adherence to social values is deemed positive whereas deviations from norms are usually sanctioned. However, this effect will become stronger when answering a questionnaire that is linked to rewards. Because in this case it is – consciously or subconsciously – assumed that meeting the expectations may improve the chance of winning. Meeting the (assumed) expectations means in this case praising the service quality. Accordingly, the result of the study will likely be biased. But this bias can at least be controlled when comparing the data with a control sample of questionnaires that were not linked to any reward.

Indeed, it is an intellectual challenge to realize that for a company that is really interested in improving its service, critical answers and comments can be much more helpful than flattering statements. But who knows if this is really the idea behind the questionnaire? After all, many alleged service studies are little more than a ritual instead of getting to the core of service performance.

Unfortunately, the alternative is not much better. Who can actually be expected to answer if there is no reward? Most likely, these will be first of all those people who feel called upon to speak up. And these are usually those who have a lot of sympathy for the organizer of the study. Or these are people with clearly negative comments who want to take this opportunity to make their point at last – to say what they always wanted to say but nobody wanted to hear. However, when the majority of ambivalent respondents keep silent, this effect will have an impact on the distribution of the data and hence impact on the results of the study.

Researchers cannot easily escape this dilemma. It becomes even worse because of a growing number of questionnaires and their omnipresence on the Internet. One can hardly escape from this harassment and after a while, even well-meaning people may get tired of this kind of opinion poll and eventually spoil research designs regardless how meaningful they are by simply refusing to answer. Enough is enough.

That demands convincing arguments for why someone should participate on the one hand and a thorough comparison of the respondents with the originally targeted group on the other. Even a sophisticated research design is no guarantee that the ultimate sample is unbiased. But this is a crucial element of the validity of the research results.

The best protection from a biased sample is to check if relevant characteristics show significant differences between the statistical population and the actual sample of returned questionnaires. In case of major deviations, one should be careful with any statements and conclusions because the actual sample may simply not be representative for the targeted population. Such results would likely be artefacts instead of facts. And sometimes this difference between the originally targeted population and the ultimate sample of respondents may even provide interesting hypotheses and insight into the research topic as well as the study design. Why are certain individuals more willing to respond than others?

Even the most convincing arguments for participation in a questionnaire may be futile if the questionnaire itself shatters all efforts to persuade people to participate. Especially with online questionnaires, it is easy to annoy respondents to an extent that they exit the questionnaire before it is completed. Often, the promised short interview – please take ten minutes of your valuable time – drags on and on and is still not finished after 20 minutes. Or you are forced to tick categories that do not make much sense and do not reflect what you would like to say. Other questionnaires may not have translated the theoretical concept of the researchers into the cognitive structures of their target group. As a result, the respondents find themselves in a cognitive world that is not theirs and the answers have no link to the reality that they experience. Furthermore, there may be questions that one does not want to answer. Income, age or status are typical questions that many people are not willing to answer truthfully. Nevertheless, some online questionnaires insist on an answer because otherwise one cannot continue to the next page. These are flaws that could have easily been avoided if the questionnaire had undergone a pretest. One can be sure that such methodical weaknesses have an impact on the results. Either the respondents give up at an early stage and exit the questionnaire before it is completed or they tick answers that are actually not applicable just because they want to satisfy the system. Respondents learn from that experience. They will remember the encounter with methodically weak or even annoying data collection when they are invited for another study – and may simply decline.

It is in the good hands of the researcher to avoid such blunder. No study has to fail because the questionnaire drives away those who were prepared to answer. The real hurdle is to overcome the initial reluctance to fill in a questionnaire. The right wording and an attractive design are important. Convincing arguments, relevance of the research topic to the target group, familiarity with the subject as well as reasonable expectations regarding the required time are essential elements of a successful questionnaire. Last but not least, a contact address for possible feedback should be provided that gets the interview out of the anonymity of a black box. And even if all these requirements are met, it is important to check the ultimate sample if it is possibly biased.

The difficulties of finding participants for a study are not limited to interviews. While it is most obvious in studies that are based on questionnaires, it is also a common problem of all other reactive research approaches. For example, it is inherent in focus group discussions as well as in experiments although not as obvious as in opinion polls because of the usually smaller number of participants. In all cases, the research design must pay proper attention to the question of how the targeted sample can actually be convinced to accept the invitation to the survey. As much as the number of studies is increasing, the reluctance to participate is also growing.

If all efforts fail, there could still be the alternative of a non-reactive research approach. It requires some creativity but it is worth the effort. For example, instead of asking customers about the service quality of a manufacturer one can analyze their complaint rate and the actual complaints. Many customer service centres advise the callers that their calls will be recorded for training purposes. These calls provide excellent data for an analysis of customer service quality. It is a slightly different perspective that requires more efforts. Different from the ticked categories in a questionnaire, an analysis of customer calls makes it necessary to listen to customers and requires a sometimes tedious categorization and coding of what was said. But when it comes to quality, it is worthwhile listening to customers. And it prevents possible bias resulting from the difficulty in convincing the target group to participate in the study because in a non-reactive research design the researcher is not at the mercy of the participants.

4.6 Refusal

Despite all efforts, almost all research will face the problem of missing data. Relevant data is not available or not accessible, some people cannot be approached, refuse to participate in a study or decline to respond to particular questions and sometimes information is simply not recorded correctly. There are many reasons why a researcher faces the problem of missing data. The effect is always the same – where relevant information is expected, the researcher will find nothing but blanks. So what to do? As usual, it depends. The crucial question is: what is the cause of the missing information?

The researcher is in a comfortable situation as long as he can rightfully assume that data are not missing systematically but solely at random. In other words, the likelihood that information about a certain variable is missing is neither related to its value nor to the value of any other variable that is relevant in the context of the research question. But this is actually a tricky assumption. In practical research, one may be inclined to generously claim that missing data are caused by chance even if on closer examination there are some doubts. The idea of randomly distributed missing data is simply too tempting because, in this case, nothing else has happened but a slight reduction of the sample size, which should not cause too much trouble.

In fact, the decision is more delicate than it may appear at first glance. Look for example at a survey dealing with the after-sales service of a manufacturer of hi-fi home audio equipment. One of the questions to customers who have contacted the service desk refers to the equipment that has malfunctioned and requires technical support. Everybody knows that the model designations are often rather confusing. So one would not wonder if this information is not provided, causing missing data in the questionnaire. It looks like a typical case of data that are missing at random. But then you have to consider that this survey is related to hi-fi equipment, which in its high-end product range is not a mainstream product but targeted at audio enthusiasts.

To them, two slightly different models can make a major difference. And having a better model means at the same time having a higher status within the community of hi-fi devotees. So one can expect that they know the correct designations. On top of that, these enthusiasts will have different expectations compared to buyers of equipment that is not in the top range. Suddenly, what looks like data that are missing at random turns out to be a likely bias.

This example also makes it obvious that it is not necessarily the same if an answer is not known or if it is declined. Nevertheless, the respondent may claim that he forgot the model designation although, in fact, he does not want to name it after he felt embarrassed standing with his simple stereo in a queue with hi-fi experts.

The situation is similar when not only individual questions are rejected but participation in the study is declined. One could assume that the common excuse that unfortunately there is not enough time to take part in the study can well be distributed at random. After all, everybody is busy and most people are not waiting for an interviewer with some questions that are not really dealing with what one deems important. But there are some who think differently and have a high interest in the research topic. And that is exactly the crucial point that makes the difference. In most cases, it is not easy to decide if such refusal, which is also described as unit non-response, occurs at random or not.

A special type of missing data are intentionally false answers to interview questions. Sensitive questions in particular are exposed to such bias. Instead of rejecting the answer, the respondent chooses an answer that is deemed appropriate in the interview situation and socially desirable. Questions regarding income are a typical case that does not only result in missing data but often in false answers. So the long overdue salary increase that the boss never approved appears at least in the answer to the respective question. And the responses may be similarly biased when it comes to educational level, profession or other variables that are related to social status.

Unfortunately, it is rather difficult to find out why some people decline to participate in a survey. Does it depend on the interviewer? Does a pretty young girl get more interviews than an overweight man radiating body odour after climbing too many stairs? Of course, one could simply ask why an interview is declined. But one would probably get an answer that is just another non-response – either openly or nicely wrapped as a little white lie. What does it mean having no time? Sufficient time is a matter of priorities. Can the interviewer come back when the candidate has more time? Oh so sorry, I'll go on a very long vacation. Or what does it mean not to be interested in a survey? Is it only this topic or surveys in general? What does lacking interest say about the research topic? Before getting an answer, the door may already be closed or the phone hung up. One could just try to record some obvious data like gender, estimated age, living environment or similar and check if the non-respondents differ significantly from the total population. But this only makes sense if these variables are relevant for the research topic. And even if there are no significant differences with regard to these variables there can still be major differences in other variables. On the other hand, as long as there is no obvious reason to assume a bias one could enlarge the sample by selecting more people in order to make up for the missing cases.

Whenever it comes to touchy questions one can expect a high number of missing or false responses. While religion or political preference will hardly play a role in quality studies, income and age can be relevant variables. So what to do? One possibility is to find obviously false answers by means of control questions that allow some plausibility check. In face-to-face interviews, missing data allow at least the tactful inquiry why someone does not want to answer. Yet it will be questionable if the answers provide any new knowledge. It could even spoil the atmosphere for further questions. Or the respondent decides to answer the question simply in an obliging manner but with limited truthfulness. So inquiries into the reasons for missing data will in many cases not contribute to a better understanding of the research topic. After all, false answers are not better than missing ones.

There is a third category of data that can cause a headache – the outliers. Outliers are measurements that lie far outside the distribution of the vast majority of data and hence do not meet expectations as defined by the normal variance of a variable. While outliers may reflect reality, it is generally more likely that they depend on either particular phenomena or measurement errors. Based on the actual circumstances, the researcher will have to decide how to proceed with these outlying observations. If one can assume that they are not measurement errors, one has to keep in mind that they can have a major impact on statistical parameters like in the case of an arithmetic mean. So the median would probably be the better alternative because it is rather robust against outliers. However, if outliers are nothing but measurement errors, one would have to handle them like missing data.

A common approach to deal with missing data is to simply exclude these cases from the analysis. This is known as listwise deletion and reduces the sample size while increasing the sampling error. It is the simplest approach to missing data and a very pragmatic one – provided one can assume that the data are missing at random. However, if this is not the case, listwise deletion will cause a bias.

Instead of deleting complete cases although only few data for certain variables are missing, one can delete these cases solely in analyses that comprise variables with missing data. If, for example, age and customer satisfaction are reported but information about income is missing, this case would be included in the correlation between age and customer satisfaction but would be excluded in analyses that refer to income. As a result, the various analyses would work with different samples, sample sizes and hence sampling errors.

A third way is to deal with lacking answers in the way of just another answer category. However, this would only make sense if one can rightfully assume that the decision not to answer establishes indeed a distinct and reasonably homogeneous category following the same cognitive structure as other answer categories, which will only be appropriate in exceptional cases.

Smart researchers may have heard that under the heading 'imputation', mathematical statistics has various methods ready that allow the substitution of missing data. For example, one could replace all missing data with measures of the variable's central tendency like arithmetic mean, median or mode – depending on the level of measurement. The possible side effects are obvious. In case the data are not missing at random, this approach will result in a bias. Furthermore, the standard deviation of the affected variables will be underestimated. Also, other concepts of imputation come along with side effects. What has some logic in mathematical statistics and perhaps measurements in physics or chemistry is hardly more than some crutches when it comes to practical research and human behaviour. The researcher will have to consider carefully what impact missing data and possible imputation will have on the research results. This is in the first place not about a mathematical procedure that can be left to computer systems but requires decisions that have to consider the research context and the meaning of the data.

4.7 To the Point

The world of services is a complex world. Terms that sound so simple and plausible like customer satisfaction or service quality turn out to be highly complex once they are measured. Of course, there is some vague common sense in what is meant. But then you dig a little deeper and suddenly, there is a big question mark. What does it mean to provide good service? What is customer satisfaction? What makes up quality? In fact, there are many concepts along the research process that provoke a simple straightforward question: what do you mean?

It is the fate of social research that probably all interesting variables cannot be measured directly. Unlike measuring a distance, mass or pressure, there is no meter that measures service quality directly. Service quality is a theoretical construct that is made up of a multitude of criteria or factors. Competence and friendliness are just two factors of service quality. And there are many others. But once again, there is no direct access to these variables. Also competence and friendliness are theoretical variables that cannot be observed directly but comprise of various factors. So we have to find a way that makes them measurable.

Theoretical variables are also described as latent variables, which makes their character more obvious. 'Latent' derives from Latin *'latere'* meaning 'hidden' or 'concealed'. Accordingly, latent variables hide from direct measurement. The only access is to assume or to postulate relations between a concealed latent variable and other variables that are accessible by direct measurement such as, for example, age, waiting time at a counter or the number of complaints about a specific issue. Such empirical variables are also described as manifest variables. The roots of 'manifest' go back to Latin *'manifestus'*, which means 'clear' or 'evident' or – straight to the point – 'caught in the act'. Since the direct access to latent variables is concealed, we make a detour and look for manifest variables that can provide the necessary evidence. So we assume that the latent variables are somehow related to manifest variables, which are accessible by direct measurement, and we infer from the measurement of the manifest variables on the latent variables.

This process of defining the relations between latent and manifest variables is described as operationalization. For example, the competence of a customer service hotline can be measured in terms of the number of calls until an issue is finally settled. In other words, the number of customer service contacts related to the same issue is considered an indicator of competence – do it right the first time. Also the duration of a call can be an indicator. Or one could ask the caller to what extent the answers solved the problem. Obviously, there are various possibilities for how a theoretical variable can be operationalized. And in cases of complex latent variables like service quality, it will not be sufficient to limit the operationalization to just one manifest variable but a bundle of manifest variables will be required together with assumptions about their interrelations.

The operationalization of a theoretical concept is a major step in the research process. Nevertheless, it is a step that often shows substantial weaknesses because it is, to a large extent, based on plausibility and the defined relations are in many cases rather vague or implicit. Furthermore, operationalizations are not compelling. It is at the discretion of the researcher how to operationalize, for example, a complex theoretical concept like 'service quality'. Depending on the research question and the chosen operationalization, the results can be rather different. To some extent, these differences are meaningful because, despite similar basic criteria, the operationalization of service quality in a hotel and in a hospital would probably look quite different. But even if two researchers deal with service quality in hotels, they may arrive at different operationalizations. There is no underlying automatism that makes a specific operationalization compelling.

Therefore, it would be inappropriate to work with categories like right and wrong when it comes to operationalization. Instead, the crucial question is if the operationalization is adequate or not. This is subject to a scientific discourse and, eventually, the recipients of a study will have to come to their own conclusions regarding adequacy. So it is essential to disclose the chosen operationalization for this discourse. The researcher must make it understandable what service quality or any other theoretical constructs actually mean in the context of his study.

Theoretically, there can be a high number of manifest variables that are somehow related to the latent variable. In most cases, it will be impossible to consider all elements as part of the operationalization. And it is not even required as long as the manifest variables cover the variance in the latent variable sufficiently. The very point is to choose relevant variables whereby it is the result of a discourse and perhaps additional supporting research to decide what is actually relevant.

Indeed, it is not that easy to define what latent variables make up a complex theoretical construct. Some researchers try to escape this question by simply using a theoretical construct as a manifest variable. So instead of operationalizing and hence defining a latent variable like customer satisfaction, they simply put the straightforward question: on a scale from 1 to 7 with '1' representing complete dissatisfaction and '7' representing complete satisfaction, how satisfied are you with our service? For sure, most people will make their tick somewhere between 1 and 7 and it would be a big surprise if someone stumbles over such question asking: what do you mean with satisfaction? It is a phenomenon in empirical research that even meaningless questions will in most cases be answered. In fact, these questions are not meaningless to an interviewee because he has a particular understanding of a theoretical construct like customer satisfaction. But this meaning may be very different from the understanding that others and the researcher in particular have. So the response that is meaningful from the perspective of the interviewee may become rather meaningless once responses from very different individual perspectives are aggregated. However for this step, it is not the respondent but the researcher who would have to be blamed.

As a result, what looks like elaborated empirical research may not be more than camouflage of an incomplete research design. One could also describe it as rather meaningless operationalization because it lacks intersubjectivity. Apparently, neither the researcher has an explicit concept of customer satisfaction nor does anybody know what understanding is underlying the answers from the respondents. In such cases, what may appear as empirical research is actually nothing but a smokescreen with little epistemological value. It remains unclear in what context the results can claim relevance – if they are relevant at all. The problem is, however, that this will not prevent the researcher from presenting some breakthrough results. Meaningless research easily develops some momentum of its own.

Some consultancy companies like to highlight how many criteria they supposedly measure to come to quality judgements. The more variables the more accurate the results – that's at least the credo when they publish their studies. But then you want to know how they reduce several hundred observations of a particular service performance into a test result that service providers eventually use for their public relations work – and learn that this is a secret that will only be revealed to the management of the participating companies. You are baffled. Any attempt to receive additional information is futile. You may even be asked to abstain from related inquiries because they will not be replied to anyway. The message is clear. If you are a reader of the results you should be contented with the mere explanation that the results are a summary. In other words, believe it or not – but don't ask. Such research may be commercially successful but it is epistemologically useless.

As much as it is understandable that consultants are reluctant to reveal their methods and methodology because it is their intellectual property that they want to protect from being copied, this has nothing to do with a scientific discourse and scientific principles. Results that are not comprehensible cannot claim relevance. It does not become better when these researchers refer to many years of experience and hundreds of thousands of participants in a survey if the basics behind the results are not revealed. The only answer is to either limit the publication of the results to those participating companies that receive full details of the underlying theoretical concept as well as its operationalization and to abstain from using them for advertising purposes, or to open up for a discourse and to provide information about the research concept to an extent that allows the recipients to judge its adequacy. Of course, so much openness could be sobering. And that may be exactly the reason why some researchers prefer to abstain from disclosing the methodological background of their studies.

What has been described so far as a manifest variable can also be described as an indicator. The meaning of an indicator – deriving from Latin '*indicare*' – is to point out. It is a variable that can be measured directly and is assumed to point out a theoretical construct. We can distinguish different types of indicators. Definitional indicators are a one-dimensional definition of a theoretical construct. This type of indicator is rather rare in social sciences because social constructs are usually multidimensional. They are described by indicators that correlate highly with the concept whereby these correlative indicators do not represent the latent variable completely. Whenever a theoretical construct cannot even be observed partially, such as, for example, in the case of attitudes, one will have to work with deducible indicators that allow the deduction of attitudes from observed behaviour.

For example, measuring the service quality of a hotel, the number of staff – which from the perspective of a hotel operator is first of all a cost factor – in relation to the number of rooms can serve as an indicator of the service level. But it is not the only possible indicator. The number of restaurants, the size of the rooms and many others can be named that do also 'point out' at the service level. Complex variables like service quality cannot usually be represented by just one indicator. They require several indicators that are combined with the intention to adequately reflect a more complex theoretical construct. The result is an index. But how to combine indicators and what does the result mean?

The crucial point is that the construction of an index is not a mathematical exercise but must be guided by theoretical considerations. Indeed, it is a theoretical exercise to select the indicators that are considered relevant. It is also a theory-based decision how various indicators are combined into an index. This can be a logical or arithmetical combination. The very point is the meaning behind the operation. Mathematically, it is no problem to add or multiply two indicators. The question is, however, if this operation is meaningful. And that is not a mathematical but a theoretical decision.

Furthermore, the combination of indicators and the development of indexes are not a deterministic procedure but depend on the theoretical concept. That means that different researchers can arrive at different indexes representing the same social situation. This has consequences. The researcher must not only disclose the theoretical assumptions that have resulted in a specific index, he must also analyze to what extent the index actually measures what it is supposed to measure.

In fact, what has been said about latent and manifest variables are at the same time inherent elements of common steering mechanisms in business. Managers use just a slightly different terminology when they talk about success factors or even critical success factors (CSF) on one hand and key performance indicators (KPI) and benchmarks on the other. In many companies, CSF and KPI have become common catchwords that dominate the business culture. CSFs describe theoretical constructs that make or break a business strategy. It is the answer to the question why one should choose that very service provider and not any of its competitors. In this context, benchmarking is the process of comparing actual business performance with the targeted performance, which can reflect the best performer or some defined business targets. It is the natural desire to know where the business stands in comparison to the targets. And this will normally not only focus on the cost structure but on quality levels in particular.

From a methodological perspective, KPIs are nothing but operationalizations of supposed business success. A latent variable like responsiveness to customer requests that may have been identified as a CSF of a business is operationalized by means of manifest variables like the number of rings until a phone call is answered. It is a simple logic. Service quality means responsiveness. Responsiveness means reacting quickly. Therefore, it is mandatory to pick up the phone as fast as possible whenever a call comes in. This can be measured by the number of ringing tones. State-of-the-art telephone systems can even record the performance and provide related analyses. So far so good.

Indeed, KPIs can be quite powerful. Once they are defined and some initial moaning has been overcome, the behaviour of staff will quickly adjust to it. Knowing that how fast the phone is answered will be measured, they may develop some signs of paranoia but nevertheless ensure that it will not ring longer than three times – before they answer in a grumpy manner because a KPI for friendliness has not been implemented yet. Oops!

That is exactly the effect of an inappropriate operationalization. If the manifest variables can explain the variance of a latent variable only insufficiently because they do not reflect its complexity and focus solely on a certain aspect whereas others are neglected, the results will be biased as well. The effect is that research supposed to measure a complex variable like service quality will actually provide a rather distorted view. This will become obvious as long as the operationalization is disclosed. However, if that is not the case, as in many commercial studies, one will not even know what has actually been measured and how meaningful the results are.

In the case of success factors and KPIs, the situation is basically the same. Quality is a complex construct and many aspects resist simple measurement. Unfortunately, managers prefer to look for simple straightforward indicators. They do not want to be bothered with multidimensional theoretical concepts. They want it simple. The simpler the better. A one-dimensional world would be best. Measuring responsiveness based on the number of rings until the phone is picked up has some natural charm. It can be automated, it looks plausible and it has the potential to change behaviour. But then you recognize that quality is more than responding to a ringing telephone and suddenly, things become difficult. How to measure friendliness or credibility? It is not easy to develop indicators for these and other variables, which are undeniably part of service quality.

The effect of a KPI that does not reflect a concept sufficiently is the same as it is with inadequate operationalization in research – the company possibly moves in the wrong direction. While it may develop into a competition to pick up the phone faster than anybody else, the reactions to the caller may become increasingly paranoid and unfriendly. Some people could even make it a sport to reduce the KPI to absurdity – lousy service despite an excellent KPI. Only if KPIs are understood as some kind of permanent quality research and follow essential research criteria do they have the potential to provide meaningful support to the steering of a business. In fact, this is to a large extent a matter of adequate operationalization.

4.8 Please Tick

Please read the following statements and rate how strongly you agree or disagree with each of the items by marking the respective category:

This book ...	strongly disagree	disagree	undecided	agree	strongly agree
	1	2	3	4	5
... provides interesting information	☐	☐	☐	☐	☐
... looks at quality research from a different perspective	☐	☐	☐	☐	☐
... will be helpful when dealing with quality research	☐	☐	☐	☐	☐
... is worth a recommendation to my colleagues	☐	☐	☐	☐	☐

There are hardly any questionnaires that come without items like these. Instead of agreement, they may focus on frequency, importance, likelihood or quality. There may be more or less categories. And it may be an odd or an even number of scaling points. In any case, your judgement is requested as an indicator of your attitude. Please tick.

What looks at first glance like the ultimate answer to the measurement of customer satisfaction and perceived quality is known as a Likert scale. It was Rensis Likert (1932) who developed this one-dimensional scaling method for the measurement of attitudes.[20] Likert defined attitudes as 'dispositions toward overt action' (Likert 1932: 9), which highlights their relevance for social action. The concept assumes that the extent of agreement or disagreement to statements reflects the attitude of the respondent towards the underlying theoretical variable.[21] It was an idea that turned into a great success. Likert items have become a standard element of almost every questionnaire – and nevertheless, they come along with some unease.

To avoid misunderstandings, it is necessary to first clarify the terminology, because what are often described as Likert scales are actually Likert items. Likert items are statements that the respondents shall rate with regard to their level of agreement or disagreement. Commonly, this rating is done on a scale from 1 to 5 or 1 to 7, which – in addition to numerical values – is also described verbally.[22] When it is about agreement, the description could comprise labels like: strongly agree/agree/undecided/disagree/ strongly disagree. Similarly, when the items refer to quality one would use terms like very good/good/average/poor/very poor. Of course, this gradation represents a scale but it is not what a Likert scale refers to. A Likert scale is actually the sum of all responses to Likert items dealing with the same theoretical construct. In the example above, the Likert items range from 1 to 5 but the Likert scale ranges from 4 (strongly disagree to all items) to 20 (strongly agree to all items), which explains that Likert scales are also described as summated scale.

The above examples make obvious how important it is to find category labels that do actually represent equidistance as an interpretation at interval level would require. In order to avoid the possible bias of unequal distances between the points on the scale, sometimes only the extremes are verbalized and the description of the categories in between is left to the figures. Alternatively, all categories could be marked only with figures or just shown as a line with radio buttons at equal distance. Furthermore, instead of using figures from (usually) 1 to 5, the categories could be represented as -2, -1, 0, +1, +2. This looks more balanced and highlights the centre of the scale more clearly. But it does not prevent other unwanted effects that may lead to biased results.

Responses to Likert items are likely to be affected by a tendency to agree rather than to disagree.[23] After all, respondents do not want to disappoint the researcher. Social desirability is a driving factor when rating Likert items. And when things become critical, one can find refuge in the central category, which is not usually what a researcher wants

---

20   Organizational psychologist Rensis Likert was the founder of the Institute for Social Research at the University of Michigan in Ann Arbor.

21   While Likert scales are the most popular approach to the measurement of attitudes and opinion, there are also various other concepts like Guttman or Thurstone scales. In fact, the Thurstone scale was the starting point for Likert's work.

22   Likert used originally a five-point scale. Some studies recommend a seven- or nine-point scale whereas others advocate even-numbered scales.

23   This effect is known as acquiescence bias. See also section 4.4.

to see. So one could try to be smart working with an even number of categories that mitigates the effect of central tendency. But forcing the respondents to make decisions that they actually try to avoid is a questionable cure. It suppresses factual indecisiveness and in written questionnaires one may eventually find the tick somewhere in the middle even if there is no box to tick. Or the respondents decide to distribute their answers equally left and right of the lacking radio button in the centre or they simply decide not to make any tick and instead move on to the next item. In the end, the researcher has the choice between indecisiveness and missing data.

Despite all unwanted side effects, Likert scales have the image of being simple to develop. This may apply to the trivial use of unrelated items but things become more complex when developing a meaningful Likert scale. It is much more than just writing down a statement like, 'All in all, I am satisfied with the service performance' and asking the respondents to rate it without knowing if this will actually measure what it is supposed to measure.

Often such items are not even one-dimensional. For example, how to comment if an item reads: the customer service staff was competent and friendly? If both apply the rating may be easy. But how to assess the item if the staff were very friendly but unfortunately also pretty incompetent? Developing an elaborated Likert scale, such shortcomings would hardly occur. However, many researchers just develop some statements that are distantly related to something like Likert items. Sometimes this happens to an extent that questionnaires eventually comprise nothing but items with a rating scale that have only the effect that the respondents start to yawn after they have made a number of ticks. One should expect that after the first few items were rated carefully, the later ones will be ticked without much consideration. A long list of Likert items can be rather tiring.

In the same way as every empirical research approach, Likert scales must be based on a clearly defined research question. A vague interest in knowing something about customer satisfaction is not a particularly sound basis for the development of a research method. So what is the actual interest? How is a customer defined? And how is customer satisfaction defined? Furthermore, the question arises if customer satisfaction can indeed be understood as a one-dimensional concept. After all, Likert scales are one-dimensional. It would be an inadequate approach for the measurement of a multidimensional concept. At least some factors of customer satisfaction would not be sufficiently reflected.

Following a clear definition of the research question, the next step is to generate the items that are to be rated. These items can be worded either in a positive or negative way. At the initial stage, a high number of items will be created that are rated as part of a pretest. Based on the results of the pretest, those items that turn out to be ambiguous or incomprehensible will be eliminated. The same applies to items that have insufficient selectivity. The target is to work with those few items that are a reliable and valid indicator of the attitude that will be measured. In terms of statistics, this is the decision to sort out items that show only a low correlation with the summated score.[24] Alternatively, for each item the 25 per cent highest and lowest scores are selected and it is tested if the average score of the high- and low-scorers show significant differences.[25] Those items that

---

24   To sum up the total score, it is prerequisite that all items have the same direction and use the same scale. If items do not have the same direction, the numerical values must be adjusted for the purpose of summation.

25   This is usually done by means of a t-test. The t-test is a significance test for the comparison of two samples of interval scaled data. Assuming ordinal data, the Mann-Whitney U-test or Wilcoxon signed-rank test would be appropriate.

discriminate best[26] will be chosen for the final Likert scale. So constructing a Likert scale is actually much more than just throwing an item before the respondents and asking to what extent they would agree.

In the end, there is still the question which level of measurement Likert items and Likert scales actually represent. This is crucial with regard to the decision on appropriate statistical models. Ordinal or interval – that's the question and to some extent a matter of faith. Likert targeted the measurement of attitudes on a metric scale – measuring attitudes like temperature. Meanwhile, more than 80 years have passed since Likert first published his proposal and yet arguments are exchanged as to which scale level is the 'right' one. At the same time, this ongoing discussion could not spoil the success of Likert's approach.

Strictly speaking, assigning figures with equal distance to verbal expressions does not have the normative power of defining equal distances in the mind of the respondents. There is no proof that, for example, the semantic distance between 'strongly agree' and 'agree' is the same as between, let's say, 'undecided' and 'disagree'. And what would be the arithmetic mean of 'agree' and 'undecided'? These simple questions make it obvious that assuming the interval level of the ratings would indeed be rather daring. On the other hand, one could argue that the questionnaire presents the items visually at equal distance and even if the assumption of equidistance is not proven, it may be a reasonable approximation of the actual distribution.

Of course, ordinal statistics have various models in store for a meaningful analysis of Likert items. At the same time, a metric scale is assumed once the ratings are summed up across the items. Furthermore, metric statistical models are often easier to impart. Median or mode are not as easy to grasp as an arithmetic mean. It may be confusing that ordinal data allow only for a bar chart whereas interval data can be presented as histogram although both graphics look almost alike.[27] And in most cases the recipients of the results will not even care about such methodological subtleties. So the very point is that regardless at what conclusion the researcher ultimately arrives, the decision must be disclosed and should be justified.

With so much transparency, the recipients of the results may decide if they deem the approach adequate or not. Just rate the following statement on a scale from strongly disagree to strongly agree: assuming metric data when dealing with Likert items is appropriate. Please tick.

4.9 To be on Top

It is the common law of the jungle – everything turns towards the light and soars upwards. Struggling to be on top of the competition, being more service oriented, more responsive, more understanding, more friendly, more reliable – in a word: being better. How to prove superiority in a more convincing manner than by means of a ranking? It is like stripes on the shoulder and decorations on the breast. Rankings meet the natural demand for a clear-cut pecking order. And the winner is …

---

26   In statistical terms: having the highest t-values.

27   Contrary to histograms, bar charts have spaces between the columns because the distance between the values does not contain empirical information. In the case of nominal data, the sequence of the columns also has no empirical meaning.

Many rankings come along with a claim for the absolute. Claiming to have found the best university, best transport operator, best hotel, best cruise ship, best airport, best airline – you name it. One could just ignore these hit parades but it is more. CEOs rush to the award winners' celebration where they collect their trophy with warm words of gratitude. Thank you for making us a winner! The press will report – and politely abstain from the critical question of how meaningful all these rankings are. Facing the gospel of service excellence, who would really dispute the methodology behind the supposed findings? So much disrespect would only cause disillusion.

Rankings can be powerful. They can catapult nobodies into the limelight as well as nosedive a hitherto successful business. But what is a rather clear statistical approach becomes in reality often a miraculous black box. In many cases, this is understandable because revealing a dreadful methodology would easily spoil the trust in any seriousness of these rankings. Those who publish the ultimate rankings of service performance will know why they hide behind meaningless and stereotype explanations of their wondrous survey methodology. Obviously, it does not damage the ranking business. Rankings have a momentum of their own. Winners will not question the results. And so do the hopefuls of future rounds of awards. Nobody wants to be a bad loser in this perpetual game of alleged excellence.

There are various business models when it comes to the order of service excellence. Sometimes rankings are presented as a one-man show. This concept is preferably based on proclaiming yourself a guru and selling your supposed wisdom as ultimate truth.[28] This works even better when adding some mysticism to the ranking. A few hundred criteria that are allegedly measured, analyzed and mysteriously summarized into a few categories are sufficient to promise scholarly standard. Who would dare to argue against so much intricacy? Just keep it sufficiently mysterious. This can still be topped by establishing an institute with an impressive-sounding name – perhaps something like Services Evaluations Institute – and making yourself the President. This adds weight to your judgements. And then sell your ranking as *The Ultimate Guidebook* and don't be shy of calling it *The Bible*. Solid self-confidence is, however, prerequisite when it comes to this type of rankings.

Also as a consultant, one can easily be in on rankings. Just look for a niche and start to publish rankings. A high number of cases are as important as secrecy about the methodology. The first one pretends a scientific approach whereas the latter one prevents critical questions. Where hundreds of thousands have voted and the analysis is apparently so complicated that one has to limit explanations to some sibylline catchwords like nomination balancing, data weighting or interview screening, any doubts are out of the question. Never bother the readers with details. Successful rankings are true by definition. Just call them official, professional, trusted, distinguished or – even better – prestigious. Simply praise them as a global benchmark of service excellence. The name of the consultancy firm serves as proof of the ranking's trustworthiness. And the ranking adds to the reputation of the consultant. That is true synergy. Just make it a glamorous award ceremony. But ensure that everybody can bring a trophy home – at least almost everybody. Because next year the same show will start again and some surprise winners are always good for the headlines.

---

28   This and the following descriptions do not refer to specific rankings but describe archetypes of published rankings. Spontaneous associations with actual rankings may, however, prove the relevance of these patterns.

Journalists are grateful for rankings. Such charts of supposed excellence are always good for an article with a table and some colourful pictures. Tables are associated with scientific methods and accuracy. Journalists love rankings and they can be sure that their readers hop on it. Immediately they will flood the forum with their comments – adding their own stories in consent – or proving that the ranking is utter rubbish because their personal experience is totally different. Rankings have a high recognition value and they are highly communicative. Everybody has something to contribute. You think that airline A is better than B? I think both are bad but C is really good. And then you can hear a wild story about air turbulence during a flight or complaints about the caviar portion that was much bigger when flying another airline.

Service providers also love rankings. As long as they are on top, rankings are the stuff that makes public relations campaigns. Thank you for voting us best in the world – but please do not question the methodology. The good thing is that there are enough rankings to ensure that almost every company can be a winner. Just split the market into segments and do not worry if all this makes sense. In the end, you can even give an award to the most improved service provider – even if the performance is still not satisfying. It is not about finding the truth but about marketing. Take, for example, airlines. You can rank them overall or according to cabin crew, seats, catering, in-flight entertainment, lounges, check-in, on-time performance, safety, sustainability or whatever you like. Furthermore, one can split all this into first, business and economy class. Then break it down into long-haul and short-haul flights as well as regions and do not forget to separate common carriers, leisure and budget airlines. So who is the best? And what is such honour good for if you fly the award-winning airline of the year but are framed by two heavyweights that hardly leave space for you to breathe and make your journey a horror trip?

The answer is simple. Rankings are a business model that will work as long as service providers join in this game and are prepared to contribute directly or indirectly to the results and the readers of these rankings do not ask how meaningful the results are.

Indeed, one could live with these rankings if they would at least meet some basic scientific standards. But in many cases, one can only guess how the self-proclaimed custodians of service excellence have arrived at their findings. It will be futile to ask for more than the vague explanation that the awarded laurels represent a summary of dozens of items – please note that further details are only available to the top management of participating service providers. All others have the choice between believing the alleged results – or not. There is no chance to decide if one would consent to the criteria of the ranking because this kind of research is like a black box.

Sometimes one can guess how the results were calculated. Take for example a ranking of the service onboard cruise ships.[29] Let's assume that the results are based on a questionnaire to readers of a travel magazine who rate a number of criteria like cabins, food or entertainment on a five-point scale from excellent to poor. And when the questionnaire is finished, you cannot escape the question if you would like to receive occasional special offers and would perhaps even like to subscribe to the magazine. As said, rankings are a business model.

With thousands of questionnaires returned, a few hundred ships will be rated and those that receive more than a minimum number of votes will join the ranking. What

---

29   The following example is fictitious. It is inspired by assumptions about published rankings, which cannot be verified because of insufficient information about the underlying methodology. Insofar, it has only illustrative character.

were originally ratings on a five-point scale will be converted to a hundred-point scale, which awakes some associations with percentage figures. As a next step, for every ship and category the average score is calculated. From there it is only a short step to an overall rating – adding the individual scores and calculating the arithmetic mean. It's done. One digit behind the decimal point ensures an impression of accuracy. And to be fair, the list is split according to the type of ships before the Top 25 in every category are published as 'Best Cruise Ships in the World'. Paper doesn't blush.

That is in many cases the stuff that makes rankings. But a study is not representative just because thousands of people have ticked a number of items in a questionnaire. What does it mean if a passenger rates a ship as excellent without knowing that there are much better ships because he has never been on any other ship? And what is the meaning behind the sum of, let's say, very good food, average entertainment and reasonable shore programmes? Is it perhaps 58.7 points? Does that really justify a higher ranking compared to another ship with 'only' 58.6 points? And then you recognize that the proclaimed best cruise ships in the world operate all in the same region – also home to the magazine. Best ships in the world? What relevance can such results really have?

This is just an example. It is not criticizing a specific ranking but the underlying principle of many rankings. It is a trivial arithmetic that does not question the meaning behind the figures and mathematical operations. Figures are assigned to some more or less meaningful ratings and disappear in a black box where nobody questions any longer if the arithmetic corresponds to the empirical world. In the end, a figure comes out and meaning is assigned. But the crucial question if this meaning is still related to the empirical world is not put. Instead, the 'result' develops some almost unstoppable momentum. Newspapers will report and, eventually, readers will believe the results. After all, it must be true if so many papers have reported it. It is a wondrous perpetuation of meaninglessness.

Despite all bewilderment around rankings, one cannot deny that they meet demand and affect social behaviour. Rankings are hierarchies that come along with supposed scientific legitimization. That makes them powerful. Externally, they can affect markets because flying with the world's best dressed cabin crew onboard the world's best airline from the world's best airport eases the burden of making a decision and is simply more glamorous than travelling onboard a lacklustre airline that has not yet made it to the top of the charts. Internally, rankings can steer a business when KPIs are presented as rankings. It is the natural desire to be on top that can turn rankings into an amazing accelerator of performance. But this demands a sound methodology – and that is exactly the crux of rankings.

Generally, all data that are measured at ordinal or higher level can be arranged as ranking. This can either be done after the data is collected or as part of data collection, asking respondents to rank, for example, their satisfaction with a particular service performance in relation to others. In any case, rankings allow only the interpretation of the relations equal/unequal and larger/smaller. The difference between two ranks has no empirical meaning. This is a crucial point that does not only apply to the original data but of course also to the final rankings that are based on the original data. Arriving at a supposed quality ranking of a few hundred airports will only provide the information that airport A is rated better than airport B. There is no information how much better A is in comparison to B. The difference may not even be significant but could simply be caused by sampling errors.

Nevertheless, common practice looks rather different. Without any hesitation, ordinal data are interpreted as metric data and undergo a miraculous metamorphosis. What started with a few ticks on a five-point scale from excellent to poor eventually turns into a ranking of 100 service providers that breaks free from its humble data base – figures behind the decimal point instead of meaning. Only when you come across another ranking of the same service sector do you wonder why the results are so different. Oops – how come?

Rankings deal with complex theoretical constructs. The simple question, 'How satisfied are you with the service of our airline?' does not specify the manifold elements that determine customer satisfaction. And measuring these individual elements does not say much about their interactions and how they are eventually integrated into a construct like customer satisfaction. This demands for a theoretical model that explicates the underlying assumptions and the role of the various variables as indicators of service quality, their weighting and interactions. Is the semantic distance between 'good' and 'excellent' the same as between 'poor' and 'fair'? Is service quality 30 per cent wellbeing, 10 per cent responsiveness, 20 per cent communication and 40 per cent competence? Or is it something else? Can competence make up for lacking wellbeing? Or should one better present the results for the various factors separately without combining them?

Such questions prove how important it is to explicate the basics of the theoretical model. Otherwise, a ranking is not understandable and hence meaningless. Yet this does not constitute an ultimate truth. But it allows a discourse on the adequacy of the underlying theoretical and methodological approach and a decision on the relevance of the results. It is a discourse that contributes to the development of common sense and an understanding of what factors make up a theoretical construct like service quality. Of course, this essential requirement of an explication of the research assumptions and decisions applies also to any other empirical research results. But the power of rankings that derives from their supposed simplicity and straightness makes it necessary to stress this aspect.

There are a number of issues that make rankings much more complex than one may expect when looking at a straightforward pecking order. What is usually easy to measure in sports – Citius, Altius, Fortius[30] – becomes much more difficult when dealing with social variables that cannot be measured directly like time, height, distance or mass. But already in sports it becomes obvious how difficult it is to combine two or more criteria into a ranking that decides between victory and defeat. Look for example at ski jumping, which is not only about distance but also about style. Distance can be measured in metres whereas the style is assessed by judges. So a model is required that combines both measurements. The expected average distance from the ski jump is converted into 60 points and, accordingly, longer or shorter jumps result in more or less points. Five judges will rate the style and award up to 20 points each. The highest and lowest score is cancelled in order to reduce the variance and avoid outliers so there is a maximum of 60 points for style. For the final score, the points for distance and style are added assuming metric data. This looks like both criteria have the same weight but in fact, distance has a higher weight because it is possible to achieve more than 60 distance points whereas the points for style cannot be higher than 60. Nevertheless, neither the farthest but clumsy jump nor a short jump in perfect style makes a winner. Instead, a long stylish jump is

---

30   Faster, Higher, Stronger – the Olympic motto.

required. Yet the question is not if this approach is right or wrong. It is a model that has been agreed and everybody may decide if one likes it or not, deems it fair or not and joins this sport or watches it or not. In any case, it is an approach that is understandable and open for a discourse.

When it comes to service quality, the choice of criteria becomes even more complex. What are the relevant factors of service quality that a ranking has to take into consideration? It depends. It depends on the service sector as well as the target group. Scientific and practical research may have different perspectives and the business perspective may be different from the customers' view. The very point is relevance with regard to the research question. If theoretical knowledge and experience do not provide a sufficiently reliable and valid answer, one could make this question the subject of a pre-study or build it into the survey and ask for decisive factors of the quality of a particular service or a ranking of such criteria. This can help to develop a relevant model of service quality that is more meaningful than some hardly empirically substantiated arithmetic.

Another major issue is the question of to what extent respondents to surveys are actually qualified for such ratings. In ski jumping one would not work with amateurs as judges. Many published quality rankings have less scruples. What they sell as 'best of the world' with a decent claim for the absolute is usually based on ratings from people who would be described in sports as amateurs at best. That practice raises some spontaneous questions. Have these judges sufficient experience to compare? How homogeneous are their expectations? Do they share a common understanding of what is fair, good or excellent? A small variance in the ratings would be an indicator of expertise of the respondents but most rankings do not provide any related information. Moreover, it may well be that what is presented as 'accurate' ranking of service quality is rather a ranking of the images instead of the actual performance of service providers. It depends on the research question if such focus can be considered adequate.

The crux is that many rankings of theoretical constructs like service quality comprise multidimensional and to a large extent subjective evaluations without sufficient consensus regarding their weighting. And even if we deal with variables that are not exposed to subjective assessments but understood as 'objective' data such as, for example, blood pressure, time, length or number, subjectivity is an issue because these supposedly objective data are elements of indexes that demand for subjective weighting. So there's no getting away from some subjective elements in rankings. In fact, there is no 'true' and 'objective' ranking.

Imagine the simple – and fictitious – case of a ranking of the service onboard two cruise vessels A and B and let's restrict the analysis to so-called 'objective' data, which are easily available. Ship A has 1,100 crew members for 2,400 passengers in 1,000 cabins whereas B has a crew of 200 for 500 passengers in 250 cabins. A cruise costs 150 dollars per day onboard A but 180 dollars on ship B. The cabin size on A is 22 m² and 20 m² on B. The occupancy rate on cruise A is 95 per cent and on cruise B 80 per cent. All data can easily be measured and there should not be any dispute regarding the accuracy of the data. So what does all this tell us about service quality? And which ship offers the better service quality?

No doubt, A has the better crew/passenger ratio than B. On the other hand, B is the smaller ship and less crew may be required for a personal service. But the nautical and technical personnel should be about the same on both ships, which would reduce the number of staff attending directly to the passengers on B relatively more than on A. However, considering the occupancy rate, B has actually more crew per passenger than A, which speaks for B. But a day onboard B is also more expensive, which could point at a better service while at the same time the expectations are higher. On the other hand, the cabins onboard A are bigger and should offer more comfort. However, the average number of passengers per cabin is lower onboard cruise B. Furthermore, it is not only the cabin size that determines the service level but also the suitability and comfort of the cabins. In fact, A has a higher occupancy rate, which lets us assume that the service quality is better because it seems to attract more passengers than B. On the other hand, a high occupancy rate may come along with some inconvenience that results in lower experienced service quality. So how does the actual ranking look? Which is the 'Top Cruise Ship in the World'?

To make it yet more difficult, even seemingly 'objective' data like the number of crew or passengers or the price per day are not as simple to measure as it appears at first glance. Should one count all crew or only those who deal directly with passengers? Is the maximum or the actual number of passengers relevant when it comes to service quality? How to count young children who travel in their parents' cabin? What does the price per day comprise? Again, there is no answer that would result in a 'true' and 'objective' ranking. Things just become more complicated.

Moreover, one has to consider that service quality rankings comprise usually more service providers and variables than this extremely simple example. So what looks already rather confusing is in reality by far more complex. Nevertheless, actual rankings come along with the proud claim of covering dozens of factors that each comprise numerous variables.

One should further consider that something as complex as the service performance onboard a cruise vessel comprises a number of factors with rather different relevance to a specific passenger. So depending on actual travel expectations and requirements, the interpretation of 'best' cruise vessel will vary substantially. It is of little interest if a children's play area is provided when travelling without children. The show programme is not relevant if you join the cruise because you just want to gamble in the casino and the same applies to shore programmes if you prefer to enjoy the ship when most passengers have gone ashore. So how relevant is a ranking?

The only way out of this dilemma is to disclose the methodological approach including the variables that are used as operationalization of service quality as well as their weighting and interactions. Without such information, rankings have no epistemological value. This becomes obvious at the latest when there is more than one ranking dealing with the same subject and readers rub their eyes in surprise wondering why all rankings arrive at different results.

The quality of university rankings, for example, is an area where not only several rankings compete but the proximity to science awakes expectations of particular accuracy and reliability – and leave puzzled readers behind in view of sometimes substantial differences in the results. Just look at some results of three leading worldwide university rankings as presented in Table 4.2. Considering the differences, the almost unavoidable public reaction is the question which ranking is right and which is wrong – 'Ranking university rankings' as *The Straits Times* of Singapore once titled (Davie 2010). 'With so many different league tables, it's hard to tell which is reliable,' they lamented and found that 'all use different grading measures. Some are more credible than others.'

Table 4.2   Comparison of the overall rankings of selected universities

University	QS World University Rankings 2012 Top 500	*Times Higher Education* World University Rankings 2012–2013 Top 400	Academic Ranking of World Universities (Shanghai Ranking) 2012 Top 500
Harvard University	3	4	1
Stanford University	15	2	2
Massachusetts Institute of Technology	1	5	3
University of California, Berkeley	22	9	4
University of Cambridge	2	7	5
California Institute of Technology	10	1	6
University of Oxford	5	2	10
University of Tokyo	30	27	20
University of Michigan, Ann Arbor	17	20	22
University of Heidelberg	55	78	62
National University of Singapore	25	29	101–150
University of Hong Kong	23	35	151–200
Peking University	44	46	151–200
Nanyang Technical University, Singapore	47	86	201–300

Note: See: www.topuniversities.com; www.timeshighereducation.co.uk/world-university-rankings; www.shanghairanking.com/index.html.

It is just another example for the never-ending search for the ultimate truth. It is the centuries-old (and long overcome) idea of an universal empiricism that just has to refine its methods to find the objective reality. In fact, the search for the objective reality will be futile. Instead, the crucial question is what the rankings target at and how adequate and relevant the underlying theoretical model and its operationalization are. But looking at respective websites, the targets of the rankings remain sometimes rather nebulous although the differences between the rankings make it clear that one can approach the quality of universities from rather different angles. For example, help for students to make them understand which universities are ranked the highest is mentioned as well as self-praise for covering more factors than other rankings. Or they highlight with which international organizations they cooperate. But a clear research question would be more helpful when judging the methodological approach. On the other hand, providing information about the underlying variables and weightings is already more than what many other ratings provide. And indeed, all three rankings define the quality of universities in a rather different manner as shown in Table 4.3.

So which university is 'really' the best? Or perhaps: which ranking is the best? The cited *Straits Times* article argued that 'it all boils down to the credibility of the ratings'. So which approach is most credible? On which ranking can a student rely when choosing his alma mater? A big Singapore university found a rather pragmatic answer to the question why one should choose them. They simply refer to that very ranking where they have come off best. But what is understandable from a marketing perspective appears to be somehow questionable from a scientific point of view.

Table 4.3   Comparison of the methodology of some leading university rankings

	QS World University Rankings	*Times Higher Education* **World University Rankings**	**Academic Ranking of World Universities (Shanghai Ranking)**
Reputation	Academic reputation (survey) 40%	Research excellence (survey) 18%	Alumni of an institution winning Nobel Prizes and Fields Medals 10%
	Employer reputation (survey) 10%		Staff of an institution winning Nobel Prizes and Fields Medals 20%
Research		Research: volume and income 12%	Papers published in Nature and Science 20%; Papers indexed in Science Citation Index-expanded and Social Science Citation Index 20%
Citations	Citations per faculty 20%	Citations: research influence 30%	Highly cited researchers in 21 broad subject categories 20%
Teaching	Faculty/student ratio 20%	Teaching: the learning environment 30%	
Knowledge Transfer		Industry income: innovation 2.5%	
International Aspects	International student ratio 5%	International outlook: staff, students and research 7.5%	
	International faculty ratio 5%		
Academic Performance			Per capita academic performance 10%

Note: This is a summary based on the websites of the rankings. The Shanghai Ranking does not consider 'Papers published in Nature and Science' for institutions specialized in humanities and social sciences and distributes the weight to other indicators. *Times Higher Education* has a separate ranking by reputation.

It is not more convincing when the *Straits Times* writer comes to the conclusion that 'at the moment' the Shanghai Ranking 'is one that is more trusted by academia' because 'it uses objective measures'. No, neither do rankings become better because they are built on 'objective measures' nor are categories like right or wrong, better or worse appropriate to distinguish between different approaches to rankings.

Assuming that data collection and statistical analysis follow basic scientific standards, the very point is adequacy in the context of the research question. As a student, one may not really deem it relevant how many Nobel Prizes have been won at the university of choice. However, as a professor this may look different. Teaching and researching at a university that produces Nobel Prize winners will add to one's own reputation even if such great honours will be denied most academic staff. Students may deem the faculty/ students ratio and learning environment more relevant. Similarly, one can discuss all variables of the rankings and their weighting and come to a conclusion regarding their adequacy. Such consideration is not about better or worse, it is about relevance in a specific context. It is an essential discourse that is only possible if the basics of the rankings are available.

4.10 Trendy

When it comes to quality, short-termism would be a rather questionable approach that could make a service provider short-winded. Successful service performance demands that the long view is taken. After all, the non-material character of services and their dependency on human behaviour sets natural limits to a standardization of service performance and makes service quality volatile.

Having said this, it is to some extent surprising that many quality studies are designed as a one-shot approach that provides a snapshot of service quality but does not reflect a long-term development. Things may look different tomorrow. And once a study has come to the conclusion that the service performance meets high quality standards, it would only be human to lean back a bit further – until rude awakening is looming.

Depending on the design, empirical social research distinguishes between cross-sectional and longitudinal studies. A cross-sectional study makes a straight cut through a statistical population at a certain point in time. It is the common one-shot approach that provides a snapshot of the research topic. By contrast, longitudinal studies deal with change over time. The same study is performed at different points in time and the results are compared in order to analyze developments. In comparison to a snapshot that a cross-sectional study provides, longitudinal studies are more like a movie although it may be stuttering because it is usually not a continuous measurement.

Longitudinal studies can be either trend or panel studies. A trend or repeated study performs the same measurement at different times on different – but structurally identical – samples. For example, this could be a representative sample of customers of a service provider whereby every time different people make up the sample but each sample represents the same target group. A panel study, on the other hand, deals with the same sample made up of the same people at different times – following people through parts of their life cycles. Trend studies work with – apart from the underlying statistical population – independent samples whereas the samples in panel studies are dependent. This is an important difference that has not only an impact on the choice of an adequate statistical model when it comes to further analysis but is particularly important with regard to the interpretation of data. Both approaches are an appropriate approach to changes between the repeated studies but only panel studies allow an interpretation of these changes at an intra-individual level.

This difference makes panel studies more powerful than trend studies. Nevertheless, panel studies are relatively seldom in practical research – for good reason. Panel studies are expensive because of the efforts that are required to maintain the sample over a long time. And they are exposed to all kind of mortality. Panel members may lose interest in the study, have passed away or moved and cannot be found or they simply do not meet the definition of the target group any longer. The effects of panel mortality become the stronger the longer a panel study lasts – and this can well be several years. So before the researcher finds himself lonesome in the midst of a panel that has faded away, it makes sense to start with a larger sample in order to have enough 'survivors' at later stages. Things become yet more complicated because one cannot assume that panel mortality is a random effect. Instead, there may be structural effects that eventually result in a distortion of the sample design. Furthermore, one has to consider the impact of repeated surveys on the behaviour of the respondents. After all, members of a panel assume to some extent the role of recognized experts, which can make their judgements more critical or comes along with other effects of reactivity. As much as this approach can provide information about time-related effects and intra-individual changes in particular, there are a number of constraints and effects that cause some reluctance when it comes to panel studies in practical research.

In comparison to panel studies, trend studies are less expensive and easier to design because they are not affected by mortality and learning effects. In trend studies, identically defined but independently drawn samples make up the group of respondents – different people who represent the same statistical population at different times. As long as a study does not target at intra-individual effects but just wants to follow up on developments over time, a trend analysis will usually be the more practical approach to the measurement of variables that are relevant for customer satisfaction and service quality.

Usually, not all questions of a questionnaire will be identical over the lifetime of a panel or trend study. While some variables are measured as time series, other variables and their measurement may change. However, it has to be ensured that these changes do not influence the measurement of the time series. If repeatedly measured variables suddenly appear in a different context, supposed changes may eventually not be an effect of time but an artefact of changes to the questionnaire. Only if direct comparability of measurements along a timeline is ensured, will it be possible to determine the time factor.

Longitudinal studies were so far described in conjunction with interviews. This largely reflects the research reality but is not at all inevitable. Also, other methods of data collection can be designed as panel or trend studies. Non-reactive models like content analyses especially offer opportunities for longitudinal studies and even allow retroactive analyses of time effects. Written or otherwise recorded customer feedback as well as repeated standardized measures of all kind of variables that are relevant in the context of service quality are obvious sources of empirical data for time series analyses.

Trend studies are a good starting point for discussions about the development of service performance over time. But it is not only the service performance that may fluctuate. Times will change in a way that a service performance no longer meets customer requirements although it may be consistent. This is not an unusual phenomenon.

As Machiavelli worded it half a millennium ago: 'All this arises from nothing else than whether or not they conform in their methods to the spirit of the times ... But a man is not often found sufficiently circumspect to know how to accommodate himself to the change, both because he cannot deviate from what nature inclines him to do, and also because, having always prospered by acting in one way, he cannot be persuaded that it is well to leave it' (Machiavelli 1532: Chapter XXV). Longitudinal studies can guide the way out of this dilemma.

4.11 Meaning

Imagine a study on the quality of transportation services with hundreds of thousands of respondents from all over the world. Readers of the results are deeply impressed and bow down in awe before so much cosmopolitanism. Wow! A truly global study. Such a study one can trust – they think – until they have a closer look at the questionnaire that is available to everybody on the Internet. It is written in English. Translations into other languages are not provided. Suddenly, what started as a wow! turns into an oops!

What does doing a worldwide survey with a questionnaire that is only available in English mean? Apparently, what appears like an international approach narrows down to recipients who are proficient in English. One could argue that this is acceptable because English has become an international language and so many people around the world speak English well enough to understand a short questionnaire. Maybe.

But it is not only about language. It is about culture. Talking about the service of transportation, you will probably face an item in the questionnaire that deals with 'punctuality'. Please rate the punctuality of your most recent travel on a scale from 'poor' to 'excellent'. No problem, one may say. Really no problem? Obviously, what looks relatively simple within a homogeneous society becomes a complex issue once a study deals with different cultures. In fact, punctuality can have a rather different meaning depending on the cultural context. So the question arises if British 'punctuality' is actually the same as German 'Pünktlichkeit' or Italian 'puntualità'? Probably, the British, Germans and Italians would agree that regardless of the language, it is about being on time. But what is the actual understanding of being on time? Irrespective of the actual translation, the meaning of punctuality may differ substantially depending on the cultural context. This is the difference between the denotative and connotative meaning of a word. The denotative meaning is its 'official' meaning as it is defined in a dictionary – to be on time. In contrast, the connotative meaning goes beyond the denotation and describes a specific meaning depending on experience and cultural context. From this perspective, some delay may be deemed 'normal' and in some situations it could even be impolite to be punctual in the sense of the agreed time. Connotations make the difference between punctuality in different cultures. And the same applies to many other variables. That makes studies across cultural differences difficult – and interesting.

So a study with respondents from 100 countries – and hence many different cultures – may look impressive but the question remains what the actual meaning of the results is and how relevant they can be. In our example, the situation becomes more difficult because the restriction to an English questionnaire will already result in a biased sample and impact on the representativeness of the study. Even if this bias would be negligible and one could argue that the composition of the sample reflects the customer structure sufficiently, the question arises what relevance an average rating can actually claim? What is the epistemological value of the information that transport operator A receives a better punctuality rating than B if the different rating can be explained with a different cultural understanding of the respective respondents as the confounding variable? Controlling the cultural influence as an intervening variable, the situation may look very different. Perhaps there is no more difference in the rating or the rating turns around in favour of B. Facts or artefacts? It may even be that both companies operate in completely different markets and a comparison is not relevant at all.

This is just an example that demonstrates how strong the cultural influence on research results can be and how important it is to consider cultural factors in a research design. This does not only apply to research across cultural boundaries but even to a society that appears rather homogeneous at first glance. For example, air travel insiders have their own understanding of punctuality and consider up to 15 minutes delay as an on-time arrival.[31] Nevertheless, travellers may be more demanding. So if a complex and culturally related term such as punctuality is not scrutinized but just interpreted from an innocent perspective, one may transfer data into a context where they cannot claim validity and the study arrives at artefacts instead of facts.

Considering the global focus of many service providers on one hand and the dependence of service quality on people on the other, one should not underestimate the impact of cultural differences on practical research. Again, this demands for an explication of the research process in order to ensure an adequate interpretation of the results. In some cases, this will change the focus of research. Instead of looking for some overall quality assessments, it could be much more interesting to understand the actual differences between the 'cultural' groups. This leads straight to the inherent dilemma of an international brand in the service sector. On one hand, offering a product that is standardized across the world and creates a brand identity. On the other hand, being aware that the individual demand and expectations can be quite different depending on the cultural context. Intercultural comparisons could answer the question of how much corporate identity is required in order to maintain the identity of the brand and how much variability can be granted in order to meet customer expectations – with the ultimate target of delivering high quality in different cultural contexts.

Intercultural comparisons highlight an aspect of research that becomes obvious particularly in content analyses[32] and is actually a latent issue of all research. It is all about the reconstruction of meaning. It is the key question of how to understand and interpret observations that are made in the course of the research process. This should justify a discussion because only when the understanding of the researcher and the respondents to a questionnaire is largely congruent, can one expect meaningful results. The reality is, however, that in many research projects, this essential step is reduced to technicalities. A tick behind an answer is understood as an 'objective' and 'accurate' result. When such results are deemed superior to content analyses or open-ended questions in interviews where the process of assigning meaning to data is not hidden behind a tick but becomes necessarily obvious and hence understandable, one misses

---

31   See for example the analyses by Flightstats (www.flightstats.com) or United States Department of Transportation and Research and Innovative Technology Administration (RITA) (http://www.transtats.bts.gov/OT_Delay/OT_Delay Cause1.asp).

32   See section 6.3.

the crucial point that research is always about the reconstruction of meaning – regardless if implicitly or explicitly.

In quality-related studies one cannot simply assume common sense that makes it unnecessary to consider such cultural aspects. In fact, the perspective of service providers and customers is usually rather different and so is the terminology. Every industry has its technical terms that have a different meaning to experts and non-experts. Research that is done too much from the perspective of the service provider and neglects the consumer perspective is prone to fall into the gap between these two worlds and will end up in an epistemological no-man's land.

CHAPTER 5

Samples and Generalization

Anyone who has been to the boardroom and presented the results of the latest trailblazing study will have gone through this experience. You have worked hard to make it a presentable study although budget constraints made your life once again difficult. And then the boss sweeps aside all results with ardent conviction. No, he says and claims that his experience would be totally different. You engage in some lukewarm defence, mutter something like representative – and give up. What to say? He is the boss. Trying to explain the difference between personal observations and a scientific study would probably be futile. In fact, such discussion could become rather difficult because the researcher cannot claim the ultimate wisdom for his research results. Where the boss points at his experience and position – I'm the boss, I know the business – the researcher can only refer to probability.

Empirical research questions target populations that in most cases cannot be analyzed in their entirety. Dealing with customers of a service provider, participants in education programmes, documents reflecting customer reactions or any other source of information about service performance, in almost all studies the workload, time and cost of a complete analysis would be unreasonably high and in many cases simply beyond feasibility. So instead of analyzing all elements of the statistical population, we limit our analysis to a smaller sample and try to come to conclusions regarding the total population in the sense of a generalization of our observations and findings. And this inference brings probability into play – because it will be unavoidable that the sample will not reflect the total perfectly but will show some deviations. This makes the sampling procedure so crucial.

As a first step, it is necessary to clearly define – with regard to the research question – the relevant statistical population in terms of its function, location and time. It can be all passengers of an airline above the age of 18 on flights between Singapore and London or all patients of public hospitals in London above the age of 15 who have been admitted in 2013 for more than a week, or any other clearly defined group for which the research results shall be valid. This is the statistical population from which we draw our sample, which will eventually be analyzed in greater detail.

The examples already make it clear that the total population can be finite or infinite. If the total is defined as customers of a car repair shop in the month of August 2013, the total would be finite because there is only a limited number of customers. But who is really interested in such limited population? So the customers in August 2013 would probably be considered representatives of all – and also future – customers. After all, our research results shall not only be valid at the time when the sample is drawn but shall be a projection into the future. This means that in social research, we usually deal with infinite statistical populations although the factual total at the time of sampling will be finite.

Furthermore, even in the rare case that a complete list of all members of the statistical population at the time the sample is drawn would be available, we have to expect that some people cannot be contacted or may decline participation in the survey. And even if participation would be compulsory, false responses can become a specific form of non-response. So again, there are differences between factual and targeted population when drawing a sample. One may deem these differences negligible but they have the potential to affect the sample that is actually drawn as representatives of the statistical population and cannot simply be ignored.

The purpose of a sample is to generalize about a defined population by inferring from a much smaller group of elements under consideration of the research question. For such generalization, it is required that the sample reflects the total population as much as possible. The sample should be a scaled down model of the statistical population that reflects all – with regard to the research question – relevant characteristics 'true to scale'. In other words, a representative sample is needed. In the eyes of recipients of research results, representativeness is often something like the accolade of social research. Claiming representativeness means claiming the truth – and nevertheless, often misses the very point that even a representative sample allows only for assertions that have some likelihood of being wrong.

This chapter will discuss what representativeness means and what common misunderstandings come along with that concept. Furthermore, we look into sampling procedures and their impact on the sampling error and the cost of research. And of course, we put the crucial question of how large a sample should be in order to be representative, allowing generalization. But representativeness is not the only road to knowledge. So we also look into concepts that do not claim representativeness and nevertheless can contribute to a better understanding of research topics.

5.1 Delegates

Representativeness – that is the magic formula in empirical research. It is the make-or-break of a successful study. A representative study lays claim to be genuine research and our researcher will have a knowing look in his eyes when he declares the results of his study representative. Every syllable stresses the importance – rep-re-sen-ta-tive. Now the world will be explained at last and everybody nods with pleasure. Until someone puts a nasty question: excuse me, representative of what? Oops! Such a question indeed has the potential to stall a great presentation.

What appears so catchy at first glance turns out on closer examination to be a complex concept. In fact, there is no representativeness as such. Describing a sample as representative has to keep the research question and related variables in mind. The concept of representativeness assumes that a sample represents the total population in all relevant variables – and what this means depends actually on the research question and the underlying theory. Provided a sample can be considered representative, sample parameters allow projections on respective parameters of the statistical population – with certain likelihood and without systematic error. This induction or inference of empirical phenomena is based on mathematical theory and can be described as representational conclusion.

The crucial point is the link between abstract mathematical theory and the empirical world, which is mainly based on plausibility. It is easy to demand that a sample reflects the statistical population with regard to the distribution of all relevant variables. But which are the relevant variables? Theoretically, there are an infinite number of variables that may be more or less relevant with regard to the research question. So what does 'relevant' mean?

Relevance is more than a fashionable term. It goes back to an old Scots term meaning legal pertinence. Something is relevant if it has an important influence on related social behaviour and attitudes. Accordingly, relevance depends on the context. What may be relevant in a particular context may be irrelevant in a different context. Eventually, it is a largely theoretical decision which variables are deemed relevant in the context of a specific research question, related hypotheses and the defined statistical population. It is the nature of such theoretical decisions that they can be more or less adequate. That makes it essential to disclose these decisions to a scientific discourse.

Analyzing, for example, the quality of the after-sales service of a furniture store where people come to complain about some missing screws or parts that do not fit, the first question would be what the statistical population is. Is it all customers of the store or only those who contact the after-sales service? The first group would at least have to be considered in order to understand the importance of the topic. But the latter one could define the statistical total that the representative sample shall reflect because only they have experience with the after-sales service and can judge their performance. Everybody else will have some expectations and assumptions at best.

So what are the relevant variables with regard to representativeness? Is it relevant if the customers who approach the after-sales service are male or female? Perhaps. What about age? Likely. Does one have to consider their political orientation and religious belief? Rather unlikely. The distance to the place where they live? After all, they have to come a second time because something went wrong with their purchase. The mode of transport, which can make it more or less troublesome to come again? What about those who have to come a third time or even more often because the problem is still not settled? And is it important if they are one-time or regular customers? The list of potentially relevant variables is long and the decision is not always easy.

It may be possible to check the distribution of a few variables because the parameters in the total population are known. But in most cases, there will not be any information about the distribution of relevant variables in the statistical population. So the only way out is a random sample –randomly picking a number of customers who approach the customer service counter over a defined period of time. If the sample is large enough and drawn at random, the law of large numbers[1] will allow the assumption that the sample is an adequate model of the statistical population. But some questions arise immediately. What about those customers who do not contact customer service face-to-face but via telephone or Internet? How to deal with those who decline an interview? And what period should be chosen? Are there differences during the day or depending on the weekday? Or even over the year?

Apparently, what looks so straightforward in the context of abstract mathematical theory is burdened with uncertainty, assumptions and – conscious or subconscious – decisions when it comes to the empirical world. Furthermore, many decisions are governed by budget constraints that may eventually overrule scientific reasoning.

---

1   See section 5.2.

Perfectionists who are lucky enough to have a big budget could be tempted to analyze not only a representative sample but the total population – simply doing away with all difficulties of inference and the troublesome uncertainty of probability. But this will not solve the problem. Instead, they will get lost in infinity because what looks like the total population is actually nothing but a sample in time.

Imagine a study that deals with, let's say, customer satisfaction in the private banking sector in the UK. So what would be an adequate definition of the statistical population? The simple reference to everybody who has a bank account in the UK would result in millions of people and, nevertheless, this would not cover the population appropriately. A researcher would not only struggle with the fact that this total changes already in the short period of data collection, he would also come to the conclusion that a snapshot of reality at a particular point in time is actually rather irrelevant. Practical research targets at the future. Based on observations at a specific time, research wants to come to conclusions that are not only valid at the time of data collection but allow prognoses for the future. And this also applies, of course, to research in the field of quality in the service industry. It is not particularly interesting if customers express dissatisfaction with today's investment consultancy as long as this has no relevance for the future. What has caused concern is anyway over and provides no more than a historic view. Only if the information about this experience of dissatisfaction affects future developments because it is spread among other actual or potential customers resulting eventually in behavioural changes – like withdrawing money and moving to the competition – do the research results become relevant.

So research that is based on today's sample from today's supposed total population tries to gain knowledge about future behaviour and developments. This extends the understanding of a total population from a snapshot at a certain point in time to a steadily changing but structurally stable statistical population. So the random sample that a researcher draws in the process of a project is drawn from a total that again is a sample from a statistical population that develops over time. In this context, quality research comes with the underlying assumption that tomorrow's customers will not have substantially different attitudes, expectations or behaviour because the elements of a sample can of course only be chosen from the present total population.

The samples that have been described so far are simple random samples. They follow the rather straightforward principle that all elements of the total population have the same chance to be selected as an element of the sample. But this is not as simple to realize as the term simple random sample suggests. Provided a complete list of the members of a statistical population is available, the choice could be based on random numbers. However, having access to such a list is rather an exception than the rule. Either it does not exist or it is subject to restrictions because of data protection. So one will have to look for alternatives. If it is a customer survey, one could pick every, let's say, tenth customer – provided it can be assumed that their appearance does not follow any system. Or one could think of other procedures that draw sample elements in a way that can be deemed sufficiently at random. In practice, it can be quite tricky to develop a sampling procedure that can rightfully claim representativeness.

Even if all conditions are met and there is no uncontrolled bias, a sample may still come along with some error. After all, it is a model of the statistical population and some flaws are unavoidable. That's the nature of probability. However, we know from the law of large numbers that the likelihood of a certain sampling error will be smaller the larger the sample is. And that can make attempts to reduce the sampling error a rather costly affair. Calculating the sampling error, one will see that, for example, in the case of a simple random sample and a dichotomous variable,[2] it will require a four times larger sample to halve the sampling error – which can easily spoil the research budget. But there is some remedy.

Instead of working with a simple random sample, the sampling error can be reduced using a stratified sample. For this purpose, the statistical population is split into subgroups according to the characteristics of a variable that is considered relevant with regard to the research question. From these subpopulations, samples are drawn according to the distribution of the variable in the statistical population. The result is a proportionally stratified sample, which avoids some uncontrolled accidental effects of a simple random sample and comes with a reduced sampling error. Unfortunately, this approach to a reduced sampling error cannot be increased as much as one may like. There is a natural limit. However, one can optimize the effect if the stratification does not follow the underlying distribution of the statistical population but is based on the question at what size of the subsamples the sampling error is minimized. The result is in most cases a disproportionally stratified sample whereby the disproportional distribution of the underlying variable has to be considered in the process of data analysis. Such a disproportionally stratified sample can also be appropriate when certain characteristics of a relevant variable have only marginal frequencies but will nevertheless be used for comparisons.

The problem is, however, that the – with regard to the sampling error – optimal sample is not necessarily optimal with regard to the research costs. This is for example the case when the selected people live far apart and have to be reached for a face-to-face interview. So it is rather likely that one has to seek a compromise between a small sampling error on one hand and economic viability of the sample on the other. This can be achieved by means of combining a stratified with a staged sample.

Multistage samples offer a less costly alternative. The stages refer to different hierarchical levels of the statistical population like states, counties, cities and ultimately individual persons. So instead of selecting individuals who are spread all over the places, one would go for a random sample at every level – until eventually those people are selected who make up the sample. Of course, what reduces costs will at the same time increase the sampling error and this effect will be the stronger the more stages are chosen. Back to square one.

Another possibility to reduce costs are cluster samples, which are actually a special type of a staged sample. A cluster is a subpopulation that contains numerous individuals. So instead of going for individuals as elements of a sample, clusters or groups of individuals are selected, which makes the access easier and more economical. The effect is obvious. Also cluster samples save costs at the expense of a larger sampling error.

Especially in commercial market research, quota samples are also used to make surveys less costly and time-consuming. The researcher will define quotas and ask the interviewer to go for a certain number of interviews with people showing specific characteristics. For example, the interviewer is asked to conduct ten interviews with female respondents aged 25 to 35 years. It is left to the interviewer to find such persons, which gives the interviewers great influence on the sample and the research results. It is obvious that

---

2   Dichotomous from Greek '*dikhotomos*' means to cut into two and describes a variable that has exactly two categories like yes–no or male–female.

contrary to stratified and staged samples, a quota sample is not a genuine random sample. It is chosen consciously and can only claim representativeness with regard to the quota variables. So the advantage of higher efficiency comes at a price. Even worse, there are only a limited number of variables that can be used to define quotas because these variables must not only be easy to recognize, they must also be relevant for the research question and their distribution in the statistical population must be known. Furthermore, combinations of characteristics that are difficult to find are exposed to manipulation and sometimes quotas can cause amazing metamorphoses. Eventually, the 90-year-old grandfather turns into a young female respondent or vice versa.

The decision as to which sampling method is most appropriate and eventually chosen depends on the research question and the research method as well as time and budget constraints. Special questions may require special models. Take, for example, the common question if one would recommend a certain brand to a friend, which is often used as an indicator of customer satisfaction or loyalty. This is usually a very non-committal question. Please tick on a scale from 1 to 7. Only the respondent will know if he has really made any recommendation. So why not ask for a name to whom the respondent has actually made a recommendation? And then follow up with the recipient of the recommendation. From whom did you hear about this brand? Have you tried it yourself? To whom did you recommend it further? This snowball sample could result in a complex picture of a diffusion process that cannot be covered by any random sample. It is not representative but it is relevant.

This is just an example that proves that when it comes to sampling, it is worthwhile to think beyond the common approaches and sometimes even forget about representativeness. Representativeness is not an end in itself. It is essential for inferential statistics when drawing conclusions from a sample that can be generalized about a larger statistical population. But this is not the only way to better knowledge and understanding of social situations, behaviour, attitudes and expectations.

Being in the service industry and targeting better service in the sense of meeting customer expectations, one could ask if it is really worthwhile to go through all the hassle of representative samples that are costly, time-consuming and provide a good overview but seldom go into details. Of course, a consumer organization that compares the service of various companies could not simply come with a few cases that are hardly comparable and for sure not representative. Such comparison would quickly turn into a court case and eventually spoil the reputation of the consumer magazine that would publish such biased results. But for companies that want to know more about their service quality and potential room for improvement, it is a valid question if it is worthwhile to pay tribute to the ideal of representativeness. After all, representativeness has its price. If research in service quality is not only an alibi but an expression of serious interest in potential for improvement, labelling a study generously as representative despite a biased sample can only mislead and result in inappropriate decisions. In such a situation, an elaborated case study can provide much better knowledge than a dubious representative study.

Case studies can provide deep insight into backgrounds, relations and perspectives – provided the cases are chosen in a smart way. There is no reason to overestimate representative studies as the one and only way to a better understanding. In fact, one of the greatest studies of management and working procedures is based on case studies – Niccolò Machiavelli's *The Prince* (1532). Written half a millennium ago, his analyses are still valid. Machiavelli did not base his analysis on representative surveys but derived at his timeless conclusions from a number of case studies thus providing *Ancient Wisdom for Modern Management* (Lisch 2012).

Being familiar with the business, one does not always start from scratch but usually has a largely reliable and valid understanding of the market as well as one's own position in relation to competitors and customers. So the target is in many cases not so much to support this general understanding with some digits behind the decimal point but to look behind the scene and dig deeper into motives, attitudes, expectations and – most important – room for improvement and innovations. This is the strength of case studies.

Case studies can deal with individuals, groups or institutions. They can be based on group discussions, in-depth interviews, observations, content analyses, experiments or other methods of data collection. In any case, they have in common that the analyses go into detail. Particulars instead of generalization. Where representative studies look for averages, case studies look into peculiarities. Instead of looking for a 'typical' or 'average' case, which may not have much news value, they often go for extreme and therefore likely untypical cases or they deal with key cases that are essential for specific working or decision-making processes and provide insight into mechanisms behind particular behaviour and attitudes. So the selection of a case is not based on representativeness but solely on assumed relevance, which makes it so crucial.

Often, case studies are linked to more general and usually representative studies. In that context, they can either precede or supplement another study and have explorative or illustrative character accordingly. As explorative study, they play an important role in the development of a basic understanding of a so far widely unknown research topic. In many cases, they are used to generate hypotheses that are subsequently tested as part of a representative study. Alternatively, case studies can follow a representative study and target at a better understanding of its outcome.

Many case studies are independent analyses. In particular, this can be a meaningful approach when it comes to extreme or critical incidents[3] because such individual cases usually provide more complete information and hence a better understanding of details, structures, problems and possible solutions than a generalized study. Looking at the story behind service failure can be more inspiring than going for an average rating of service performance. It doesn't matter if it is representative. The very point is that such insight is relevant.

5.2 How Many Cases?

At some stage in the course of a research project, a researcher faces the crucial question of how large the sample should be. The answer is simple: it depends. Indeed, it depends on the complexity of the research question as well as the variance of the data. The more complex the research question and the higher the variance of the variables the larger the sample should be. Moreover, the sample size also depends on the sampling method.

In practical research, another factor also has a substantial impact on the sample size: the research budget. The financial controller will come and highlight that the smaller the sample size the lower the project costs. This will quickly be identified as some austerity potential and makes it necessary to find a reasonable compromise between theoretically desirable and economically justifiable sample size.

---

3   See also section 6.6 on the critical incident technique.

Interestingly, some mysterious figures are named when talking about representative samples. Sometimes, 100 or 200 cases are deemed representative. Others demand for 1,000 or even 2,000 cases before they give a thumbs-up when it comes to representativeness. And some supposed experts have done a calculation and arrived at a figure like 1,013 or some other odd figure. The best way to deal with these figures is to simply ignore them. In fact, inferring representativeness directly from sample sizes is a misconception that cannot be wiped out.

Unfortunately, things are more complex. Representativeness is more about quality than quantity. The very point is if a sample meets scientific criteria. A huge sample of several thousand respondents to a trivial pop-up questionnaire on the Internet is most likely a less representative basis for a survey than a few hundred people who have been selected by means of a classic random sample. After all, nobody knows who makes up the group of respondents to that online questionnaire, what statistical population it actually represents and if this population is in any way relevant in the context of the research question. In fact, it is more likely that relevant target groups are systematically excluded from the survey because they have not gone to the website or do not have Internet access or simply reject to respond to this kind of surveys. The researcher does not know anything about the motives of why some have responded and others have not. Furthermore, in many cases it is possible that the same person responds more than once. So what and how many people are actually behind the proudly presented number of responses to an online questionnaire?

These misconceptions about representativeness have a long history. *The Literary Digest* disaster is the classical example that reflects in many aspects the problems of pop-up questionnaires on the web although it dates back to a time long before the Internet was established. *The Literary Digest* was a well established and renowned weekly in the US with a circulation of more than a million copies. Five times they forecast the results of presidential elections correctly. In preparation for the 1936 presidential election, they once again initiated an opinion poll to predict the winner of the presidential election – Democrat Franklin D. Roosevelt or Republican Alf Landon – who would make the race? *The Literary Digest* spared no efforts and costs when they sent their written questionnaire to about ten million voters asking them about their voting intentions. About 2.3 million responded whereof 60 per cent were in favour of Landon. The prognosis was clear. *The Literary Digest* predicted that Landon would win 370 out of 531 votes of the College of Electors. But when the result was official it looked different from the prediction. Landon won a mere eight electoral votes while all remaining 523 votes were for Roosevelt.

Obviously, even 2.3 million replies are no guarantee for representative results. In fact, *The Literary Digest* had overlooked an essential element of representativeness. It has been said that in the absence of a complete list of all American voters, the sample was based on subscribers to their magazine as well as car and telephone owners who would have hardly represented the average voter during the time of the Great Depression. While this sounds plausible, it has actually been refuted by *The Literary Digest*. The actual reason was apparently much simpler. It was the necessary reliance on voluntary response to the questionnaire. Even if the initial sample was representative of all voters, the ultimate sample of respondents was not. Obviously, political interest played an important role in the willingness to respond to the questionnaire with the effect that Landon supporters were more outspoken than Roosevelt voters. In other words: the net-sample was significantly biased (Bryson 1976).

American sampling pioneer George Gallup (1901–1984) worked differently. He is one of the pioneers of opinion polls in the US. In the 1936 presidential election he worked with a sample size of 'only' 50,000 and forecast – contrary to *The Literary Digest's* prognosis – that Roosevelt would win. This triumph was a turning point for opinion polls. Subsequently, the sampling methods became more elaborated, the sample sizes smaller and the results more reliable and valid.[4]

However, Gallup also went through defeat. Prior to the 1948 presidential election, he predicted – like many others – the victory of Thomas Dewey but it was Harry S. Truman who won. And in 1976, Gallup saw Gerald Ford ahead of Jimmy Carter who actually became President. This does not necessarily speak against Gallup and his research methods but is almost natural fate. After all, any generalization from conclusions based on parameters of a sample comes along with uncertainties that expose the results to the risk of errors. That is no reason to abstain from such inductive inference but refers straight to the law of large numbers, which builds the bridge between the abstract mathematical probability theory and the real world. French mathematician Siméon Poisson (1781–1840)[5] developed this theorem and described it as *'la loi des grands nombres'*.[6] With this law of large numbers, Poisson established the theory of representative samples that made it possible to infer from relatively small but representative samples on large statistical populations.

The basic thoughts behind this theorem are rather simple. Just imagine a number of independent random experiments like throwing a dice. We want to know what the likelihood is of throwing a '6'. Assuming an ideal dice (which will not exist in reality), we know that every possible result has the same likelihood of one-sixth. Going for only one experiment (one throw of the dice), the outcome cannot represent the equal likelihood of all possible results. So we have to throw the dice more often. But even after six throws of the dice, not all six possible results may have come out of the experiments. So we continue our experiment and will arrive at the experience that with a growing number of experiments, the likelihood for certain deviations from the expected relative probability becomes smaller – as demonstrated in Figure 5.1 (overleaf). Nevertheless, deviations will still happen even after many experiments. Mathematically, one can prove that with the number of experiments approximating to infinite, the likelihood for any given deviation between expected and observed relative frequencies approximates to zero. In other words, the larger a sample is, the smaller the likelihood for a particular deviation between observed and expected parameters.

Basically the same process takes place when research deals with representative samples instead of the total population. It is very unlikely that an interview with just one person can provide valid information about parameters of the statistical population – even if that very participant was selected at random. However, based on the law of large numbers, it can be assumed that with a growing number of interviews the likelihood for substantial deviations becomes smaller.

---

4   Not long after the disaster, *The Literary Digest* first merged with two other weeklies and eventually ceased publication in 1938.

5   His name is among the 72 names of French scientists and engineers that are engraved on the Eiffel Tower in recognition of their achievements.

6   Already earlier, Jacob Bernoulli (1654–1705) had proven the law of large numbers for the special case of a binary random variable. The underlying experiment can be demonstrated as the repeated tossing of a coin.

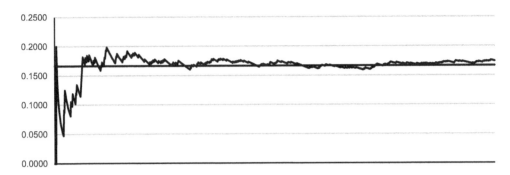

Figure 5.1 Development of the empirical (observed) relative frequency of throwing a '6' in comparison to the theoretical relative frequency of one-sixth over 1,000 experiments

The critical point is that the law of large numbers is often misunderstood and interpreted in a way that with a sufficiently large sample size, the parameters of the sample are very much the same as the parameters of the total population. This is wrong. In fact, in exceptional cases, even with a large sample size, the parameters of the sample and the total population can still show substantial deviations. It is only the likelihood of such deviations that becomes smaller with a growing sample size. This is an essential distinction.

Researchers as well as recipients of research results have to live with some sampling error, which is an inevitable side effect of a limited sample in comparison to a much larger or even infinite statistical population. But it depends on the researcher to keep the sample free from bias as much as possible and the sampling error at bay. Contrary to a sampling error that is the result of a biased sampling procedure, sampling errors caused by chance are beyond control and their likelihood can only be reduced when working with a larger sample – as we have seen from the law of large numbers.

So how large should a sample be that allows representative results? Considering that service-related quality research will hardly go beyond topological (nominal and ordinal) data, one could derive a reasonable estimate of the required sample size from looking at the most complex hypothesis of the project and counting the number of categories of each variable. From there we arrive at the number of cells of a (possibly multidimensional) matrix or spreadsheet that would be used to test the hypothesis. Assuming a (rather unrealistic) equal distribution of the data across all cells, the number of cells multiplied with the required minimum frequency for each combination of the categories of the variables will provide the minimum number of cases in a sample.

Take for example the hypothesis that the perceived quality of service in a hospital depends on the quality of the food that is served. We assume that the quality of the service as well as the quality of the food are rated on a seven-point scale. So our contingency table has 49 cells. Considering that a simple chi-square test comparing empirically observed with theoretically expected frequencies demands for a minimum observed frequency of five cases in each cell, a random sample of at least 245 respondents would be required. The actual figure would be even higher because assuming an equal distribution of observed frequencies is rather unrealistic. Actually, many hypotheses are much more complex and the required number of cases will steeply increase with growing complexity. Furthermore, other statistical models may have different requirements.

In any case, such consideration cannot be more than basic guidance because some uncontrolled factors may also have an impact on the sample. Indeed, the actual sampling error can only be estimated once the data collection is completed. And even that will not consider factors like mistakes when recording the answers, the non-availability of selected elements of the sample or the refusal to answer. These are sources of sampling errors that are not covered by any formula.

So the usually prominently presented margin of error as a measure of how well the results based on a sample reflect the characteristics of the statistical population oversimplifies the theoretical concept behind the figure. In fact, the sampling error depends very much on the sampling method, the sample size, the number of categories of a variable as well as their distribution and the confidence level that a researcher has chosen. So there is not one simple straightforward answer to the question of what margin of error a survey has. Nevertheless, the media like to state a margin of error of so and so many percentage points when they report on a survey. As much as it is righteous to highlight that sampling errors are inherent to all survey results, the recipients of such information should simply be aware that empirical research does not claim to have the ultimate truth ready but provides results and knowledge that have a certain likelihood – which includes the possibility of failure.

The above example of *The Literary Digest* disaster highlights that representativeness does not simply depend on sample size but also on the response rate and a potentially related bias. Obviously, it is not sufficient to select a large sample even if it would fulfil all requirements for representativeness. The researcher would get his sums wrong if he did not consider the impact of the non-respondents. Only if one could rightfully assume that the individual decision to answer or not to answer is taken at random – meaning that there is no systematic bias – there would not be any impact except that one would have to live with a smaller sample size. However, this assumption will in many cases contradict experience. Usually, there are valid reasons why someone refuses to participate in a survey. It may be a lack of interest in the research topic as probably occurred in *The Literary Digest* case. Moreover, it can be assumed that subscribers to *The Literary Digest* were more willing to respond than others. Also social acceptance of the research topic as well as social proximity to the research institute play an important part in the willingness to participate.

There are many potential reasons that can have an impact on the response rate and, eventually, the elaborated representative sample that was selected in style is marred by an uncontrolled bias. In general, one can say that rejecting participation in a survey is easier in case of written interviews than in a face-to-face situation with an interviewer. Response rates of 10 per cent can already be considered a success when it comes to written interviews. And a response rate of 24 per cent as in the case of *The Literary Digest* would be unusually high and was probably caused by the respondents' considerable interest in the research topic. The problem was, however, that this interest was not distributed sufficiently equal among the supporters of both candidates. Personal interviews, on the other hand, have the advantage that an interviewer can give some feedback about possible reasons why participation is declined. With such information, the researcher has a chance to recognize the bias that comes hand in hand with the response rate.

Regardless of what method of data collection has been chosen, as long as a researcher is working with reactive methods, he will face cases of refusal and possibly low response rates. So in order to avoid the missing data trap, the researcher should not only try everything to make participation in a survey attractive but should also perform a thorough check of relevant parameters in the actual sample in comparison to the statistical population – provided that information is available.

Unfortunately, the problem of low response rates has become bigger over recent years because people are less and less willing to respond to questionnaires. This is to a large extent caused by the flood of surveys that hardly deserve this name. In fact, many so-called surveys do not meet basic scientific standards and some are even used as a particularly subversive and insidious marketing swindle. As a result, many people do not distinguish any longer between serious research and dubious wheeler-dealers but simply refuse to participate in a study. The situation becomes even more critical since many people have become very concerned about data protection. All these effects have reduced response rates to an extent that jeopardizes the, for many studies, indispensable concept of representativeness. Serious researchers will have to look for ways of how to differ their projects from trivial and junk surveys. Here, well-known brands and companies have an advantage over fly-by-nights. But this advantage can only be realized when their research meets the high expectations that are linked to their names.

6 *Collecting Data*

It was in early 2012 when MS Costa Concordia, a large cruise vessel with more than 4,200 people onboard rammed into a rock near the Tuscan island of Giglio in Italy and capsized. Newspapers claimed that the captain who was in command of the ship had tried to practice '*un inchino*' – an attempt to sail past the island with minimum distance 'bowing' to the people of the island that is home to many of the seafarers onboard. For many months after the disaster, the wreckage of the cruise ship in shallow waters off the coast of Giglio documented that something went dramatically wrong. Disasters happen but things turned worse because newspapers reported that Il Capitano did not go down in style together with his ship, standing upright with a hymn on his lips – Nearer, My God, to Thee – as should be good tradition since the Titanic disaster at the latest. Instead, it was reported that he fell into a lifeboat long before the ship was evacuated. And journalists knew of even more supposed peculiarities that made the headlines. A mysterious blonde on the bridge, a captain who forgot to wear his spectacles and other stories that have the making of a scandal – no matter if they were true or not.

This story had it all and touched a raw nerve. The cruise industry had enjoyed growth rates for many years that other branches of the tourism industry could only dream of, but suddenly the safety of cruise vessels became the focus of public attention. Where the perception of service quality had until this point been limited to wine and dine, entertainment and shore excursions, the vital question was now: how safe are cruises? Journalists jumped on this question and cruisers had second thoughts before going on a pleasure trip. Even after other cruise lines claimed that such a disaster would never have happened with their vessels, some were rushing to improve their safety precautions. Nevertheless, the question remains: how do cruise operators deal with the issues of safety and security onboard? After all, safety and security are crucial elements of their service offer.

A clean safety record is important for cruise operators who want to position themselves in a competitive market. It is also important for cruise passengers who are concerned about their safety and security during a pleasure trip. Furthermore, consumer organizations should be interested in that question in an attempt to represent the interest of the travellers. And of course, journalists love this topic because it has the potential to make headlines. Last but not least, this question serves as an example for the various methods of empirical research, which will be discussed in the course of this chapter.

Safety and security are an essential part of the service that a cruise operator offers its passengers. After all, passenger satisfaction comprises more than the entertainment onboard and the quality of food and accommodation, the spa and swimming pools, the excursions in the ports, the cleanliness of the ship or the friendliness of the crew. Passenger satisfaction depends ultimately on their safety and security. As long as everything goes well, this aspect is usually neglected and passengers may experience the compulsory muster or lifeboat drill[1] rather as a nuisance than a necessary preparation for the unlikely case of an emergency. But when worst comes to the worst, safety and security measures suddenly have the highest priority and determine the quality of the service onboard.

So it is worthwhile looking deeper into the issue of safety and security onboard cruise vessels to see how the various cruise operators deal with this issue and where they stand in comparison to their competitors. But what is the best approach to data collection? The answer is simple: there are many possible approaches but there is no best approach. Every approach provides a different aspect of reality. And every approach has its specific characteristics, advantages and disadvantages. The starting point is always the research question, which in the course of the project will be further specified and possibly developed into hypotheses.

In this chapter, we use the question of how cruise operators deal with safety onboard their dream ships as an example of a study in the service sector and discuss the major methods of empirical research and their potential in conjunction with their specific characteristics.[2] The major focus will be on interviews, observations, content analyses, group discussions and experiments. These would all be appropriate approaches to the topic of safety and security, yet they focus on different aspects of reality. It should, however, be noted that the research design that is outlined in the following sub-chapters has solely the purpose of a discussion of various research methods. Within that limited context, it will neglect some aspects that would be relevant in the case that such a project would actually be realized.[3]

For the sake of a more complete discussion, we'll also deal with some methods that were developed specifically for the analysis of service quality. Finally, we look at multi-method studies, which have the potential to overcome some limitations of the individual methods.

6.1 Asking

Interviews have often been described as the 'royal way of empirical research'. Actually, this sounds a little too euphoric in view of a number of methodological problems that come along with questionnaires but it reflects at least the dominance and popularity of interviews in comparison to other methods of empirical research. In fact, the supposed superiority of interviews as a method of data collection is at the same time a curse because it is not obvious at first glance that a scientific interview is quite different from putting a question in everyday life. As a result, almost everybody feels competent enough

---

1   A muster drill is an exercise that prepares crew and passengers for an emergency situation. Major features of the exercise are the familiarization with the alarm signal, life-saving equipments and escape routes. According to the International Convention for the Safety of Life at Sea (SOLAS), on a voyage where passengers are on board for more than 24 hours, the drill must be conducted within 24 hours after their embarkation.

2   In addition to safety, security is also an important aspect of a cruise which is often underestimated. Hence, an empirical study of safety issues should also deal with security matters. However, considering that this chapter has the purpose of demonstrating methodological and methodical decisions and their implications in the research process, the following examples have been limited to the aspect of safety.

3   The author would be pleased to assist in a realization of this project.

performing interviews and drawing sometimes abstruse conclusions from questionnaires that can be described as amateurish at best.

Journalists do not hesitate to pounce on passersby, ram a microphone into their face and ask them their opinion on the latest political development. And when they feel at least obliged to mention that these interviews are not representative, it is usually followed by a little subordinate clause: but you can see. No, one cannot see anything from such interviews except that journalism and empirical research have little in common. And the same applies to many questionnaires that are cobbled together from everyday knowledge and have nothing to do with scientific interviews.

On the other hand, reliability and validity issues of interviews have probably been examined more extensively than related issues of other approaches to data collection. It is obvious that the supposedly royal way of empirical research is actually plastered with a number of reliability and validity concerns that often are swept under the carpet when researchers present their results although it would be the better approach to face these issues in an open and proactive manner.

Indeed, the reliability of interview data can to some extent be increased and controlled. A far-reaching standardization of questions can contribute to better reliability. One could also split the sample at random and compare the results of the two subsamples, which is known as split-half. Or one could do the interviews in two waves and compare if the results are stable or show significant differences. These are necessary measures but they are not sufficient in order to ensure valid results.

Contrary to some other methods of data collection where the issue of validity becomes almost automatically obvious, in interviews it is easily covered under supposedly clear questions and standardized answers. However, such a view neglects that the questions are nothing but operationalizations of theoretical variables. Accordingly, the validity of the answers depends to a large extent on the appropriateness of these operationalizations. Furthermore, the interview situation has a substantial impact on the answers. Even if the questions are considered clear and unbiased, the interview situation causes reactions that affect the results.[4]

This makes it necessary to discuss how the questionnaire is constructed and to make the ultimate decisions understandable. Interviews as a method of empirical data collection are not a clearly defined method but comprise a bundle of different approaches that can be more or less appropriate depending on the research question and research situation. A basic typology comprises:

- oral vs. written interviews;
- standardized vs. non-standardized interviews;
- individual vs. group interviews.

The classical approach is the oral or personal interview where an interviewer with a questionnaire approaches a person belonging to a usually representative sample and asks for an interview. The advantage of such face-to-face interviews is that interviewers can provide feedback about the interview situation, they can explain questions or deal with interview aids like, for example, cards with alternative answers that will be sorted according to importance or similar. Furthermore, face-to-face interviews can

---

4   Regarding the problem of reactivity, see section 4.4.

usually be longer than other interview types. On the other hand, the process of data collection takes substantial time and the involvement of an interviewer is an additional factor of reactivity that is difficult to control. So the interviewers have to be trained and controlled. Altogether, this type of personal interview can be a rather expensive approach to data collection.

Faster and less costly are telephone interviews. They are more anonymous but it is questionable to what extent this really does impact on the openness of the respondents. At the same time, telephone interviews have to be kept relatively short because it would be difficult to keep the interest of the respondents awake over a large number of questions. How long a telephone interview can actually be will largely depend on the respondent's interest in the topics that it is dealing with. The major problem is, however, the usually high number of refusals. At times when junk calls trying to promote the most fantastic but absolutely useless offers are a common nuisance, people have become increasingly reluctant to answer interview questions on the phone. Furthermore, who can really be sure that it is a genuine research project and not a prank call? The usually low response rate in telephone interviews is even more critical because one cannot assume that the refusals are distributed at random. The impact on the representativeness of a study is obvious.

Written interviews on the other hand avoid some of the above mentioned problems but face new ones. The traditional approach to written interviews are mailings. What was once delivered by the postman – a questionnaire and a cover letter trying to convince the recipient to complete the interview and return it in an enclosed stamped envelope – is now in most cases sent by email with a link to a website with the questionnaire. This has made written interviews a relatively inexpensive method of data collection but this is at the expense of dubious samples and low response rates unless the interview topic really hits a nerve. Even if the invitation email passes the spam filter, the chances that the questionnaire will be answered are slim. There are hundreds of software tools that allow the creation of online questionnaires but references to some of their names may cause further doubts rather than trust among those who are not familiar with these programs. The question is what associations links to tools with names like SurveyTracker, SurveyMonkey or SurveyDaemon may actually trigger among respondents who are not familiar with them? Perhaps suspicion, lacking seriousness or something ominous? And even if such questionnaires are filled in, it is doubtful who has really answered and how valid the answers are unless there are dedicated control questions that make inconsistencies and contradictions obvious. Worst of all, online questionnaires bear the inherent risk that highly complex methodological issues are reduced to technicalities resulting in an automated but largely meaningless process.

On the other hand, online questionnaires provide substantial advantages. They can make some logic checks, control the input and steer the sequence of questions. For example, they can vary response categories in order to avoid response sets and control the stability of questions. Furthermore, they speed up the research process.

Instead of sending email invitations for online interviews, questionnaires are often linked directly to a website. Provided the pop-up blocker is not activated, visitors to the website will face an invitation: thank you for visiting our website! Before you leave, please spare us a minute or two and let us know your thoughts on our fantastic service. Your feedback is valuable to us. Please click to take our survey. Thank you!

Some people may follow the invitation out of curiosity or because they hope to offload some comments at last that they always wanted to make but nobody wanted to hear. But in most cases, such pop-up invitations are experienced rather as nuisance than as a welcome opportunity. The result will be a low response rate. Even worse, it cannot be assumed that the respondents are a representative sample of the total population of all users of the website. And even if that would be the case, the question would still be if the users of the website do really represent the statistical population that is relevant with regard to the research question. This is probably not the case when it comes to questions about, let's say, customer service performance, a recent holiday trip or any other topics that are not linked directly to the visit of the website. So the sample would most likely be biased. Furthermore, there is in many cases no reliable control to avoid questionnaires being answered repeatedly by the same respondent.

Only when the questionnaire deals with topics that are directly related to the website will the pop-up invitation for an interview at least target the relevant population. After all, informative websites are part of the customer service of a company and their quality reflects to some extent the customer orientation of the respective company. The weakness is, however, that in many cases the respondents do not have the necessary knowledge to answer the questionnaire. They have only just accessed the website when they are already asked to please rate the new version. How? What shall they answer? They may not even have recognized that the website is new because they have hardly gone beyond the homepage or have never before visited this website. The situation is not much better when the invitation comes only upon leaving the domain because the user may have visited only very few pages and may not be in a position to make comprehensive judgements. As a result, the answers will have more the character of obligingness than providing realistic feedback. But perhaps that is indeed wanted – research as alibi. It is obvious that the advantage of relatively low costs of written and especially Internet interviews comes at a price.

Written interviews are largely standardized in their wording and sequence of the questions. However, some variations can be made for different subsamples that would allow the analysis of the stability of the answers. For examples, one could use in one subsample scales from 1 to 7 whereby 1 = fully agree and 7 = fully disagree, while in a second subsample the allocation of the figures to their meaning is exactly the opposite. Assuming that both subsamples were drawn at random, a high correlation of the results would indicate that the direction of the scales does not impact on the responses. Nevertheless, the questionnaires for both groups would be fully standardized and force the respondent into the cognitive framework that the researcher provides. This improves the completeness and comparability but leaves the question unanswered as to what extent the responses will actually reflect the cognitive structures of the respondents. In other words, the answers may be very reliable but, unfortunately, their validity may have fallen by the wayside.

The higher comparability of standardized interviews has resulted in the term quantitative interview in contrast to non-standardized, free or unstructured interviews that are sometimes described as qualitative interviews.[5] Between these two extremes there are many gradations of more or less standardization that can be appropriate for oral interviews whereas written interviews are usually standardized, although

---

5   See also section 4.2 for a critical discussion of this rather misleading dichotomy.

Internet questionnaires allow for some flexibility depending on the way they develop. Nevertheless, they would hardly reach the character of an unstructured explorative interview.

When it comes to projects where the researcher's knowledge about the topic is very limited, one would resort to non-standardized interviews and may even equip the interviewer only with a list of items that should be covered in the course of an interview, whereas the wording and the sequence of the questions would be left to the interviewer's discretion and judgement of the interview situation. This approach is often used in expert, narrative and in-depth interviews, which mainly have an explorative character whereby the difficulties regarding the influence of the interviewer and the resulting limited comparability are obvious. So they will preferably deal with case studies.

While interviews focus in most cases on individuals, oral interviews can also deal with groups of respondents. This can make it easier to reach a large number of respondents but the effect of group dynamic processes on the answers must not be underestimated. In that respect, group interviews are closely related to group discussions.[6]

At the end of the day it depends on the research question and the context as to which research approach is most appropriate. And with this we return to our example of a research project about the service aspect of safety onboard cruise vessels. Analyzing what the concept of safety comprises, the question arises of how cruise passengers deal with safety issues and related information. The question is to what extent basic safety measures are successful and meet the passengers' safety requirements. Based on the results, better concepts for creating awareness of safety topics can be considered. The underlying hypothesis is that cruise passengers experience safety information more as an unavoidable interruption of unlimited pleasure than as an essential preparation for a worst-case scenario. Another hypothesis is that despite international conventions regarding safety measures, cruise operators handle this in a different manner.

While it goes without saying that in the context of this chapter we go for interviews, it must be noted that this is not at all inevitable. The following sub-chapters will prove that other methods of empirical research are not less appropriate in the context of our research topic but focus on slightly different aspects of reality. And talking about interviews, this does not automatically indicate that the interviews are performed with cruise passengers. For example, a very straightforward approach would be interviews with ship safety experts from classification societies or related authorities. They are involved in the development of technical rules and test and approve the designs of ships. Furthermore, they make regular inspections of the ships' safety. All this makes them a priori excellent partners for questions regarding differences in the attitude of cruise operators towards safety. One can, however, assume that they would reject an invitation for an interview that goes beyond general statements. And the same would most likely apply to any interviews with the crew or the ship's management of cruise vessels. Travel agents, on the other hand, would probably be able to provide relevant information about the passengers' attitude towards safety. They will know what the decisive factors are when booking a cruise. Is safety an issue when choosing a particular cruise? Or is it only about the itinerary and the luxury and comfort of the ship?

---

6   See section 6.4.

These possibilities highlight that there are alternatives to the, usually, first thought of interviewing customers. Nevertheless, we decide to choose in our example interviews with cruise passengers because they can cover both hypotheses. They have the experience of the recent journey and they can elaborate on their own attitude regarding safety.

At this point we abstain from discussing the definition and selection of the sample and assume that we target a representative sample of cruise passengers from a defined selection of cruise lines. We decide to work with a written questionnaire that will be handed over after a cruise is completed. If a list of cruise passengers is available one could send an invitation for a written online interview via email and provide a link to an online questionnaire. Alternatively, one could distribute questionnaires to a certain number of randomly selected passengers once they leave the ship at the end of the voyage.

Of course, all interviews that are handed over to passengers must be accompanied by a stamped and addressed envelope and a cover letter. Also for oral or Internet interviews, a cover letter helps to develop some trust, which will have a positive impact on the response rate. The cover letter should have an attractive layout, be free of grammar and spelling mistakes, it should be short and nevertheless comprise basic information about the project such as:

- What is the target?
- Who is behind the project?
- Why is it important to participate?
- How long will it take?
- Who can be contacted in case of further questions?
- How to return the completed questionnaire?

The wording should be personal and easy to understand. The cover letter is not the place to hover in higher scientific spheres. Instead, it must be short but concise and the wording should take the background and information level of the targeted sample into consideration.

Having composed a tempting cover letter, the focus is now on the questionnaire. Let's first look at some general parameters. The most obvious one is the length of the interview. In general, interviews must not take too long. While up to 30 minutes would be acceptable in a face-to-face situation, a written interview should clearly require less time. Otherwise, a questionnaire will not be answered or may be terminated prematurely once the individual tolerance level is surpassed. Printed questionnaires make it easy to judge if the assumed workload is acceptable. In the case of online interviews, it is helpful to have some graphical indicator that represents how much is done and how much is still to come. Furthermore, the cover letter should always provide a realistic indication of how much time the questionnaire requires.

Nevertheless, one cannot exclude that participants return the questionnaire incomplete and that makes it necessary to consider if some basic demographic variables should be covered at the beginning or at the end of the questionnaire. These questions refer to items like the name of the ship, duration of the cruise, cabin class, sex, age group, travelling alone or with partner or family, being new to cruising or having cruise experience. It is common to put basic demographic questions at the end of the questionnaire. On the other hand, putting them at the beginning has the advantage that the answers are available even if the questionnaire is not fully completed. Furthermore, these are easy to answer questions especially whenever categorized answers are provided that just have to be ticked. So the interview develops some momentum and possible hesitation to reply can to some extent be overcome. However, putting these questions at the beginning would only make sense if this part of the questionnaire is rather short because otherwise the respondent may be wondering what the questionnaire is actually about and quickly lose interest.

Many questionnaires comprise more demographic items and ask for more details than what is really required in the context of the research question. It is not unusual that information about income is requested in greater detail than actually needed or a question about religious orientation is included just because it is a common demographic variable and regardless of its relevance for the research question. The result will probably not be better information but a lower response rate. As a matter of principle, the curiosity of the researcher should solely be guided by the research hypotheses instead of a nice-to-have attitude. So there is no need to ask for sensitive information if this is not part of any hypothesis and one should always consider if relevant information can be collected through less sensitive questions.

In order to make it easy for the respondents, we provide standardized answers whenever possible but have to highlight – and program an online questionnaire accordingly – if only one or several categories can be chosen. It is important that the answer categories are distinct and exhaustive and cover all possible answers to the question. If this is not possible, one could offer the opportunity to add further important items to the list of categories under 'others, please specify'. Furthermore, answers must be one-dimensional and they must all deal with the same variable at the same level. Only when the possible answers may create artificial reactions that would otherwise not come or a list of answers would either be too long or the responses are not foreseeable will open questions usually be the better choice. In any case, the wording must adapt to the target group. A questionnaire is the wrong place to show off with scientific terminology if one cannot assume that the target group is familiar with it.

So let's have a look at a possible set of introductory questions and discuss them in conjunction with the chosen wording. We introduce the initial section with a phrase that makes it clear that this is just a prelude. So we can assume that the respondents will quickly go through and tick wherever appropriate while being curious to see the 'real stuff'.

Let's start with some quick general items:

1. *What was the name of your cruise ship?* _____

This information is necessary because the handling of the muster drill may be different depending on the cruise operator and ship. It can be assumed that passengers remember the name of 'their' ship. Alternatively, one could provide a list of cruise lines and move on from there to a list of all ships of that line.[7]

---

7 The comments under each question are of course not part of a questionnaire and inserted only for a better understanding of the ideas behind the questions in this example.

2.   *How many nights did you spend on this ship during your most recent cruise?*

- *1–3 nights*   ☐
- *4–7 nights*   ☐
- *8–14 nights*   ☐
- *more than 14 nights*   ☐

The hypothesis is that safety consciousness increases with longer cruises. For this purpose, a categorization instead of the exact number of nights is sufficient.

3.   *When did the cruise depart?*

Month: _____ *Year:* _____

This information will just ensure that any lack of safety knowledge is not an artefact of the time that has passed since the cruise. For this purpose, the exact date is not required.

4.   *What stateroom (cabin) did you have onboard?*
     (please tick only one category)

- *inside stateroom*   ☐
- *outside stateroom*   ☐
- *outside stateroom with balcony*   ☐
- *suite*   ☐

The question behind this information is if safety awareness is linked to the costs of the cruise, which increase with the type of stateroom.

5.   *Did you travel alone or with your family or partner?*
     (more than one category may apply)

- *alone*   ☐
- *with my spouse/partner*   ☐
- *with my children*   ☐
- *with friends*   ☐
- *with a tour group*   ☐

The question is if travelling together with family – especially with children – increases safety consciousness while travelling as member of a carefree tour group reduces safety consciousness.

6.   *Was this your first cruise?*

- *yes*   ☐
- *no, how many cruises have you taken already?* _____

This question refers to the airline effect where frequent travellers try to show off with their status when they demonstratively shun safety presentations.

7.   *I am*

- *female*   ☐
- *male*   ☐

The question is if there are differences between men and women when it comes to safety orientation.

8.   *I belong to the following age group*

- *not older than 20*   ☐
- *21–30*   ☐
- *31–40*   ☐
- *41–50*   ☐
- *51–60*   ☐
- *61–70*   ☐
- *71 and above*   ☐

Age may also have an impact on safety orientation whereby it is sufficient to deal with age groups, which makes it more convenient for the respondents to answer.

The reason why supposed 'standard questions' are discussed and justified is to highlight that actually every question has a certain function. These questions are not just included because every questionnaire comprises some demographic data. Instead, the information is collected strictly in the context of underlying hypotheses and research questions. That makes it possible to restrict the request for information to what is really required and makes answering as easy and as meaningful as possible. Such a considerate approach avoids unnecessary hiccups and will always have a positive impact not only on the response rate but also on the reliability and validity of the data.

Following these demographic data, the focus will be on the actual cruise experience. This is what the respondents are probably already waiting for. So we start with a transition but do not mention the topic of safety in order to avoid some halo effect that could impact on the responses to the following questions. One has to keep in mind that respondents interpret every question in the context of previous topics as well as some imagination of the researcher behind the study. So instead of referring to safety, we simply refer to the experience of a cruise.

Let's now talk about your most recent cruise experience:

9.   *What were the most important criteria when you chose this cruise?*
     (Please tick the three most important criteria)

- *cabin*   ☐
- *entertainment onboard*   ☐
- *itinerary*   ☐

- *land excursions* ☐
- *price* ☐
- *restaurants* ☐
- *safety* ☐
- *spa, pools and other sports and leisure facilities* ☐

Is there any other criterion that was important for your booking?

- *yes, please specify* _____
- *no* ☐

This question targets the importance that passengers assign to safety. There are various approaches for how to do this. The straightforward question: how important is the safety of a cruise for you?' or even 'Is safety onboard a cruise ship important? is very suggestive and only potential suicides would seriously reject it. As an alternative to the above wording, one could ask the cruise passengers to provide a ranking of all categories from most important to least important. However, this becomes increasingly difficult with a larger number of categories. After all, N categories allow for N! permutations – which is in the above example of eight categories already $8! = 1×2×3×4×5×6×7×8 = 40,320$ different sequences. This may not only be overly demanding on the respondents but will cause also difficulties when analyzing the data. Alternatively, one could turn every item into the question of how important that criterion is on a scale from, let's say, 1 to 7. However, the effect may be that everything is described as important and the various categories do not discriminate sufficiently.

Another possibility is to make it an open-ended question and simply ask what the most important criteria were when choosing the cruise, whereby one could limit the number of criteria to three. In comparison to closed-ended questions, open-ended questions have the advantage that the respondents can answer freely and no stimuli are provided that trigger responses that otherwise would not have come. Furthermore, the respondents are not restricted to categories that are defined by the researcher and may not reflect their cognitive structure. This is particularly advantageous when the spectrum of possible answers is not known. However, the categorization that has been done *before* data collection with the definition of a list of answers in closed-ended questions will have to be done *after* data collection when working with open-ended questions in order to reduce the complexity of the actual responses.

For the above question where certain categories are obvious, closed-ended questions appear to be more practical. But since these categories are probably not exhaustive, an open-ended question has been appended that allows the respondents to add any important categories that they feel are missing. One should, however, keep in mind that an answer like 'safety' would most likely less often be added if it would be missing among the given categories than it will be ticked as part of a list of given alternatives. This makes obvious to what extent the structure and wording of a question impact on the answers and how important it is to consider alternatives before a decision is made.

That also becomes apparent when looking at the answers that in this case are sorted according to the alphabet. Other questionnaires provide possible answers – sometimes probably subconsciously – according to the expected likelihood starting with the most likely response. One should, however, consider that it is likely that the sequence of categories has an impact on the frequency of the responses. Furthermore, the longer the list of categories the more likely it is that the categories at the beginning of the list are chosen because answers are chosen spontaneously or simply as a matter of convenience. In order to control the effect of the sequence, one could vary it in different sets of questionnaires and compare the response patterns.

10. *At the beginning of every voyage there is a muster (lifeboat) drill. When did this muster drill take place?*
    (please tick only one answer)

    - *before departure* ☐
    - *within 24 hours of departure* ☐
    - *later than 24 hours after departure* ☐
    - *there was no muster drill* ☐
    - *I don't remember* ☐

This and the following question target the seriousness of the muster drills. While the pure information when the muster drill has been conducted could be gathered more reliably through participant observation[8] it is included here for two reasons. On one hand, it is used as an indicator for the sustainability of safety information, which should closely correlate with the answers to question 12. On the other hand, it works as a funnel that narrows down to the following questions.

11. *Did you participate in the muster drill?*
    (please, tick only one)

    - *yes* ☐
    - *no, because*
        - *I was not interested* ☐
        - *I know the safety procedures from other cruises* ☐
        - *I was not aware of the muster drill* ☐
        - *there was no muster drill* ☐

Part of the muster drill should be a check if everybody is present because attendance is compulsory. Theoretically, there should not be anybody who has not participated. While one cannot exclude that a few responses are simply wrong, a high number of respondents who claim not to have participated in the muster drill should cause concern as to how seriously the muster drills are conducted on certain ships.

At the same time, this question narrows the interview down further to the content of the muster drill, which is the topic of the following question. Logically, ticking any of the categories under 'no' should lead directly to question 13. However, these shortcuts can easily have the side effect of an unwanted impact on the response pattern. If a particular response causes less work than others, the respondents may be tempted to go the easy way. So in this case, no shortcut is offered and those who answered 'no' should simply not answer the following question. Nevertheless, some will answer – either because they responded

---

8   See section 6.2.

incorrectly to the previous question or they have the knowledge from other sources or they answer simply as a matter of politeness. Such responses would have to be handled with care.

12. *What topics were highlighted during the muster drill?*

- *where to find my lifejacket* ☐
- *how to put on a lifejacket* ☐
- *the number of my muster station* ☐
- *how children under care of the crew will reach the muster station in case of emergency* ☐
- *the signal for the general alarm* ☐
- *how to dress in case of an emergency* ☐
- *to bring along required medication when assembling at the muster station* ☐
- *what to do if someone falls overboard* ☐

Are there any other important topics that were highlighted during the muster drill?

- *yes, please specify* _____
- *no* ☐

This question covers what topics are really remembered and reflects at the same time the interest in safety issues assuming that the higher the interest the more is remembered. However, one has to consider that such a question is strongly exposed to social desirability. So it is likely that more categories are ticked than actually remembered. For that reason, there will later be some control questions. Answers to the additional open question on the other hand can be understood as dealing seriously with safety issues.

13. *Was there any safety information in your cabin available and have you studied any of the following sources?*

	available	*studied*
• *yes*		
– *on in-room TV*	☐	☐
– *on the inside of the cabin door*	☐	☐
– *in a folder on the table/desk*	☐	☐
– *somewhere else, where?*	☐	☐

- *no, there was no safety information in my cabin* ☐

This question is a further indicator of safety awareness and the interest in related information.

14. *What is the signal for the general alarm?*

- _____
- *I don't remember* ☐

15. *What is the meaning of the general alarm?*
    (more than one category may apply)

    - *to abandon ship*   ☐
    - *to proceed to the muster station*   ☐
    - *to put on a life jacket*   ☐
    - *there is a fire onboard*   ☐
    - *to wait in the cabin for further announcements*   ☐
    - *the signal is only important for the crew*   ☐
    - *I don't remember*   ☐

Question 14 and 15 analyze essential safety knowledge that every passenger must have. Both questions are closely related to question 12. They check to what extent important information from the muster drill is remembered. In order to avoid interactions between question 12 and these two questions, they were separated by another topic.

16. *Did you check the website of your cruise operator regarding safety information before you booked the voyage?*

    - *yes*   ☐
    - *no → proceed to question 18*

This question is a filter and indicates at the same time the interest in comprehensive safety information.

17. *How comprehensive was the information that you found?*
    (please tick all applicable answers)

    - *there was the same information as it is also provided*
      in a folder onboard   ☐
    - *there was a safety video explaining the behaviour in*
      case of an emergency   ☐
    - *there was a reference to the muster drill onboard*   ☐
    - *it was clarified where safety information can be found*
      onboard   ☐
    - *there was information about fire safety*   ☐
    - *there was information about forbidden items*   ☐
    - *Other, please specify* _____

It can be determined which safety information the websites of the cruise operators do actually provide.[9] This can be compared with the information that is said to be found and can be used as an indicator of the interest in safety information. At the same time it will reveal the correctness of the answers.

---

9   See section 6.3.

18. Please tell us **how many cases** you think happened **over the last ten years** that resulted in oceangoing cruise ships

- colliding with other ships _____
- grounding _____
- having a fire onboard _____
- sinking _____
- and how often did it happen during that time that passengers or crew of cruise ships fell or jumped overboard _____

This question is meant as an indicator of the respondents' risk assessment. The assumed accident rates can be compared with the actual figures. Intentionally, no answer categories are provided in order to avoid that these categories already give some indication. Unfortunately, it is too late to compare the answers to this question before and after the Costa Concordia disaster, which has probably triggered a hike in the assumed accident rate.[10]

The above questions are just examples. One could add several more questions but since it is not the intention to develop here a complete research instrument but just to highlight some crucial issues, we close the questionnaire at this point. Of course, at the end of any questionnaire it is time to thank the respondents with some nice words for their contribution to the study. So much support deserves serious appreciation – thank you for taking your time to support our study.

The questions outlined above highlight how crucial even little things can be when it comes to interviews. This makes it clear that everyday questions are rather different from questions in a questionnaire – even if plenty of trivial studies ignore this fact. A questionnaire is a complex and highly interrelated system. That's why it is essential to make the underlying intentions and decisions explicit and create awareness as part of the interpretation of the research results. Only when the recipients of a study can understand and judge the underlying approach are they in a position to deal with the results in an appropriate manner. This does not only apply to the (incomplete) example of a questionnaire that was outlined above but to all questionnaires and other methods of empirical research as well.

Textbooks provide comprehensive guidelines on how to word questions and how to structure questionnaires. But apart from the questionnaire, the social situation of an interview has a great impact on the response behaviour as well. This applies not only to oral interviews but also to written interviews. Whereas in oral interviews the influence of the interviewer is obvious, one has to realize that in written interviews the respondent will develop some imagination and expectations of the researcher and will react to it. Of course, the researcher is aware that the respondent will develop some idea of who and what is behind the study. Hence, he will try to control the situation

---

10   Curious readers may want to know what the actual figures are. Based on information from the website www.cruisejunkie.com by Ross Klein, Professor at Memorial University of Newfoundland who compiles information about accidents involving cruise ships, the figures for the ten-year period from 2002 till 2011 read as follows: Collisions (incl. collisions with the pier): 48; grounding: 40; fire: 42; sinking: 5; people overboard: 142 (27 of them could be rescued alive). The figures exclude river cruises and ferries as well as cases that are not sufficiently documented. While the above figures appear to be sufficiently complete they do not reflect the seriousness of the incidents.

through the cover letter, the wording and the professionalism of the design of the questionnaire. Like in any communication situation, it is a reflexive process that is basically not different from the situation of an oral interview where the interviewer is present and can have a tremendous impact on the situation and the outcome. But it is not only the respondent who may develop a story that determines his response behaviour. Interviewers sometimes fake answers or even whole questionnaires. And in some cases some errors simply occur.

Appearance, attitude, male or female interviewer, even minor deviations from the wording of the interview questions, tonality, supplementary explanations, sympathy and many other factors can influence the interview situation despite attempts to train the interviewers with the aim of standardizing the situation and avoiding elements of interference that result in artefacts. At the same time, one should expect that an increasing number of interviews would contribute to the development of something like a standardized or defined interview situation – in the same way as many other social situations are largely standardized. But this is so far not the case. Instead, it appears that the high number of interviews has resulted in some signs of tiredness and dropping response rates – which is to a great degree caused by trivial or junk interviews that do not meet basic research standards.

Considering the manifold elements of interference in the interview process, one may be wondering what interviews can really contribute to the understanding of service quality. Actually, the answer is more promising than one may expect after what was said. When it comes to feedback from those who can judge service quality, interviews are still a preferred approach – provided they meet basic methodical and methodological standards. None of the approaches that will be discussed in the following chapters allow the collection of complex information in a similarly economical way. Furthermore, hardly any other approach has been analyzed as thoroughly as interviews.

Nevertheless, interviews are not the automatic and simple answer to every research question. There are alternatives that may be more appropriate with respect to a specific research question and related hypotheses or add a new perspective to a research topic. In any case, it is worthwhile developing some creativity and considering alternative or additional methods of data collection. It can't always be interviews.

6.2 Observing

Empirical research means observation. Regardless of which method of empirical research is eventually deemed appropriate in the context of a certain research question, one way or another it is always about observations of a specific part of reality. From that perspective, interviews, for example, can be described as observation of verbal expressions reflecting social behaviour such as attitudes and opinions. These cannot only be manifested by way of answers to questions but can also be available as the content of some type of documents. Accordingly, content analysis as a method of empirical research deals with the observation and analysis of social interaction manifested in verbal documents. Also, experiments require observations in order to get access to behavioural reactions and changes under experimental conditions. From this perspective, observations are the basic approach to the reconstruction of social reality.

Beyond that general role in empirical research, observation is the heading for a number of systematic methods of empirical research that all target the systematic recording and analysis of expressions of social attitudes and social behaviour from the perspective of a specific research interest.

Similar to the sometimes trivial understanding of interviews, observations are also part of daily dealings with the world around us but are nevertheless very different from everyday observation of the world around us. It can make the life of a researcher quite awkward when laymen argue with their purported experience and familiarity with observations. Researchers have a difficult stance in the face of so much supposed experience. Contrary to observations in daily life, observations as a method of empirical research are a systematic approach to reality that is controlled by a defined research interest. One could describe this as scientific observations in differentiation to unsystematic observations that are part of everyday experience.

There are various types of scientific observations that can best be classified according to their characteristics into

- participant vs. non-participant observations;
- structured vs. non-structured observations;
- open vs. covert observations.

At first glance it may look like a simple question of if the observer will participate in the observed situation or not. Of course not, one may say and refer to the effects of reactivity. But on second thoughts it becomes obvious that this is impossible in many cases. How to observe a muster drill onboard a cruise vessel without being part of it? And how to get access to other situations if one does not become part of it? This would in many cases only be possible if the role of an observer is revealed – which causes new problems of reactivity that one has just tried to escape.

So the critical point is in what way should one participate in the social situation that is to be observed. This could be a very passive approach, just swimming with the tide by taking over a role that is anyway defined. So, depending on the research topic, one could join a cruise as a passenger in order to observe compulsory safety procedures, take a job in the care for the elderly or assume the role of a customer in after-sales service. These are all defined roles that allow insight into certain segments of the service industry. On the other hand, the assumed role will to some extent define the perspective and the perception. A muster drill may look different depending if one observes it from the perspective of a crew member or joined the ship as a passenger.

Whatever the role is, it can be a very passive role or one could play it actively and try to create specific situations and observe the reactions. For example, the observer could ask defined questions during the muster drill and observe how the crew deals with it. Do they have competent answers or is it handled as a disturbing interruption of a standard procedure? Do other passengers complain that such questions prolong the muster drill? In any case, such interference has an impact on the observed situation and puts the observer into a more active role. Such active participation of the observer moves observations closer to a field experiment.[11]

---

11   See section 6.5.

Regardless of if the observer participates in a social situation or not, it depends very much on the familiarity with the situation to what extent the observations can be structured. Accordingly, a more or less standardized observation protocol will be prepared similar to a questionnaire in which the observations are recorded. It goes without saying that such protocol has to reflect the research question and the theoretical approach. With little or no pre-information about the observed situation, the development of an observation protocol would require some pre-study or exploratory observations that support the development of a structure for more systematic observations, which would be required for a possible generalization of the observation results. Unstructured observations would hardly allow such generalization. In practice, even a mostly structured observation would comprise some unstructured elements, which makes the observation receptive to new and unexpected findings.

All kind of observations can be open or covert. The decision if one should reveal one's role of an observer may be driven by ethical considerations but whatever the ultimate decision is, it has an impact on the part of the observer. Only if his role is clearly defined it is possible to control and limit to some extent its impact on the research situation. In any case, in open observations an observer will have to explain his role and the objective of the observation while those who will be observed will react to it. One should not expect 'normal' behaviour after telling passengers and crew of a cruise vessel that one has come to see how the muster drill is performed. It would probably take quite a while until the observer and those who are observed become sufficiently acquainted with the situation and return to 'normal' behavioural patterns.

Only non-participant covert observations provide a non-reactive approach to data collection. But this is not possible in many cases. One cannot observe cruise passengers without being part of the cruise. And the situation would not be much different if the observer of customer service procedures was hidden behind a one-way glass panel. Even if the observer cannot be seen, the staff on the service counter would probably assume that someone is sitting behind the glass. Apart from the problem of reactivity, such observations may raise some ethical concern.

So in most cases, the observer is either participating or his role is revealed. This makes it important to reflect one's role of an observer who finds himself caught in a dilemma between proximity and distance. On one hand, it is important that the observer is familiar with the sociocultural framework of the research subject, which requires an elaborated understanding of its language, symbols and behavioural patterns because that is the key to an adequate understanding and interpretation of the observed situation. After all, the attempt to ascribe meaning to observations in the context of the research interest will be the more successful the more the sociocultural context of those who observe and those being observed is overlapping. Without sufficient familiarity with the observed scene it will not be possible to understand and interpret it. On the other hand, this proximity must not be to an extent that the necessary critical distance that is prerequisite for scientific observations suffers eventually. It is part of observer training to overcome this dilemma and clearly define the role of the observer and create familiarity with the subject.

An observation scheme defines the framework for the observations and provides the structure for their recording. It must reflect the research interest as well as the related observation items and their categories. In that respect, the observation scheme has some similarity with a questionnaire that is not filled in by the observed persons but by the observer. It is important that the scheme is easy to handle and the observer must be familiar with it in order to ensure complete, systematic, reliable and valid recordings of his observations. This requires serious observer training and pretests will also help to develop the necessary experience before the actual data collection starts. Furthermore, it is desirable to have some supervision at least during the initial stages, which will help to improve the reliability of the observation records. For example, the observations of two observers of the same situation could be compared in order to improve reliability. Ultimately, the relevance of the results of observations and the legitimacy of any generalization will largely depend on the relevance of the observed situations with regard to the research question.

Returning now to our 'study' on safety onboard cruise vessels, we are dealing with two complex variables. One is the attitude of cruise passengers towards safety issues, the other one is the dedication of cruise lines and the ship management to safety. Our approach is to check on both as part of a participant covert observation. This avoids, to a large extent, unwanted reactions to the test situation because the observer takes over the well-defined role of a passenger. At the same time, this is the easiest access to the targeted environment. So we book a cruise, join the ship, take part in the muster drill and also observe further indicators of safety consciousness.

Based on experience of the past as well as related rules and regulation, we develop an observation protocol and focus first of all on the muster drill as the most obvious manifestation of safety awareness and attitude. We can rightfully assume that every muster drill is a typical situation that allows generalization because every passenger has the same right to have a safe journey – *pars pro toto*. This justifies to limit the observations to that particular muster drill that the observer has to attend as passenger anyway.

The difficulty will be that the observer cannot bring along the observation protocol in order to protect his 'undercover' status. During the muster drill the use of cameras or mobile phones is not usually allowed. One could, however, consider recording the announcements discreetly but this raises an ethical concern. In any case, the observer will, to a large extent, depend on his memory and a good knowledge and understanding of the observation scheme, which would include some items such as the following:[12]

1. *Time and duration of the muster drill:*

   - *Name of the ship, departure port, day and time.*
   - *Day and time of the scheduled beginning of the muster drill.*
   - *Day and time of the actual beginning of the muster drill.*
   - *Duration of the muster drill.*

2. *Attendance:*

   - *Did the passengers come on time for the muster drill?*
   - *How did the crew check completeness of attendance?*
   - *Did the crew check if passengers assembled at the correct muster station?*

---

12   In the interest of practicality, the actual observation scheme would of course provide sufficient space to record the observations and it would also offer observation categories whenever possible, which makes the observation scheme similar to a questionnaire.

3. *Audibility and comprehensibility:*

- *In which language(s) were the explanations given?*
- *Were passengers who do not understand that language told how to get the necessary information?*
- *Were the explanations loud and clear enough to be understandable?*

4. *Outfit:*

- *How could the crew be identified during the drill?*
- *Did the crew wear lifejackets?*
- *Did the passengers wear lifejackets?*

5. *General alarm:*

- *Was the general alarm explained and triggered?*
- *What instructions were given on how to behave in case of general alarm?*
- *Was it highlighted that the general alarm does not mean to abandon the ship?*

6. *Safety topics:*

Which of the following safety topics were explained during the muster drill:

- *Where to find the lifejacket.*
- *What to do if there is no lifejacket at the designated place.*
- *How to put on a lifejacket.*
- *How to know at which muster station one has to assemble in case of emergency.*
- *Was there a reference to the description of the exit route inside the cabin door?*
- *In case of emergency, should one go back to the cabin to collect the lifejacket or go straight to the muster station?*
- *Where to find lifejackets for children.*
- *How children will come to the muster station in the case that they are under the care of the ship's crew when the general alarm goes off.*
- *How escape routes are marked.*
- *Were there references to lifeboats and life rafts?*
- *Has it been highlighted that there are sufficient life-saving devices?*
- *How the crew will attend to disabled passengers in case of emergency.*
- *How to dress in case of emergency.*
- *To bring possibly required medicine along.*
- *Not to use elevators in case of emergency.*
- *Not to smoke in non-smoking areas.*
- *Not to throw cigarette butts or other burning items overboard (fire hazard).*
- *Not to throw anything overboard (environmental hazard).*
- *Not to climb or sit on the ship's railing.*

- *What to do in case of man overboard.*
- *Not to run on the ship.*
- *Not to play ball in areas that are not designated for ball games.*
- *Where to find safety information.*
- *To follow the instructions of the crew.*
- *Any other topics?*

7. *Encouragement:*

   - *Did the crew invite further questions?*
   - *Did the crew encourage passengers to familiarize themselves with safety issues?*
   - *Did the crew refer to safety information in the cabin?*
   - *Did passengers ask any questions? If yes, what were the topics?*

8. *Discipline:*

   - *Did the crew ensure discipline during the safety instructions?*
   - *How disciplined were the passengers during the muster drill?*

9. *Others:*

   - *If passengers embarked in more than one port, was there a muster drill for new passengers?*
   - *When and how was it performed?*
   - *Are there any other important observations?*

This is a pretty long list of items that an observer would have to keep in mind when attending the muster drill. Afterwards he would have to quickly record his observations because their validity will depend on their completeness and correctness. It is obvious that this role of an observer is clearly different from the role of a 'normal' participant in the drill who will also make some observations and return with some impressions. Perhaps the 'normal' passenger will tell somebody what caught his eye or he may mention it in his postcard to loved ones at home. But such observations have a completely different quality. They are neither systematic nor comprehensive but pick just some conspicuous elements from an otherwise hardly actively observed event. Interviews as described in the previous chapter could help to find out what is really remembered.

The above observation topics cover two interrelated aspects of safety. On one hand, they are an indicator of the cruise line's commitment to safety. On the other hand, they reflect the interest of the passengers in safety matters. These observations can be complemented with an observation of other accessible and relevant safety elements. This is not only a further aspect of the ship management's safety attitude but also allows some kind of validation of the observations of the crew's dedication to safety during the muster drill.

While some – with regard to safety – important areas of the ship are not accessible to passengers, there are many other areas where observers can check the conditions and maintenance level of safety equipment. Like all observations, this requires related training and experience. And of course, such checks must be performed without any damage to the equipment.

Although these observations refer more to physical equipment instead of social behaviour, the condition of the equipment serves as indicator for social behaviour and the general attitude towards safety in particular. Insofar, we are not talking about a technical inspection but about social research. It is a non-reactive observation of traces of the ship management's safety attitude.

While no complete observation scheme shall be developed here, a few observation items will illustrate this approach:[13]

- *Are all escape routes clearly marked?*

Cruise vessels should provide a perfect world of relaxation and entertainment. Any reference to inherent risks can only spoil such environment. So directing the way to the casino is more profitable than directing the way to the muster station – provided nothing happens. In that respect, marking escape routes with clear signage that does not interfere with other signage reflects safety consciousness.

- *Are all escape routes accessible?*

Escape routes must be clear at all times. Blocking them intentionally or simply because of negligence puts passengers and crew at risk. So keeping escape routes clear is another indicator of safety consciousness.

- *Is all emergency equipment easily accessible?*

On passenger ships, there is a permanent conflict between easy access to emergency equipment and protecting it from abuse. Ensuring that safety equipment is accessible at all times and nevertheless in good condition and complete proves safety consciousness.

- *Have moving parts of the safety equipment been painted over?*
- *Have hinges and rubber gaskets of air shaft covers been painted over?*
- *Has the hydrostatic release of life rafts been painted over?*

These items are good indicators for safety consciousness among the crew. Seamen like to paint everything. It is a common sight on ships that moving parts, rubber gaskets and even hydrostatic releases of life rafts are painted over – with the possibly fatal effect that they do not function any longer. Air shafts cannot be closed in case of a fire, safety equipment does not move and life rafts are not released when the ship is sinking. It may look nicer when all these parts are painted but it is inconsiderate and can end in a disaster. This makes these items good indicators of the ship management's attitude towards safety.

These are just a few examples that prove how action leaves traces from which an observer can draw conclusions regarding the underlying attitude. Analyzing traces is a non-reactive approach to data collection that is little used but offers great opportunities – and requires a bit of creativity. In our case, this indirect approach is a meaningful supplement to the direct observation of the muster drill.

---

13   The author performed comprehensive observations onboard ferries in the Mediterranean as well as in North Sea and Baltic (Stiftung Warentest 1989, 1990).

Although observations have vast potential in social research and offer a great source of understanding, in practice this method of data collection is used much less than interviews. There are two major reasons for such reluctance. On the surface, observations appear to be less 'accurate' in comparison to interviews, and they make it difficult to realize a high number of cases. But these impressions are misleading.

Of course, it is easier to perform a high number of interviews than doing just as many observations. But it would be a thorough misunderstanding if one would judge the validity of the results simply based on the number of cases. Furthermore, in our example the relevant units are not the individual passengers as in the case of interviews but the ship and the ship management as representatives of a cruise line.

In fact, observations have the advantage that they make the process of assigning meaning to empirical findings necessarily explicit. However, the same process of reconstructing meaning takes place in interviews – although usually implicitly. In any case, neither an answer to a question in a questionnaire nor some recordings in an observation scheme have a meaning per se. In both cases the meaning has to be reconstructed by the researcher in the context of the research question. That makes it necessary to make the underlying assumptions and decisions transparent. So making the process of reconstruction of meaning explicit must not be interpreted in the sense of lesser accuracy. On the contrary, it should be understood as a call for similarly extensive discussions of the underlying meaning of questions and answers in interviews. This discussion and awareness of underlying decisions in the research process can only have a positive effect on the reliability and validity of the results.

Indeed, it is worthwhile developing some ideas beyond interviews when considering empirical research. Observations offer many more opportunities than it may be apparent at first glance. And they have a major advantage over interviews. As long as one has access to an environment that is relevant in the context of the research question, one will not struggle with low response rates. This may be a good reason to think seriously about observations when it comes to quality research.

6.3 Reading

Social behaviour leaves traces. This was obvious when we looked at safety equipment that is painted over or locked away in order to protect it from abuse but will be unavailable in case of emergency. Such traces are an amazing store of social scientific knowledge that also comprise a large amount of written material. Content analysis[14] deals with such documents of manifested communication processes.

In the field of services, the most obvious example for quality-related text material is mail from customers. These letters are a great source of information about a product and related services. Furthermore, many customer service hotlines advise the caller that their call will be recorded for training purposes. This should also cover an analysis of the praise and concern that is reflected in these calls. What topics are raised, what emotions are expressed, how are they handled? An analysis of the content and characteristics of customer reactions can provide comprehensive knowledge of the service quality.

---

14   Content analysis is sometimes also denoted as textual or document analysis. For a more comprehensive discussion of the methods and methodology of content analysis, see also Lisch and Kriz 1978.

These few examples prove that content analyses can contribute to better service quality. The reality is, however, that content analysis is very much on the fringes of social research methods. The number of content analytic studies is actually rather limited and also its methodical and methodological stage of development hardly reflects its basic potential. The major reason is that content analysis makes assumptions and decisions of the research process explicit that usually remain implicit in other methods such as, for example, interviews. That gives the wrong impression that content analysis would be less 'accurate' than other methods of data collection. But this is simply a misconception.

In fact, one should look at content analysis from a different perspective and describe it as the very model of social research. Like any other empirical approach to social behaviour, content analysis deals with the reconstruction of meaning. But in the case of content analysis, this process of assigning meaning to verbal expressions becomes necessarily explicit whereas in interviews it is often concealed behind ticks in the box next to standardized answers. This suppresses the process of reconstructing meaning. The meaning of a tick behind a standardized answer is no longer questioned but simply taken for granted. Content analysis, on the other hand, exposes the assignment of meaning to an open discourse. This necessity of a disclosure of assumptions and decisions along the process of data collection can only have a positive impact on the reliability and validity of a study.

In related literature one can often find a distinction between quantitative and qualitative content analysis. In this context, quantitative content analysis is usually understood as frequency analysis of certain text elements whereas qualitative content analysis deals with texts in the sense of a hermeneutic or interpretative way of understanding. Actually, that distinction is rather misleading. On one hand, quantitative content analysis without interpretative or hermeneutic elements would be rather pointless because the simple counting of words or other text elements would not have any social scientific relevance as long as it is not associated with a distinct meaning. On the other hand, the hermeneutic analysis of a text would probably not reject any word count or other quantitative elements provided they contribute to a better understanding. So quantitative content analysis always requires elements of qualitative content analysis and vice versa.

It is a major difficulty of content analysis that the meaning of text elements depends to a large extent on their context. This is most obvious when it comes to homonyms – words that are spelt and pronounced the same way but have a different meaning.[15] Simply counting words without looking at the context would hardly contribute to a better understanding of the meaning of a text. However, considering the context requires proximity to the social situation from which the text derives. In other words, the reconstruction of meaning will be more successful the smaller the cultural gap and the greater the common sense between the researcher and the author of a text is.

It is like in any conversation, when the sender and receiver of a message each assumes a different context misunderstandings are almost inevitable. Some basic parameters will be rather obvious as long as it is not a secret message encoded by a spy. For example, one can assume that in a message the content is represented by the black letters on the white paper and not by the white areas around the black characters. Furthermore, there should be a common understanding as to which language will be used to decode the message and

---

15   For example 'vessel', which can be a ship, a container or a canal conveying blood. Words that have the same spelling but different pronunciation are called homograph (for example, lead – to be in command or a heavy metal) whereas words with identical pronunciation but different spelling are called homophone (for example, four and for).

if the text should be read from left to right or from right to left. But beyond such basic assumptions, the meaning of certain expressions cannot simply be taken for granted. The researcher has to develop the necessary empathy and cultural understanding of the context in which the text has been developed. This dependence of meaning on a certain context is actually not different from what has been said about interviews and observations and will basically also apply to the research methods that are discussed in the following chapters. In any case, social research deals with the reconstruction of meaning.

The basic steps of a content analysis are not different from other methods of data collection. Also, it applies here that all steps are interdependent and have implications for the further research process. The beginning of a content analysis is marked by a research question that can be further specified in the form of hypotheses. At the same time, the research question and hypotheses narrow down the relevant text material. The theoretical variables of the hypotheses have to be operationalized by means of empirical variables. For example, customer orientation as a theoretical construct that cannot be observed directly would have to be operationalized by means of empirical variables such as availability and accessibility of relevant contact information, indicators of competence and so on. These variables and their interrelations have to be specified further. How does a text express accessibility? What text elements indicate competence? Eventually, the operationalization results in a system of content analytical categories that compile text elements under consideration of the research question and their assigned meaning as indicators of theoretical constructs such as service quality.

It is essential that these categories are not only based on the research question but also on the actual text because the scientific categories of the researcher are not necessarily identical to the relevant category system of the communicator. It is actually the function of the operationalization to define the link between both systems. If this link is not made explicit, it is exposed to implicit decisions by the encoders of the text material, which will jeopardize the reliability and validity of the results. After all, the system of categories defines the framework of the content analytic study and its results.

Depending on the research question as well as statistical aspects of the further analysis, a usually representative sample of the relevant text material is chosen and analyzed. The simplest case would be a frequency analysis of text elements assuming that their frequency reflects their importance or relevance in a certain context. But there are more elaborated content analytical models that try to reflect the complexity of a text more adequately.[16] However, research reality is that these models are actually hardly ever deployed. The reason for so much reluctance is rather simple. The possible knowledge gain does in most cases not really justify the necessary efforts. Computers can offer only limited support. Once the analysis focuses on more complex verbal structures, computer programs would have limited capability to ensure the necessary context recognition despite substantial progress over recent years. So the vast majority of the anyway rather limited number of content analyses hardly goes beyond frequency analyses of text elements. At the same time, the great advantage of content analysis is that it does not face the manifold problems of reactivity, which is a great advantage over many other methods of data collection.[17]

---

16   For example, evaluative assertion analysis (Osgood, Saporta and Nunnally 1956), Contingency Analysis (Osgood 1959), Bedeutungsfeldanalyse [semantic field analysis] (Weymann 1973) or Assoziationsstrukturenanalyse [association structure analysis] (Lisch 1979).

17   Assuming that the text material was not purposely and knowingly developed for a content analysis.

When it comes to quality issues in the field of services, content analysis can indeed offer new perspectives beyond the normal interview approach. That makes it worthwhile to have another look at our topic of safety onboard cruise vessels, although in this context the analysis of text documents as a source of relevant information would probably not come immediately to one's mind. Indeed, apart from formal safety certificates that do not allow further differentiation with regard to the safety attitude of a cruise line but define just a minimum requirement, there are actually other manifested communication processes that can provide more distinctive answers.

The most obvious area of communication between a service provider and a consumer is the Internet where service providers present themselves and consumers search for information. The website of a cruise line is for many passengers the first contact with the service provider and it is a source of information about schedules, itineraries, prices, excursions, services, terms and conditions – and of course safety and security onboard. It makes sense to provide safety information on the website because once a passenger comes onboard and dives into the carefree world of a cruise, a muster drill is pretty much a nuisance to days of pleasure, entertainment and luxury. So a safety and security-related analysis of the content of the web pages of cruise operators can provide valuable information about the underlying safety attitude. This is based on the hypothesis that the safety attitude of a cruise line is better and more dedicated if more relevant safety information is provided and the more prominently and systematically it is presented. Ideally, a passenger should be able to find all relevant safety information on the website of the cruise operator before going onboard – and the booking confirmation should highlight where to find this essential information.[18]

Our category system is based on safety topics that are deemed relevant for passengers of cruise vessels. For every topic, several items are mentioned that describe the category further and help to code the information reliably and valid. For most items, it would just have to be recorded if the respective information is provided, which should in some cases be supplemented by further specifications. For example:[19]

Muster drill:

- *compulsory participation;*
- *timing and duration;*
- *where to meet;*
- *what to bring along;*
- *where to find information about the muster station;*
- *where to find safety information;*
- *reference to safety training and experience of crew.*

18   The reality looks, in many cases, different. Once the booking is made, the passenger is advised to make the most out of the cruise – and reserve excursions, spa treatments or dining pleasure. Numerous cruise operators provide little and sometimes almost no information about safety. But some cruise lines prove that this can be done much better, which confirms that a content analysis of cruise websites can be used as indicator for the underlying safety attitude.

19   This is not a complete category system but serves only the purpose of illustrating content analytic categories.

Location and handling of life jackets:

- *where to find life jackets;*
- *features of the life jacket (light, whistle);*
- *how to put on the life jacket.*

General alarm:

- *signal (seven short, one long);*
- *meaning (and what it does not mean).*

Behaviour in case of emergency:

- *dress code (warm clothes, no high heels, life jacket);*
- *carrying essential medication;*
- *where to collect life jacket;*
- *proceeding to muster station;*
- *waiting for further announcements.*

Safe behaviour onboard:

- *not to sit or climb on railings;*
- *not to run onboard.*

Fire safety:

- *forbidden items;*
- *not to throw cigarette butts or other burning items overboard;*
- *what to do in case of fire.*

Man overboard:

- *throwing a lifebuoy;*
- *alarming the crew;*
- *trying not to lose sight of the victim.*

Specific safety information with regard to children and handicapped passengers:

- *availability of children's life jackets;*
- *how children under crew's care will proceed to the muster station;*
- *how to ensure that handicapped passengers get assistance.*

For every item it is recorded if it is covered. In addition, for every major category it shall be rated how concise and relevant the safety information is. This is done separately for written and – if provided – video information. The coding could, for example, be done on a five-point scale from no information to comprehensive information whereby the basis of such coding could be either the best performer or a defined optimum. Any incorrect information would have to be recorded separately.

As an additional item, we analyze the accessibility of safety information because the information would be useless if it cannot easily be found on the website.

How easy is it to find safety information?
(more than one category may apply)

- *the topic of safety is presented prominently on the home page;*
- *the home page contains an unobtrusive link to safety information;*
- *safety information can be found via search function;*
- *safety information can be found as part of FAQ (keyword: safety);*
- *safety information can be found among general information (specify);*
- *safety information is presented as a separate section of the website;*
- *safety information is scattered in an unstructured manner over various pages of the website;*
- *safety information is dealt with as part of the terms and conditions or cruise contract (specify);*
- *safety information can rather be found by chance (specify).*

It is obvious that the category system of a content analysis has some similarity with an observation scheme as presented in the previous chapter. The major difference is that content analysis describes categories in terms of verbal expressions whereas observation schemes define categories via behaviour, which of course can include language.

Also in this case, the established category system will probably not cover all aspects of the analyzed texts because every service provider follows a different logic of presentation – and sometimes there is not even an apparent logic. So in order to avoid that relevant characteristics, which are not part of the category system but recognized in the course of data collection, are eventually missed out, we add an open category for any kind of relevant information that is not covered under the defined categories. An example for such supplementary information could be that the information about tipping onboard comprises more than three times the space of the safety information. Or that safety information is hidden under headlines like 'behind the scenes' and 'customs onboard' – safety as an excursion into the wondrous peculiarities of the culture of seamen, presented in close neighbourhood to the captain's dinner.[20]

Based on such a category system, the websites of the selected cruise operators will be analyzed and coded. It is a tedious process that requires some practice in order to get familiar with the category system and to ensure reliable and valid data collection. Although the above list is not at all complete, it illustrates the complexity of a content analytic category system. In this case, the understanding of the categories is rather self-explanatory. In other cases, further elaboration on the individual categories and compilation of verbal expressions that represent each category may be required. If the coding is to be done automatically, one would have to develop a detailed dictionary that represents the category system and contains all

---

20   These examples are based on an actual (but so far unpublished) content analysis of safety and security information on the websites of 31 cruise operators in April 2012. The study revealed substantial differences in the safety attitude of cruise operators.

words that a certain category comprises. In addition, the system would have to be able to analyze the context in which these words occur in order to deal with homonyms. In practical research, the workload that is linked to these steps has often a rather prohibitive effect.

In any case, the researcher will eventually sit before a mountain of data and face the task of reducing the information to the relevant aspects with regard to the research question. In this case, one may go for a ranking of the completeness and appropriateness of the provided safety information. But how to condense the complex information that is left from the coding process after all websites were analyzed? It depends on the research question. Perhaps one will resort to statistics. Although content analysis deals with spoken or written language, any statistical analysis of, for example, frequencies of words or content analytic categories would probably demand the clearly defined and logical language of mathematics. So one would have to look for appropriate statistical models that can reduce the complexity of the collected information.

In our case of the analysis of the websites, it would be more appropriate to compile a table that lists all relevant elements of safety information, what information each operator provides and how complete and appropriate the information is. This provides a detailed overview that can be of great assistance for experts who look for room for improvement. Readers of a magazine would, however, look for a rating. So one could go a step further and develop a model that combines the individual results and delivers an overall rating of the provided information with regard to appropriateness, which covers elements like completeness, conciseness and comprehensibility. It is a theoretical decision how such a model looks. It is based on a definition of the safety information that a website should provide in preparation for a cruise. And of course, the model would have to be developed before the data were collected. It is a step like in any other research process.

Content analysis also deals with readability research. Good readability of product, safety and other information is part of a service promise and an expression of service quality. One could ask how readable the safety information that cruise operators provide on their websites actually is. Readability is a key factor of comprehensibility. In the field of public services, readability has even a democratic component because it decides on accessibility to information. This becomes obvious when, for example, tax laws are so difficult to understand that learning about saving potentials demands for expensive tax experts. As a result of such lack of readability, people with low incomes may pay relatively higher taxes.

Readability must be distinguished from intelligibility, which has an impact on reading speed and depends on factors like font, size, weight and colour of the text as well as its contrast in relation to the background. Readability, however, depends on the verbal structure of a text, which can be measured in terms of complexity of vocabulary and linguistic structures on one hand and the linguistic abilities of the reader as well as familiarity with the topic on the other.

Readability research had its heyday in the middle of the twentieth century and was an important issue in journalism and pedagogy in particular. It was an attempt to find a formula combining linguistic elements of language that are deemed essential for its understanding into an index of readability. Typical indicators were, for example, the average number of words per sentence, the percentage of 'simple' words or the number of 'difficult' words, the percentage of different words, the number of personal pronouns or the number of sentences per paragraph. While the numerous readability formulas differ in some linguistic components, the result is always an index that describes how 'difficult' it is to comprehend the analyzed text.

It is obvious that such formulas depend very much on the language they are applied to. For example, a readability formula that is based on the average word length would always result in lower scores for German in comparison to English texts. This is simply due to the fact that the German language allows the combination of several nouns into a new noun. The famous Donaudampfschifffahrtsgesellschaftskapitän (Captain of the Danube steamship company) is just an extreme example that would skyrocket a readability index that is based on word length or number of syllables. Accordingly, the underlying formula of readability indexes will have to be adjusted according to language.

A very common approach to the readability of English texts is the Flesch Reading Ease index (Flesch 1948), which has gained additional popularity because it can be automatically calculated as part of Microsoft Word.[21] This makes it worthwhile having a closer look.

The index is based on the assumption that readability depends on the average sentence length in number of words per sentence (asl) and the average word length in number of syllables per word (asw) and is calculated according to following formula:

Flesch Reading Ease = 206.835 − 1.015 asl − 84.6 asw

Looking at the formula, one may be impressed in view of so much supposed accuracy and may be satisfied or not with the assessment of a particular text but it is rather unlikely that a user of the index will analyze the meaning behind the mathematical expression. Indeed, it is worthwhile having a closer look at the index, which is supposed to result in values between 0 and 100 whereby 100 would indicate a very simple and 0 a very difficult text. An index between 60 and 70 is supposed to represent a 'normal' text.[22]

Already at first glance, everybody who has ever dealt with social research should become suspicious in view of such a formula. Three digits behind the decimal point usually indicate a mathematical calculation rather than a reflection of the underlying meaning.[23] Furthermore, the formula suggests that short words are more important than short sentences when it comes to readability. A text made solely from words with only one syllable would reach an index of 100 even if the sentences comprise about 22 words on average. On the other hand, an average word length of 1.26 syllables would make it impossible to reach the highest level of readability regardless of the length of the sentences. These examples make it obvious that the index can easily go beyond the defined range. In fact, there is no natural range for the values. This leaves serious doubts as to what extent the formula is appropriate to indicate readability. Furthermore, one would have to see what variance of readability the average length of words and sentences could really explain. After all, these are not the only variables that influence reading ease and other readability formulas are based on different indicators.

---

21   Contrary to the dependence of the Flesch Reading Ease index on a particular language, MS Word seems to work with the same formula in the English and German version. The effect would be that the English version of a text would most likely show a higher score than its German equivalent. Interpreting this in the sense of better readability of the English text would be a classic case of a research artefact.

22   Based on the analysis in MS Word, this book has a Flesch Reading Ease index of 38.9, which – according to the interpretation – is deemed a difficult text although it does not require academics. The reader may judge if this is an appropriate description.

23   From a mathematical perspective, the formula is a regression equation based on the correlation of the length of sentences and words in some reference texts that were developed for the test of reading ability. It is, however, questionable to what extent reference texts from the middle of last century can still claim relevance for the measurement of readability.

MS Word also provides the Flesch-Kincaid Grade Level which is supposed to convert the Flesch Reading Ease index into years of school in the US education system that are necessary to understand a certain text.[24] Its problems are similar to the peculiarities of the Reading Ease index. Many other readability indexes that follow the same approach, although they may use different variables, face basically the same problems. Apparently, readability formulas are a somehow questionable approach. But there is an alternative.

The Cloze Procedure chooses a very different concept (Taylor 1956, 1957). Its name is an abbreviation of the term 'closure', which describes in gestalt psychology[25] the ability to perceptually complete known but incomplete items. For example, an incomplete circle will still be identified as a circle because it is so well known that even incomplete information is sufficient to recognize it. The same phenomenon applies to language. One has an idea how a sentence will continue although one has only heard its beginning. And one understands a sentence even if part of it is missing. The Cloze Procedure makes use of this ability, which is largely independent from a specific language. Instead of calculating a formula based on characteristics that have always a limited explanatory power and are also limited to a specific language, in Cloze Procedure a certain number of words of a text are deleted at random. The missing words are replaced by spaces of a given length in order not to allow conclusions regarding the length of the missing word. Then a number of readers representing the target group are asked to replace the missing words in the text. This will be more successful the more readable a text is and the better it is understood. Accordingly, the share of correctly replaced words is used as criterion for readability – the more words are replaced correctly, the easier it is to read and comprehend the text.

Of course, this index depends on the number of deleted words as well as the target group. If too many words are deleted, it will become impossible to replace them. If too few are deleted, the exercise may be trivial. Furthermore, the more familiar the target group is with the topic of the text the more words will probably be replaced correctly. So the Cloze Procedure relates readability to the target group of a message. However, the number of replaced words as such does not say much. Only the comparison of various texts with the same share of deleted words and presented to representatives of the same target group allows a meaningful interpretation in the sense of higher or lower readability. This allows the differentiation of various versions of a text with regard to readability. Or working with different groups of readers, one could find out for which target group a text is most appropriate. One would, however, have to keep in mind that a maximum number of correct replacements does not necessarily indicate easy readability but is more likely an artefact of an insufficient number of deleted words.

The potential that the Cloze Procedure has for practical research, especially in the context of the development and analysis of customer information, is obvious. But the major reason why it is mentioned here is that it proves how important and necessary it is in practical research to get off the well-trodden paths and develop innovative ideas. In that respect, content analysis has still great potential.

---

24   Based on the analysis in MS Word, this book has a Flesch-Kincaid Grade Level of 12.5, which means that it requires more than 12 years in the American school systems to understand it.

25   The German word 'Gestalt' denotes a shape or appearance. Gestalt psychology explains perception as ability to recognize structures and systems rather than by analyzing its individual elements.

6.4 Discussing

It is a normal situation in management. A problem is identified but the knowledge is too limited to have answers. What to do? The first reaction is to set up a working group. That proves a proactive management style and to what extent the results will actually be used can still be decided at a later stage. So some people are selected who are expected to be able to contribute something to the topic. Of course, a group needs also a leader. So someone is chosen to conduct the group. And before the discussions may go haywire, the moderator will receive some more or less structured guidance that serves as a central thread on the way to presentable results. The outcome of all the efforts shall be some new knowledge and better understanding of the subject. That's the expectation.

What has been described as a rather normal working group in business is basically not so different from a discussion group in social research. Explorative studies in particular make use of this approach to reality. Their objective is to structure a research area and develop some basic insight into opinions and attitudes as well as backgrounds and developments in order to generate hypotheses. Group discussions are also beneficial as a supplementary study to other approaches because they can help to deepen knowledge and gain a better understanding.

Discussions have their roots in the Latin word 'discussio', which stands for an official investigation or examination. It refers to the elements 'dis' and 'quatere' meaning to break apart. Accordingly, a discussion group examines an issue by breaking it into pieces.

In market research, the term 'focus group' is often used instead of talking about group discussions. The Latin word 'focus' denotes the hearth or fireplace and assumes on analogy of the burning point of a lens the meaning of concentration and emphasis. So a focus group concentrates on a hot topic and looks for the point of convergence of various perspectives. The underlying assumption is that group discussions represent the everyday process of the forming of an opinion.

Returning to our project about safety onboard cruise vessels, it could be worthwhile bringing together a group comprising nautical experts as well as people with and without cruise experience who are requested to discuss what kind of safety information they would actually expect and deem necessary in preparation for a cruise. The moderator of the group will not only be equipped with the basic stimulus that will trigger the discussion but will also have a checklist of topics like fire safety or the risk of falling overboard that will be touched on in the course of the debate. It makes sense to first let the discussion develop some momentum and to see into what direction it will develop on its own. Only thereafter should further stimuli be introduced that may otherwise not be covered. So we try to create an environment that reflects the setting of a 'normal' opinion-forming process.

Provided the group members consent, one could record the discussion. That makes it easier to analyze the conversation but it may affect its openness. Usually, one would not conduct only one discussion group but go for several. Nevertheless, this would still not allow the claim of something like representativeness but it would at least allow for an impression of the reliability of the results – which on the other hand is no guarantee for their validity.

Group discussions and focus groups are a form of group interviews. The topic functions as stimulus that initiates a discussion representing the process of opinion-forming. The idea is that this open discussion process reveals the values, attitudes and motives of its participants. Furthermore, it is assumed that the group setting is more natural and relaxed than a face-to-face interview. Ideally, listening to others triggers associations and stimulates ideas. In management, one would describe it as synergy effects. But what sounds so nicely like an enjoyable research setting is in fact laden with many limitations regarding the reliability and validity of the results.

Usually, group discussions comprise not more than ten to 12 people. Some publications recommend even smaller groups. That makes it clear that this approach does not target generalizations in the sense of representative studies. It is a rather misleading idea that group discussions would be an efficient way to increase the number of cases in a study because one can talk to several people at the same time whereas face-to-face interviews are more costly and take more time. In fact, the results of a discussion group do not refer to individuals but to a group. After all, the results represent the opinion-forming process of a group. Furthermore, the contributions of the individuals who make up the group are highly reactive and influenced not only by the moderator of the group discussion but also by group dynamic processes.

The group members are chosen under consideration of the research question and the stimulus that is given to initiate the discussion process. A crucial question is how homogeneous the discussion group shall be. One can expect that a heterogeneous group will be more lively in comparison to a rather homogeneous group that may have little to say except an exchange of commonplaces. On the other hand, a homogeneous group could discuss a topic more in depth whereas a heterogeneous group may better reflect the scope of a topic. In any case, the structure of the group will have an impact on the discussion and its results.

When the group discussion aims to explore the ins and outs of a research topic, a group made up of experts can contribute substantially to the development of the concept of a subsequent study that will deal with the research topic in a more appropriate and skilled manner than would have been possible without such expert knowledge. Some consumer organizations that do comparative testing of services have institutionalized this approach. In order to ensure professional tests, every study must be combined with a group discussion that brings representatives of consumers, service providers as well as independent experts together. So in the case of our study of safety onboard cruise vessels, we would invite relevant stakeholders like representatives of a few cruise lines, perhaps a captain who was in command of a cruise vessel, a representative of a classification society that carries out regular surveys to ensure compliance with safety standards as well as some passengers and travel agents selling cruises. When they discuss the topic of safety from their individual perspectives, there is a good chance that new knowledge emerges that can be extremely valuable for the design of a subsequent representative study.[26]

The usually relatively small number of group discussions that are conducted in the course of a study makes them largely dependent on individual participants. Accordingly, group discussions are sometimes classified as a qualitative research method in contrast to quantitative methods but it was already highlighted that this polarity is rather misleading than helpful. Considering that the unit the results refer to is the group

---

26   It would have to be ensured that such expert discussion does not affect the results of further research into that topic by means of alerting the industry of imminent research activities. Especially in the service industry, it is relatively simple to adjust the performance at short notice.

(and not its individual members), group discussions are actually case studies – with all related limitations. But at the same time, this is their strength when they are used as an explorative pre-study that targets the development of hypotheses, which are subsequently tested based on a representative sample. Or they are performed as a post-study focusing on an elaboration and better understanding of research results from a larger and usually representative study.

The character of a case study underlines the importance of a careful choice of group members. Group discussions do not allow researchers to resort to the law of large numbers. Choosing participants who one way or another hamper the discussion has a much stronger impact than having an interview with an outlier in a large representative survey.

A special group in every discussion are the taciturn people who are too shy to speak up. Either they see their opinion already reflected in contributions by other participants and do not want to repeat what others have said – nodding at best when others speak – or they have an opinion that deviates from the prevailing thoughts within the group but surrender to peer pressure and avoid expressing their opinion because they are afraid of isolating themselves within the group. This shows that to some extent the taciturn members of a group illustrate that the openness of the discussion is at the same time its limitation because, contrary to holy promises in conjunction with interviews, whatever is said will be public. Any promise of confidentiality will be rather limited. And that may keep some people silent.

The other extreme are the self-styled opinion leaders. They have a loud opinion on each and every thing regardless how well it is founded. They quickly seize the discussion. Who would dare to disagree with their opinion? It is the task of the moderator to encourage the taciturn members of a discussion group to speak up and to control the dominance of the self-styled opinion leaders to avoid that the discussion process stalls. In a badly conducted group discussion, the results are often rather an artefact of group dynamic processes than a reliable and valid reflection of values, attitudes and opinions. This assigns substantial responsibility for the outcome of the discussion to the moderator.

In fact, the moderator has a major impact on the results. He will have to find the right 'tone' to initiate the discussion process and keep it going while at the same time, the moderator should restrain himself in order to limit his impact on the outcome of the discussion. It is part of the nature of group discussions that they are highly exposed to reactivity. Eventually, the results may be more a reflection of the group members' assumptions regarding the moderator's expectations than what the participants do 'really' think. And also the moderator cannot fully escape his expectations and prejudgements. This role demands for comprehensive training and considerable self-restraint. In that respect, focus groups in the field of market research that are established to gain feedback regarding the market acceptance of new service concepts or other ideas can easily develop a pseudo-scientific alibi function. Even worse, they may hinder innovations because they persist in the mainstream just because nobody wants to offend with deviating opinions.

The problems of limited reliability and the questionable validity of group discussions are obvious. This is to some extent understandable when considering the background of this approach to reality. One simply has to keep in mind where group discussions have their roots. They were once developed to study the impact of group dynamic processes on members of a group. These studies were not so much interested in individual group members but in the processes within the group. So the design of these studies followed more the design of social-psychological experiments. The approach of some subsequent group discussions was though different. They were designed as an alternative to representative studies based on a high number of interviews that ignore the process of opinion-forming and present opinions without considering their development.

Group discussions can prove their potential when this contrast is overcome. In fact, they are not so much an alternative to interviews of larger representative samples but a supplement. Group discussions have substantial explorative and explanatory potential and can help to develop an initial understanding of a research topic as well as to deepen the understanding of research results. But when trying to generalize their results one will quickly reach their limits.

6.5 Experimenting

Having a particular research topic in mind, it is obvious to ask if it would not make sense to go for the real thing instead of taking a detour though answers to many questions, long discussions, detailed text analyses or similar approaches. Why not to just try it out and see what happens? Make it an experiment. After all, experiment comes from the Latin word '*experimentum*', which is related to '*experiri*' meaning to try. That describes the purpose of an experiment best. It is no coincidence that experts, experience and expertise all have the same roots as experiments. Experiments create experience and make experts with expertise.

Quality research offers many opportunities for experiments. Just think of the service that public transport companies offer with their ticket vending machines. Some users of public transport may even hesitate to talk about service in that context. But of course, the functionality of the machines as well as the guidance that a user experiences on the way to the required ticket are an essential part of the service of a public transport company – although some vending machines prove that transport operators easily ignore the importance of this aspect. So one could develop an experimental design with different ticket vending machines and ask users of public transport to get the correct ticket out of the machine. The result, the elapsed time, apparent displacement activities like head scratching or cleaning of the spectacles and other indicators of indecisiveness would be used to determine the machine that offers the best service and to find weaknesses of the service performance of these machines.

Or imagine a test of the service offers provided by nursing homes for the elderly. Visiting them and providing a story of a relative for whom one is looking for nursing care. The described symptoms that demand for permanent care are in every case the same but the social and financial background of the supposed patient is described differently. The question would be to what extent these variables influence the service offers.

The examples suggest that experiments have some similarity with observations. While both deal with the observation of social behaviour, the major difference is the role that the researcher plays in the observed situation and to what extent he controls those variables that are relevant for the test of the underlying hypothesis. In observations, the researcher will try to minimize his interference in the observed situation as much as possible. In experiments, however, the researcher initiates a certain situation and observes the effects of this manipulation. The experimental design will be developed in a way that allows the control of those variables that are deemed relevant for the test of the underlying hypotheses.

Of course, one can also design an experiment as an exploratory study. Instead of developing specific hypotheses, one could simply try to alter some factors of a certain situation and see what will happen. In physics and chemistry, this has generated many ideas and inventions and in social and market research it is legitimate to use such an experimental playground as a source of new ideas. However, these results are just hypotheses that will still have to undergo a test.

In a classical experimental design, one has to distinguish between dependent and independent variables.[27] The dependent variable is the one that is under study whereas the independent variables represent those factors that are supposed to have an impact on the dependent variable. The hypothesis will make a statement about the assumed effect on the dependent variable when the independent variables are altered. In other words, the independent variables shall explain the variance in the dependent variable. Such experimental design allows a causal–analytical approach in a way that changes in a dependent variable can be explained by alterations of the independent variables. In many empirical studies, such explanatory power is preferably awarded to demographic variables. So it is assumed that (independent) demographic variables like age, sex, marital status, education or social status are relevant for the explanation of the variance of a dependent variable. But of course, any other variable can also serve as an independent variable for the explanation of a dependent variable.

Let's take a simple hypothesis stating that seasickness pills suppress not only dizziness from the rocking ship but also a passenger's perceptive faculty, which would be disadvantageous during a muster drill because the passenger would not be prepared for an emergency.[28] The perceptive faculty should be measured in terms of a passenger's recollection of individual topics of the muster drill. Testing this hypothesis, we work with two groups of passengers. We have on one hand the experimental group that will be exposed to the treatment. All members of that group will receive a pill against motion sickness. It must be defined at what time they should take the pill in order to avoid that different timing can cause some variance in the test results. Furthermore, one would have to ensure that the pill is indeed taken and that there is no contraindication with any other medication that the participants possibly take. Contrary to the members of the experimental group, the members of the control group will not be exposed to the treatment and do not receive the pill.

Before we start our experiment and send both groups for the muster drill, we have to ensure that there is no uncontrolled influence from variables that are not part of our experimental design. For example, if the experimental group is significantly younger than the control group, it cannot be excluded that the 'true' influence on the perceptive faculty is not from the seasickness pills but caused by age. Or some passengers have cruise experience whereas for others it is the first cruise. So we have to 'match' both groups.

In an experimental design, there are basically two approaches to matching. One can either allocate the participants to the experimental and control group at random or both groups can be parallelized with regard to certain variables that are not part of the hypothesis but may affect the results of the experiment. In our example, this would mean that one would have to ensure that both groups have the same distribution with

---

27   Instead of dependent and independent, sometimes the terms endogenous and exogenous are used.

28   This example was chosen because this kind of experimental design is common in pharmaceutical testing.

regard to variables such as, for example, age, gender, education level or cruise experience. Alternatively, one could try to have elements in both groups that match pairwise with respect to these variables.

Eventually, the members of both groups will attend the same muster drill. Shortly after the muster drill, all participants are tested with regard to items that they remember from it. Based on the hypothesis, one would assume that the members of the experimental group who received the treatment remember significantly less items from the muster drill than those who were in the control group and did not receive any treatment.

Unfortunately, things are not that easy. Already at this point, it is obvious that there are some factors that could easily spoil our experiment. First of all, all participants are aware of the test situation. For sure, this will trigger reactions and their behaviour will probably change. Furthermore, one could rightfully argue that everybody knows if they belong to the experimental or to the control group. So they assume a specific role and develop assumptions regarding the expectations that they face in this role and react to it – consciously or subconsciously.

One could try to avoid this effect by not telling the participants to which group they belong. Everybody would get a pill and all pills look and taste alike. Some are seasickness pills while others are just placebos. But nobody is told who received a seasickness pill and who got a placebo. This is called a single-blind experiment. And one could go a step further and make it a double-blind experiment by also keeping the researcher unaware of who belongs to the experimental group and who is part of the control group. In practice, things become yet more difficult if one would also try to keep those who do the data analysis unaware of its purpose, which is difficult to realize. Nevertheless, it would still not solve the problems of reactivity completely because all participants including the researcher will interpret the experimental situation in some way and develop expectations that are likely to influence the results. These are effects of experimental designs that cannot fully be excluded but should be considered when designing experimental studies.

Furthermore, we have to distinguish between two major types of experiments. In psychology as well as in market research, laboratory experiments are a common approach. Theoretically, laboratory experiments allow the control of all variables that are relevant for the result of the experiment, which usually ensures high internal validity. But that comes at a price. In fact, the external validity can be rather doubtful because variables that have an impact in the 'real' world may have been excluded in the controlled environment of a laboratory. As a result, the relevance of the results is sometimes rather questionable. After all, it is not the artificial world of a laboratory but the real world that the researcher is interested in.

The alternative are field experiments that take place under natural conditions and in the normal environment of the subject of research. Sociology, social psychology and also market research work with field experiments. They create a research situation that is not as artificial as in a laboratory experiment and the results are generally more relevant to real life. But these advantages also carry a price tag. Indeed, it is difficult to control all relevant variables in the natural environment of a field experiment. As a result, the potentially higher external validity comes along with lower internal validity. In a nutshell, the advantages of a field experiment are the disadvantages of a laboratory experiment and vice versa.

The steps of both types of experiments are basically the same as in any other method of data collection. We have a research question that is specified further by means of hypotheses. An experimental design is developed and an adequate sample is defined. To ensure the appropriateness of the research design one would do some pretests before the actual data collection takes place. The data will be analyzed in the context of the research question and specific hypotheses and the results will be interpreted. Despite all basic similarity with other methods of data collection, the issue of research ethics is never as obvious as in experiments because the researcher interferes in the social situation. This makes an essential distinction.

In an experiment, the researcher assumes particular responsibility for all participants. They rely on the honesty and integrity of the researcher when they declare their willingness to take part in an experiment. From the perspective of research ethics, a field experiment testing the quality of matchmaking services would not allow working with people who are married or have no intention of marrying. Exposing test participants without their consent to potentially dangerous, indecent or embarrassing situations would be unacceptable as well. Of course, it would not only be unethical but also pretty much overdone to sink a cruise vessel just to see if passengers have understood the safety instructions and how well the crew is trained. Such an experiment would not help to predict if the captain may fall, in the midst of a disaster, into a lifeboat instead of standing on the bridge commanding the rescue operations. But there are experimental designs that can provide interesting knowledge about safety awareness of passengers as well as the safety attitude of the crew.

For example, one could remove the life jackets from some cabins and see to what extent passengers take action and ask for their life jacket prior to the vessel's departure. Such a field experiment highlights the importance of research ethics. Of course, not only the passengers who complained about the missing life jacket in their cabin would get one before the vessel departs but also those who did not complain. In order to protect the cruise line from an unjustified image of negligence when it comes to safety, it would also have to be explained why there was no life jacket. This could eventually be combined with a short interview about safety topics. And in order to make up for the inconvenience, the passenger could get a free drink or similar. Handling the experiment in such a considerate manner could ultimately even contribute to more safety awareness among passengers. Nevertheless, it would be a rather critical experimental approach.

Testing the safety attitude of the crew, one could stay away from the muster drill and see what will happen. Is the crew really following up on attendance or do they tolerate it if passengers do not join the muster drill? In case they really follow up, one could argue that one is aware of the safety procedures from previous cruises and see if it is accepted – although it must not be tolerated.

Or moving from the field into a laboratory, it would be worthwhile to see how passengers of different age, sex or educational level are able to put on a life jacket correctly. Some cruise lines do not ask their passengers to put on a life jacket during the muster drill but just demonstrate its handling. This is in line with normal practice onboard an aircraft. On the other hand, the likelihood that a life jacket is required is higher onboard a ship. So it is a valid question if passengers are really able to correctly put on a life jacket in case of an emergency although they have no practice. Depending on the results of such experiments one could decide if the rules would have to be changed making it compulsory to practice the use of a life jacket instead of just demonstrating it.

These few examples illustrate that there are many areas in the service sector where experiments can provide a better understanding of interrelations between relevant factors. From there, it is often only a small step to improved services.

6.6 More Approaches to Reality

So far, this chapter has dealt with common methods of empirical research. They were not developed specifically for service studies but are used for all kind of social research. We said earlier that service is about social behaviour and attitude. So these empirical methods of sociology and psychology are at the same time appropriate methods for the measurement of service quality. Nevertheless, some authors have gone a step further and developed models that are dedicated to the measurement of service performance. This section will discuss some of the best known approaches.

SERVQUAL examines service quality by means of a rating of quality-related statements and compares the ratings of a particular industry on one hand and a specific firm on the other. Critical Incident Technique (CIT), on the other hand, chooses a very different approach. It deals with service performance more in the sense of a management tool. Interestingly, both approaches are relatively old and have undergone little changes since their initial proposals. This may speak for the concepts but it shows at the same time that there were few innovations in the field of quality research – until the Net Promoter Score was presented as magic formula of customer loyalty, service quality and business success. We will take a closer look at all three models as well as some related approaches.

The not particularly creative but nevertheless fitting name SERVQUAL derives – guess what? – from a combination of service and quality and describes a standardized approach to the measurement of the quality of services in conjunction with customer expectations and satisfaction (Parasuraman, Zeithaml and Berry 1988 and Parasuraman, Berry and Zeithaml 1991). Since its development in the 1980s, it has become one of the most widely used concepts for the measurement of service quality.

SERVQUAL describes service quality in terms of the discrepancy between customer expectations related to a particular service sector and the experience of the service as it is actually performed by a specific business. That means that quality is not defined as something 'objective' or irrefutable but depends on customer perception in terms of the gap between general expectations and a specific experience. The authors of SERVQUAL describe it slightly nebulously as 'a form of attitude, related but not equivalent to satisfaction' that 'results from a comparison of expectations with perceptions of performance' (Parasuraman, Zeithaml and Berry 1988: 15).

According to some exploratory studies undertaken by the authors, consumers use ten – possibly partly overlapping – criteria to assess service quality: tangibles, reliability, responsiveness, communication, credibility, security, competence, courtesy, understanding/knowing the customer and access. These criteria were later reduced to five factors (Parasuraman, Zeithaml and Berry 1988: 23):[29]

---

29   The sequence of the categories has been adjusted.

- Reliability: Ability to perform the promised service dependably and accurately.
- Assurance: Knowledge and courtesy of employees and their ability to inspire trust and confidence.
- Tangibles: Physical facilities, equipment, and appearance of personnel.
- Empathy: Caring, individualized attention the firm provides its customers.
- Responsiveness: Willingness to help customers and provide prompt service.

As a pleasant side effect, the initials can be read as RATER, which is easily associated with rating, scores and quality assessment. In fact, that's what it is all about.

SERVQUAL consists of a list of 22 items on a seven-point scale from strongly agree (7) to strongly disagree (1). Each item is divided into two statements whereby one refers to general expectations about firms in a particular industry and the other one to the perception of the service performance of a specific firm. Items related to expectations of firms in general read for example: customers should be able to trust employees of these firms. Or: their employees should be polite. As second part of the rating, the respective perceptions with regard to a specific firm XYZ read accordingly: you can trust employees of XYZ. Or: employees of XYZ are polite. The gap between expectations and perceptions is interpreted as quality of the particular service provider.

According to the authors, this can be interpreted for each of the five categories. Furthermore, an overall measure can be calculated as average of the five categories. This can be the starting point for the development of marketing measures that aim to close apparent gaps. Alternatively, it is possible to change the perspective and categorize customers according to their perceived quality level.

That looks promising and may explain why SERVQUAL has been used in a number of studies. The authors highlight that SERVQUAL shows 'good reliability and validity' and can be used 'across a broad spectrum of services' (Parasuraman, Zeithaml and Berry 1988: 30). Furthermore, they point out that the items can be adjusted or supplemented according to the specific requirements. They don't say, however, that this may have a negative impact on the supposedly 'good reliability and validity'. Unfortunately, things are more complicated and also some other weaknesses of the model are obvious.

The authors already recognize that not all items as indicators of the five factors discriminate sufficiently. While an item like 'employees of XYZ have the knowledge to answer your questions' is used as an assurance item, one may agree that it also stands for responsiveness, empathy and reliability.

In fact, the situation is even more complex because customer perception is not independent from the service offer but the result of a reflexive process of past experience, expectations, price and the service offer. Against this backdrop, one can assume that expectations being measured only *after* the service was actually provided are most likely biased. It remains questionable if consumers have any explicit service expectations at all. Instead, their perception may be steered by some fuzzy gut feelings. This could easily inflate service expectations. Furthermore, how is it understood when customers are asked to what extent firms offering certain services should possess the features described by the statements? Does this refer to ideal, minimum or realistic conditions? One could argue that the recipients have no problem with this because they deliver answers. But then one should ask what is the meaning underlying these answers?

Moreover, it is questionable if the five factors are actually relevant for consumer decisions and related to customer satisfaction. In other words, do the five categories indeed describe the underlying factors that determine the perception and judgement of service quality? Or does quality evaluation perhaps follow completely different structures and criteria? After all, a related approach under the rather clumsy name SERPVAL[30] suggests four very different dimensions that are supposed to determine service value: living communications, peaceful life, social recognition and social integration (Lages and Fernandes 2005).

Both approaches have in common that they deal rather generously with data quality and do not hesitate to use the ordinal data of the underlying scales with statistical models that require at least interval-scaled data. Unfortunately, this methodological liberality is widespread in market research and one may deem it rather petty to highlight this issue time and again. Accordingly, any concern with regard to the impact on research results is usually buried under an avalanche of statistical parameters and the ultimate argument: but you can see.

No, one cannot see. One can only discuss if a seven-point scale from strongly disagree to strongly agree fulfils the requirements of a metric scale. Are the differences between the major points on the scale really sufficiently equal? Furthermore, some of the statistical models that are used require data that can be appropriately described with a normal distribution.[31] This is not only doubtful in view of the seven-point rating scale but much more because of the skewness of the empirical distribution. The authors themselves highlight that the service expectations are mainly rated at '6' or '7'. This means that due to the limitations of the scale, high expectations cannot be surpassed whereas low expectations cannot be failed. This is of course everyday experience but the question remains if one needs a complex model to come to this understanding? Eventually, one can go one step further and ask what it actually means when service quality is defined as the gap between expectations and perceptions. After all, a gap of +1 can occur at every level except the top level. So who delivers the best quality?

One does not have to be a statistical purist to express some doubt regarding the suitability of the results of these approaches. That does not mean that one has to dismiss the underlying ideas. To some extent, practical research sometimes requires some compromises. As long as they are disclosed, the recipients of the results may decide if they want to accept it or not. However, why not look for some more appropriate statistical models? Limiting statistical analysis to ordinal scale level is no stigma and going for factor analyses is not a mark of distinction. No doubt, there is room for improvement – and the authors do not deny this.

Interestingly, SERVQUAL triggers associations with the semantic differential that was developed in psychology for the measurement of the connotative meaning of verbal expressions as well as concrete or abstract objects and concepts even across different languages (Osgood, Suci and Tannenbaum 1957 and Snider and Osgood 1969). Contrary to the denotative meaning of a word, which describes its definition as it can usually be found in a dictionary, connotations refer to the associated affective and emotional meaning, which largely depends on the sociocultural context. The semantic differential makes use of the human ability to rate items in terms of adjectives that prima facie have little to do with one another.

---

30 SERPVAL stands for Service Personal Values scale.

31 This applies, for example, to the factor analysis that both models use.

The semantic differential comprises a list of usually up to 25 bipolar adjectives like soft–hard, passive–active, beautiful–ugly, healthy–sick, quiet–loud, strong–weak, tired–fresh, peaceful–aggressive and so on. It is obvious that these are adjectives that would not usually be used to describe the denotation of the term that shall be defined and nevertheless come along with impressions and emotions that can be used spontaneously for the description of the semantic space of a stimulus.

These polarities are the extremes on a (usually) seven-point scale. For each pair of adjectives, a given stimulus will then be rated by representatives of a defined target group. The result will be a semantic profile or polarity profile,[32] which can be compared to the profile of another item that is based on the same bipolar adjectives.

For example, one could ask a sample of bank customers to rate 'banking service' on a list of bipolar adjectives. In addition, one would ask them to rate 'banking service at X-Bank' along the same bipolar adjectives. In order to control any possible bias, one would rotate the sequence of polarities as well as the general and specific rating. Eventually, we have two semantic differentials – one for banking service in general and another one for banking service at X-Bank. This is a great starting point for discussions about service performance and service quality. Those who look for statistical evidence can compare the profiles by means of statistics. The decision which correlation coefficient or other statistical model is adequate to describe the similarity of the profiles depends very much on the assumptions regarding the underlying scale level. Opinions are divided on that. While many researchers do not hesitate to assume interval scales, it appears to be more appropriate to presume ordinal scales.

In fact, the semantic differential can be an interesting approach to the analysis of service performance that abstains from direct questions such as: how satisfied are you with the service of X-Bank? Instead, it chooses an indirect approach of describing something in terms of bipolar characteristics that are not directly related to the item under investigation. Nevertheless, people are able to deal with these at first glance rather abstract or even weird categories. It may be worthwhile looking deeper into the potential of such an approach. The very point is, however, that the semantic differential is another example that proves what opportunities open up to a researcher once he leaves the well-trodden paths and tries out new avenues.

Indeed, the following method also had a rather different background before it was adapted to quality research. It has its roots in an aviation psychology programme of the US Armed Forces during the Second World War and was originally developed to improve the selection and training procedures of combat pilots. Analyzing the hundreds of reasons that flight instructors gave for why pilot candidates failed to learn how to fly, it was found that in addition to common stereotypes, many records showed very specific observations. This was the starting point for further research into critical incidents. It was an attempt to identify incidents and related behaviour that were critical with regard to success and failure of a mission. The categorization of these individual cases resulted in 'critical requirements' that make the difference between success and failure of combat leadership.

After the end of the war, this approach was developed further and applied to others such as commercial airline pilots, research personnel or employees in the automobile

---

32   Peter Hofstätter (1963) who adapted the semantic differential to the German-speaking community used the term 'polarity profile'.

industry to name just a few. Yet its objective was to identify those situations and processes that are critical for the business in terms of performance. Eventually, this concept for the collection of behavioural facts in defined critical situations has become famous across various industries and the service sector in particular under the name Critical Incident Technique (CIT).[33]

The CIT does not provide a set of instructions on how to collect data. It is rather meant as a flexible approach that can be adjusted to the particular situation and requirements. The actual information about a critical incident can be obtained through interviews or in some cases also through observations. In any case, it is necessary to have a clear definition of critical incidents.

Data collection covers relatively few straightforward points. It starts with the request to recollect a particularly positive or negative experience with a service provider such as a restaurant, customer service, hospital or airline. Related to this incident, the following essential characteristics of that incident will be inquired either through a questionnaire or with the help of an observation scheme:

- Where and when did the incident take place?
- Who or what was involved?
- What has actually happened?
- What were the critical points?
- What made the actual experience of the situation so positive/negative?

One should keep in mind that whenever the cases are collected through interviews instead of direct observations, the stories depend on the memory and potentially selective perception of the protagonist, which may cause some bias. However, especially when the information is provided by customers, this looks more critical than it is. In fact, it is a good example for the difference between significance and relevance. While customer reports may show some significant deviations from what one would describe as 'true' description of an incident, this has little impact on the relation between customer and service provider. For this relation, the actual memory of the customer is more relevant than any 'objective' view because it is the customer's perception that the service provider has to deal with.

The charm of CIT is that it makes use of the fun of telling stories and does not restrict the respondents by means of fixed answers or other similarly standardized structures. At the same time, it depends on the underlying facts of the stories. These are the basis of the next step, which is the categorization of the incidents. One could describe it as a content analysis of the provided stories. Unless there is already a theory that can provide a system of categories, one will develop the categories inductively under consideration of the research interest. That means that a subsample of incidents is picked and discussed with regard to its 'inherent' categories. These categories may be refined further in the course of the categorization process. This turns CIT into a management tool. While it collects data and reveals problems, the management faces the challenge of providing answers to these problems.

---

33   The development of this research approach is mainly attributed to John C. Flanagan (1906–1996) who was a psychologist heading the aviation psychology programme. Flanagan (1954) also describes the history of the concept. For a comparison of various approaches to critical incidents, see Roos (2002). Gremler (2004) provides an overview and comparative analysis of CIT studies.

The system of categories of critical incidents that is developed from the variety of stories about actual cases provides a complex source for a better understanding of the strengths and weaknesses of the actual service performance. In a critical discourse, it allows identification of areas for improvement. It can help to find the root cause of weaknesses and invites a critical review of processes and an assessment of related training requirements.

One must, however, be aware that in CIT, the data are a skewed reflection of the service performance. By definition, they cover only the extremes of an actually much more comprehensive operation, which may hardly be caught when working with methods that target at a representative picture of the performance of a service provider. What is normally dismissed with a muttered apology and quickly suppressed as an extraordinary case that is 'not at all typical', becomes the centre of attention in CIT. It does not deal with 'normal' but with extraordinary cases. For that reason, the approach does not allow any conclusions regarding the relative frequency of critical incidents. It does not even allow a comparison of the numbers of positive and negative incidents because it is unlikely that both are remembered to the same extent.

Even if the CIT will usually deal with untypical cases, in the sense of a zero error strategy these cases point at room for improvement. So the analysis must concentrate on the structure of categories as well as their content. Accordingly, CIT does not measure service quality but is rather a management tool that provides guidance on the road to further improvement. After all, this can be much more relevant because it gets to the root of service quality.

In health care in particular, CIT has been further developed into a critical incident reporting system (CIRS) targeted at an improvement in the safety of patients. These are Internet-based systems for the anonymous reporting of critical incidents and near misses. Part of the reports can be proposals on how to avoid reoccurrence. A panel of experts will comment on the cases. The reports together with recommendations on how to deal with the situations are published in the system as a learning tool. Similar CIRS portals exist for rescue services and other areas. It is not their objective to collect representative information about mistakes or almost-mistakes but rather to develop a culture of turning failure into success and learning from mistakes. And that is exactly what is eventually relevant.

The Net Promoter Score (NPS) goes a step further.[34] It lays claim to provide 'the one number you have to grow' in order to be successful (Reichheld 2003).[35] Since it was proposed in 2003, it has turned into something like a secret weapon of entrepreneurial success. Customer loyalty is the magic formula. Customer loyalty is the heightening of customer satisfaction and the accolade of customer relations. Of course, one can develop customer loyalty through excellent service but at least in business-to-customer relations, the more common approach are rewards like bonus points and mileage programmes. They make it difficult to change a service provider because defection comes at a price. Changing means losing points and status. You will be downgraded from Gold Member to a nobody, from Frequent Flyer to an ordinary traveller. You will miss the great feeling of having accumulated points and reaching the next status level – no matter how much

---

34   The Net Promoter Score, Net Promoter and NPS are registered trademarks of Satmetrix Systems, Inc., Bain & Company, and Fred Reichheld.

35   For a basic overview, see www.netpromotersystem.com.

trouble it is to exchange the points for something you do not need. It is the modern version of a kickback that builds on the human primeval instinct of hunter–gatherers. Service providers strive for loyal customers. Loyal customers spread the word, they are more forgiving and reliable, require less promotional efforts and will return no matter what happens. They will even bring new customers along. Loyal customers are profitable customers. Customer satisfaction leads to business success. This is the starting point of the Net Promoter Score (Satmetrix 2009).

It is the attempt to reduce the measurement of customer loyalty to just one item: how likely is it that you would recommend company X (or service Y) to a friend or colleague? The respondents are asked to rate the likelihood on a scale from 0 to 10 with 0 meaning 'not at all likely' and 10 standing for 'extremely likely'. And since the simple tick on the scale does not say much about the reasons behind, it can be followed by one more question: why? As simple as that. It sounds like the philosopher's stone has been found at last. Or at least the manager's stone. But what is it good for?

The Net Promoter Score is based on the rated likelihood of a recommendation to friends. It distinguishes between three categories of respondents. Those customers who tick 9 or 10 are defined as 'promoters'. That is the type of customer every business is longing for. They are satisfied, enthusiastic and loyal. They paste your company logo on the back of their car and sing the hymns in praise of your business to their buddies. The 'passives' who have ticked 7 or 8 are somehow satisfied as well. But they lack the enthusiasm of the promoters and their referrals are likely to come with a 'but'. Even worse, once they find a better offer they may abscond. The third group is made up of the 'detractors' who have placed their tick somewhere between 0 and 6. They are unhappy by definition, lack loyalty and spoil the reputation of your business with critical remarks. That is the type of customers you do not want to see. Time to convert these non-believers.

The Net Promoter Score as an indicator of customer loyalty is defined as percentage of promoters minus percentage of detractors – in other words:

NPS = Promoters[%] – Detractors[%].

The passives are not considered in the calculation because they are somehow neutral and neither spoil nor move your business forward. The target is clear: increase the number of promoters and have less detractors. Just do it.

The value of the Net Promoter Score can vary between minus and plus 100 – the higher the value the higher your customers' loyalty. The authors of the Net Promoter Score claim that companies achieving long-term profitable growth usually have high Net Promoter Scores and describe customer loyalty as key to future success. The Net Promoter Score is supposed to gauge the efficiency behind a company's growth efforts and – somehow depending on the structure and some characteristics of the particular industry – is considered a highly reliable indicator of future company growth. That's in short the theory. But is it sound?

As with every score or indicator, it makes sense to scrutinize it and see how it behaves in specific situations. Obviously, the passives who do not appear in the formula nevertheless have a strong influence on the score because the total of all three groups is always 100. Furthermore, one promoter neutralizes exactly one detractor. The difference in numbers defines the extent of customer loyalty. However, the higher the share of the passives the smaller the share of promoters and detractors. Imagine a company with 80 per cent passives, 20 per cent promoters and no detractors. Considering that, according to a study of more than 400 companies in 28 industries, the median Net Promoter Score was a mere 16 per cent (Reichheld 2003), the resulting score of 20 per cent would be respectable. One would arrive at the same result with 60 per cent promoters, 40 per cent detractors and no passives. And then you ask yourself which of these two service providers you would probably choose.

Take another example. A company has neither promoters nor detractors, just 100 per cent passives. Another company has 33 per cent promoters, 33 per cent passives and 33 per cent detractors each. And a third business has 50 per cent promoters and 50 per cent detractors, no passives. In all cases, the score is zero. Looking at the figures without calculating any score, one would probably describe the first company as rather average – not bad but with some room for improvement. The second business has only half as many detractors as at least somehow satisfied customers and as many promoters as detractors, which leaves some ambivalent feelings. Compared to so much homogeneity, the third company is perceived in a very controversial manner. You love it or you hate it. Perhaps exactly that creates a market niche. But it could also be a company that does not have its processes under control, which offers extremely erratic services and is just about to lose its reputation. All companies have a Net Promoter Score of zero. And nevertheless, their future development will probably look quite different.

The best way to improve the Net Promoter Score is to get rid of detractors. That is the declared aim. There are two strategies to reduce their share. One can either ensure a service performance that makes them at least passives or one provides such a bad service that they are lost for good. They will have a last chance to bring your Net Promoter Score down but thereafter, they will not spoil your KPI any longer. Lost customers are out of the game. Let them tell your competitors if they would recommend *their* services to a friend. *Your* Net Promoter Score will go up miraculously – while the business goes down.

One should not dismiss this as nasty theory. KPIs are a challenge to all staff and it would be risky to underestimate their inventiveness when finding ways to outwit them. After all, it is the 'one number that you have to grow'. Once the Net Promoter Score is established, be sure it *will* grow.

These are only a few examples of where the 'metrics' – as the authors call it – are critical. Apparently, it is a weak point of the approach that the so-called passives are shut out from the score although they have an influence on the percentage of the remaining two categories. As much as statistics target the reduction of complexity, an obviously relevant group of customers has fallen by the wayside.

It is not only the statistics that cause concern. It is also the basic question of what information the Net Promoter Score can actually provide. A comprehensive study tried to replicate the findings of the authors of the Net Promoter Score – and failed. 'We find no support for the claim that Net Promoter is the "single most reliable indicator of a company's ability to grow"', they summarized their findings (Keiningham et al. 2007).

There is no doubt that data collection for the Net Promoter Score is fast and meets the demand for simplicity. Customers will appreciate that they are not bothered with long questionnaires, which will have a positive effect on the response rate. And bosses and controllers will be happy having a nice KPI that they can challenge every month: why has your Net Promotor Score gone down?! Such questions can make seasoned managers stumble and develop an unprecedented momentum. But what is all this good for if the methodology is apparently rather questionable?

The authors have a modest answer. 'It is not shocking news that getting more customer promoters and fewer detractors accelerates growth. All we did was quantify this common sense in a way that made sense to business leaders – the target audience for my book. These practical leaders have little interest in advanced statistical methods. Frankly, we see little value in continued debate about cause versus correlation, timeframes, or statistical methods. A more productive use of time would be to start building your own data to determine the NPS-growth relationship in your business' (Reichheld 2006).[36]

'Oops!' one is inclined to say. After all, statistics that are not meant for science but for 'practical leaders' are still statistics. They are not exempted from basic methodological requirements – regardless of how much these practical leaders are interested in statistics. Just calculating statistical parameters without knowing what one is really doing turns easily into a blind flight and ultimately into a crash landing.

One could simply ignore the Net Promoter Score as just another dubious indicator but the fact is that an increasing number of chief executives praise themselves for focusing their organization on this very score. The number of reputable companies linking their fate to a methodologically questionable parameter is growing. Against that backdrop, it was almost inevitable that a complex industry developed around the score. Meanwhile, the Net Promoter Score has grown into a net promoter system. Conferences are held, consultancy and training are provided, certification and IT solutions are offered. All this is possible because the world of the bosses is different from the world of scientifically sound research. Bosses have an insatiable demand for simplicity. But the world is not that simple.

There is still the second question following the rating of the likelihood of a recommendation to friends: why? It is an open-ended question asking for the reasons why customers have ticked a certain score. Without this information one could hardly take the necessary action in favour of improved customer loyalty. Unfortunately, the answers to this question may not really meet the desire for simplicity. Instead, the question creates complexity and new questions that require further research – in which 'practical leaders' have probably as little interest as in complex statistical analysis. Usually, focus groups[37] are recommended to look deeper into the reasons behind the score. It is just one possibility to arrive at a better understanding of the customers and why they would or would not give a recommendation to their friends and colleagues. Other approaches could also provide adequate answers. But with these further steps we are back to square one because the alleged simplicity and efficiency of the Net Promoter Score is gone and we return to the proven methods of empirical research. Much ado about nothing?

6.7 Joint Efforts

Glancing through reports on practical research, one can see that they are mostly based on only one methodical approach whereby interviews are clearly prevailing. This is understandable from a financial perspective. In practical as well as in academic research, most projects struggle with a limited budget. That makes interviews attractive because they allow, within a short time and at relatively low cost, the collection of a high data

---

36   One can be grateful for this quote because it proves perfectly how important it is to bring decent methodological awareness and some basic understanding of empirical research and statistics into the business world.

37   See section 6.4.

volume that comes with the vague promise of representative results. Furthermore, results of interviews are easier to convey to the public than the outcome of most other methods of empirical research. Interviews are perceived as a common process that everybody can re-enact in his mind and that gets a touch of objectivity and accuracy once the many answers turn into percentage figures with several digits behind the decimal point.

However, one can assume that, in many cases, it is not only budget limitations that restrict to one research method but a – probably subconscious rather than explicit – understanding of the methods of social research as a tool box. These supposed tools are used to record reality whereby the decision for a specific tool is driven by the idea of an optimized reflection of the real world. Accordingly, some tools are deemed more successful than others when picturing 'the reality'. We have already highlighted that this – as one could call it – universal empiricism is misleading. Instead of asking what method can picture reality best, the more appropriate question would read: what method provides the most adequate picture of reality under consideration of the research question? In fact, this is more than just wordplay, it is an essential distinction.[38]

One can compare it with human perception where different senses provide a different perspective of the universal reality. Every part of the potential reality provides some – with regard to our actual research interest – more or less relevant information. Take for example a restaurant tester. The dish that he has ordered is served and now he wants to know how good it is because this sample will decide how many stars the chef can paste on the door as symbols of his culinary arts. Our tester will perceive the dish with all five senses and they will all provide different although partly overlapping perceptions. Just listening to the food will probably not provide much relevant knowledge about the dish unless he ordered some sizzling hot plate. But listening can tell a lot about the ambience, which will contribute to the culinary experience. Touching the food will say something about its temperature, texture and freshness. Smelling it and looking at the food allows an anticipation of the taste although it may eventually result in disappointment. Tasting the food could be the ultimate approach to culinary delights but without the smell and look of it, the experience will be very limited. Nobody would accept a restaurant tester who based his decision on just one of his senses. Only the combination of various sensory receptors – in other words: a multi-method approach – will allow for a comprehensive understanding and provide the basis for a valid judgement.

And yet, it is the perspective of the restaurant tester. It may be a systematic and to a large extent even standardized view of the appearance and taste of the food but, nevertheless, not everybody will share this view. Furthermore, despite using all senses it leaves out possibly relevant aspects like a microbiological test. There are elements of reality that cannot be grasped by human senses. And a chemist or physician would look at the chef's creations from very different perspectives. They may be interested in molecular structures or cholesterol levels instead of tickled taste buds – at least from a professional perspective.

None of these moves towards reality is right or wrong. There is not *the* very method that leads to universal knowledge. One can only discuss if it is more or less adequate with regard to the research question. And that makes it necessary to make the decisions along the research process available for a critical discourse that allows an interpretation of the results in the context of the underlying decisions.

---

38   See also section 4.1 on the distinction between methods and models.

What has been said is of course not limited to restaurant guides but can also be applied to all empirical research and projects dealing with the quality of service. We have used the topic of safety onboard cruise vessels as an example to illustrate the various methods of empirical research. Every method can provide some answer to our research topic but some are more, others less, relevant with regard to the research question. Depending on the respective method, the answers will be different – not because they are right or wrong but because they deal with different aspects of reality. The situation is not at all different when analyzing the performance of customer service hotlines or after-sales service, the friendliness of airline cabin crews, the quality of investment consultancy, customer orientation in health care institutes, the service quality of public transportation or whatever other question a researcher is dealing with. In any case, a single-method approach means a self-restraint in the perception of the potential reality.

Apart from a more comprehensive understanding of a research topic, a multi-method approach also provides a better insight into the validity of the research results. This is most obvious with regard to face validity. Measuring safety consciousness of a cruise operator by means of observations onboard their ships, one should assume that the result should not contradict the knowledge from interviews with passengers. Or, at least, there should be a hypothesis or theory why the results conflict with one another. Otherwise, this should be a good reason to look deeper into the operationalization of 'safety consciousness' in both approaches.

Results of a study using a specific methodical approach will often allow predictions for the results of studies based on a different method but dealing with the same topic. For example, a ranking of safety consciousness based on a content analysis of the coverage of safety topics on the websites of cruise operators may not be substantially different when such ranking is built on observations onboard – provided the public relations and the operational departments follow the same spirit. In statistical terms, both rankings should have a high positive correlation. If this is confirmed, future studies of this topic could abstain from expensive observations on site and resort to a less costly content analysis of the related websites.

Choosing an approach that combines various methods and perspectives in order to deal with a greater part of reality and – that is important – to better understand interrelations in the interest of higher validity pays tribute to a methodological holism. Realizing the limitations of research concepts that deal with a rather limited perspective of a usually very complex topic, the answer can only be a multi-method design.

Of course, one may say immediately, that's what one would always have loved to do. And after a short sigh an anguished 'but' will follow: but the budget, you know. Trying to start a discussion at this point would probably be in vain so it will be better to face the facts. Nevertheless, it could still be considered if the number of interviews should perhaps be reduced or if the questionnaire could be shortened without foregoing essential information. Perhaps there is some savings potential in favour of a complementary approach. It may also be that others have already worked on the same topic using different approaches and their works can now be consulted. This applies to studies in the field of public services in particular because such studies are often supported with government funds under the condition that the results and sometimes even the data are publicly available for secondary analyses. A multi-method approach does not always have to go beyond budget.

In some cases, a multi-method approach can even help to reduce research costs. The researcher should self-critically ask how great his familiarity with the research topic actually is. Would a small exploratory study using a different approach perhaps deliver some insight that can help to make the main study more stringent and efficient? Or can a representative study be supplemented with a small case study that looks deeper into some specific results and broadens the understanding?

There is hardly any limit to the combination of various methods. They can be used sequentially or concurrently. Especially in research designs that could be characterized as exploratory or explanatory research in the sense of a pre- or post-study, the various methods will probably be used sequentially. On the other hand, if a project deals with different facets of the research question with the intention to cover as much as possible of the potential reality, the various methods will probably be used concurrently.

Sometimes a distinction is made between multi-method and mixed-method designs. In this context, a multi-method design consists of two or more part-projects that are mostly complete on their own. Each study is designed and conducted independently and focuses on different questions or hypotheses. This is a common approach in collaborative research when researchers of various institutes cooperate in a complex research programme. While the individual studies may be conducted either sequentially or concurrently, their individual results are usually put into relation only at a later stage.

Mixed-method designs, on the other hand, combine various methods over several stages of a study. For example, the muster drill on a cruise vessel is observed and subsequently some of the passengers who attended the muster drill will be invited for group or in-depth interviews with the aim of getting a better understanding of their experience and perceptions that shall be confronted with the impressions of the observer.

The crucial point is the combination and integration of the various approaches. It is a matter of the research question as well as practicality at which stage of the research process the various aspects are best brought together. In any case, a multi- or mixed-method design will allow a broader and deeper understanding of a research topic. Yet, the target is to reduce complexity and arrive at a reliable, valid and relevant understanding of its relations and structures that can provide the basis to predict future developments, support decision-making and develop necessary measures. That's what quality research is all about.

CHAPTER 7

Analyzing Data

When the data collection is completed at last, the researcher will sit before a huge amount of data and wonder how to find answers to his research questions. What was designed to reduce complexity has instead resulted in a multiplication of information that goes beyond receptivity. A call for help rings out. Studying all data records does not make it better and would rather result in even more confusion than in a better understanding. Such a detailed look may at best provide a vague idea of what it is all about but it would be a very unreliable way to deal with reality. A more systematic approach is required.

Statistics provides an answer to the dilemma. The term goes back to Latin '*statisticum*', which refers to state affairs. And indeed, the origins of statistics go back to the analysis of data for governmental purposes. The seventeenth and eighteenth century were the time of systematic comparative descriptions of states. Sir William Petty was one of the best known statisticians of that time. It was the idea of political arithmetic to derive inherent laws from the social and economical data that they collected. German philosopher and economist Gottfried Achenwall (1719–1772) who is considered the father of statistics in Germany proposed to make statistics 'a discipline compiling all data that one can get of a country and its people, from which the political science of a state will result.'[1] Unfortunately, things are not that easy but the works of Sir Petty, Achenwall and their contemporaries paved the way for empirical research and statistics.

In fact, the beginnings of statistics go back even further into history. The best known early example of statistics is a census that is referenced every year during Christmas time: 'In those days Caesar Augustus issued a decree that a census should be taken of the entire Roman world.'[2] And even long before the birth of Jesus, data about population, trading, wealth and taxes were collected and analyzed. They were important as an instrument of power and often top secret.

Today's understanding of statistics is mostly influenced by the development of probability theory and the basic concepts of estimation, hypotheses testing and decision theory that were mainly developed during the nineteenth and twentieth century. Nevertheless, some mysticism around statistics has remained. Indeed, statistics is of a rather ambivalent nature. On one hand, it awakens curiosity especially when it comes to forecasts. On the other hand, it causes suspicion when it is about generalizations from a small number of cases. Things become even more mysterious because, to a large extent, statistics is about probability and chance – something that is usually known as pretty unreliable.

Actually, things are much more rational than it may appear at first glance. In social sciences, statistics is just a system of models and related mathematical procedures that allow a systematic reduction of complex data with regard to a specific research question.

---

1   'Man mache hieraus eine Disciplin, man trage alle Nachrichten zusammen, die man von einem Lande und seinen Einwohnern auftreiben kan; so wird die Staatslehre eines Reiches daraus erwachsen' (Achenwall 1748: 6, § 4).

2   The Bible. Luke 2,1.

While mathematical statistics is based on figures and relations between these figures, one has to keep in mind that empirical social research deals with social phenomena. So the numerical data and their interrelations are actually representatives of empirical occurrences and relations. We have described this information transfer from the empirical into the numerical world as measurement.

It is obvious that under these circumstances, any operation in the numerical world is only meaningful if the corresponding operation in the empirical world is also meaningful. So despite operating with figures, we cannot unscrupulously help ourselves in the store of arithmetic. Only if we consider the underlying meaning of mathematical operations we can fully exploit the advantages of working in a mathematical statistical environment – and these are indeed substantial.

Mathematical symbols and operations are unambiguous. Contrary to normal language, they are clearly defined and free of connotations. That makes mathematical operations understandable and communicable. The language of mathematical formulas is not bound to a certain cultural context but is objective. These characteristics are a great advantage over an approach to empirical information by means of normal language and make statistics so efficient.

No doubt, statistics is a vast field that can easily be confusing when becoming engulfed in mathematical formulas. Preferably, two escape routes are taken. One leads straight to descriptive statistics because diagrams and simple parameters appear to be easy to digest. The other one goes hand in hand with an astounding ignorance of essential statistical and methodological requirements. Both ways can easily result in misunderstandings. Actually, there is no reason to be afraid of statistics. In fact, there is little need to deal with complex statistical formulas and it is only consequent that this book abstains from excursions deep into mathematics. The crucial point is rather to understand the logic behind statistical models and to avoid their pitfalls.

In this chapter, we look into the basic concepts of some important areas of statistical analysis and focus on common misunderstandings that result time and again in an inappropriate interpretation of statistical results.

7.1 Describing and Analyzing

The first encounter with data can be rather disturbing. The collected information is unsorted and more confusing than enlightening. A better overview is required. Descriptive statistics aim to structure data and present them in a way that makes it easy to grasp relevant information and allows comparisons with other data. It is an efficient and structured way to summarize the information of the collected data.

There are basically two ways to process the information. Either one does away with information that is redundant in the context of the research question while the original data are maintained in a way that makes it possible to largely reproduce them. Or one does away also with non-redundant information and focuses on selected statistical parameters. Examples of the first possibility are mainly frequency distributions and related graphs and diagrams. The second group comprises, for example, parameters of the central tendency of a set of data like mean, median or mode as well as measures of dispersion like interquartile range, median absolute deviation or variance and standard deviation – depending on the level of measurement. Of course, there are also descriptive statistics for more than one variable. Such frequency distributions of two variables can be presented as contingency tables or graphically as a three-dimensional bar chart. And in the case of more than two variables, contingency tables as well as graphic presentations can be broken down to a number of two-dimensional presentations. So descriptive statistics allow a better understanding of the structure and characteristics of data. But in any case, it is essential to consider the level of measurement when representing data graphically or choosing parameters that represent the sample data.

Official statistics is to a large extent descriptive statistics. They describe social and economical characteristics of countries and are often available to the public. International organizations like the EU or the Organisation for Economic Co-operation and Development (OECD) and others cover several service sectors and provide comprehensive data that can be a great source of background information.

In fact, descriptive statistics has a great advantage – it is easy to understand. Everybody feels familiar with means, histograms or diagrams. Programs like Excel, Numbers or Calc will assist when calculating parameters and PowerPoint, Keynote or Impress make it easy to present them with nice graphics. Just choose the colour scheme and make up your mind if you prefer it two- or three-dimensional. The choice is yours. The problem is though that these programs do not check or ask if the mathematical operations make any empirical sense. And that can make it dangerous. Because graphics may suggest information that the data actually do not contain.

If ordinal or even nominal data are represented by histograms that allocate meaning to the thickness of the rectangles or even work with lines between the data, they provide information that the level of measurement does not justify.[3] If developments over time cut off the lower portion of the y-axis, fluctuations may look more dramatic. If curves connect grouped data, they pretend a development that is not supported by empirical data. Even the colour scheme can have an impact if the most striking colours distract from what is crucial. So the risk is that graphical presentations subconsciously transfer information that the data do not justify. This may be done intentionally or by mistake. Parameters as sober figures are less suggestive but are also, of course, not as comprehensible.

Furthermore, the perception of recipients of descriptive statistics goes easily beyond the sample. Strictly speaking, descriptive statistics can claim validity only for the sample that it describes. That means that any parameters of the sample cannot simply be generalized in the sense of representativeness. Nevertheless, this step of generalization is often subconsciously on the mind of the recipients of descriptive statistics. But you can see, they will say and anticipate what would actually be the subject of analytical statistics.

Basically the same happens when descriptive statistics is used to generate hypotheses, which are subsequently tested based on the same set of data – having a look at the data and then applying statistics to confirm what one could see already without statistics. This puts the basics of statistical testing upside down. As a matter of principle, any hypotheses that shall be generalized must be generated independent of the data and based on theoretical considerations. So in case hypotheses are generated by means of descriptive statistics, these hypotheses must subsequently be tested based on a sample that is different and independent from the first one. Everything else is nothing but circular reasoning.[4]

---

3 The sequence of the rectangles can only be interpreted if they represent at least ordinal data. Only metric data allow the interpretation of the thickness of the rectangles of a histogram.

4 See also section 7.2 on the logic of inferential statistics.

Table 7.1 Overview on correlation coefficients depending on the level of measurement

Level of measurement	Nominal			Ordinal	Interval (normal distribution)
	'naturally' dichotomous	dichotomized (normal distribution)	polytomous		
Nominal 'naturally' dichotomous	Phi coefficient			Spearman's Rho (no ties);	Point-biserial correlation
Nominal dichotomized (normal distribution)		Tetrachoric correlation		Kendall's Tau (no ties)	Biserial correlation
Nominal polytomous			Coefficient of contingency C		
Ordinal	Spearman's Rho (no ties); Kendall's Tau (no ties)			Tau_b, Tau_c (ties); Goodman & Kruskal's Gamma (grouped data)	
Interval (normal distribution)	Point-biserial correlation	Biserial correlation			Pearson product–moment correlation

Going a step beyond graphical presentations of data and some basic parameters, the research interest focuses on the relationship between variables. Correlation coefficients have an answer to the question for the strength and direction of the relation. Contrary to tests of significance, which are described in the next chapter, correlation is not primarily about the question if there is a relation at all but has the purpose of quantifying the strength of the relation – which nevertheless would have to be checked if it is caused by chance or if it is a systematic relationship.

Most correlation models focus on a linear relation and the related correlation coefficients express the strength of the relationship as values between +1 and -1. Perfect positive or negative correlation will be represented by a coefficient of plus or minus one whereas zero represents statistical independence between the variables. Or in other words, in a perfect relationship between two variables every change in one variable makes the corresponding change in the other variable perfectly predictable. Accordingly, there is no systematic relation between changes in the variables in the case of statistical independence.

Between the two extremes, correlation coefficients can assume any value. The higher the absolute value of the coefficient the stronger the relation between the variables whereby the prefix indicates the direction of the relationship – which of course only makes empirical sense if the variables are measured at least at ordinal level. Table 7.1 provides an overview on some correlation coefficients depending on the level of measurement.

As straightforward as the concept of correlation looks, there are some pitfalls. Although most correlation coefficients have the same range from -1 to +1, they cannot in all cases be compared directly. A good example are Spearman's Rho and Kendall's Tau, which both deal with ranked data. But despite the same range of the correlation coefficients, Tau is generally lower than Rho and also cannot be compared with Pearson's product-moment correlation coefficient.

The most important point is, however, that correlation does not mean causation. Correlation means only that two variables are somehow related. The model does not say anything about the cause behind that relation. With two variables X and Y, there is no evidence that changes in X cause changes in Y (or vice versa). Take for example the question if a bank customer's judgement of the quality of investment consultancy is related to the yield that the consultant indicates – the higher the indicated yield the higher the customer's satisfaction. Maybe. But it could also be that these two variables influence one another reciprocally. After all, an apparently happy customer may spur on the consultant who ultimately comes with a tailor-made offer that results in a better yield. Another possibility is that the relation between customer satisfaction and yield is actually influenced by other variables like the amount of investment or the duration of the bank's relation with the customer, which are not part of the correlation model. So after introducing additional variables, the observed relation could turn out to be a spurious correlation.[5] Moreover, it can also not be excluded that X and Y vary coincidentally because good consultation is more a matter of honesty and highlighting chances and risks realistically, which will not necessarily result in a high yield. And as if all this would not already be confusing enough, one cannot exclude that the relationship between the indicated yield and the bank customer's judgement of the quality of investment consultancy is actually non-linear whereas the correlation model assumes a linear relation. After all, it is not out of place to assume that the indication of a very low as well as a very high yield will raise some doubt regarding the qualification and honesty of the investment consultant. So many explanations are possible and the correlation coefficient will not provide an answer to causation.

It is the same as with any other statistical model – a meaningful understanding of correlation models requires more than a mechanistic calculation. It must always be guided by theoretical considerations.

7.2 Significance and Relevance

What is it that actually determines service quality and customer satisfaction? That is the basic question of all quality-related research. Is quality dependent on certain characteristics of the customer service team? Does a specific training concept for service staff influence the service performance? Does after-sales service impact on purchase decisions? These are typical questions of quality research that give researchers no rest. Analytical statistics and tests of significance in particular can provide an answer.[6]

---

5   To be precise, it is not the correlation but its causal interpretation that is actually spurious.

6   Analytical statistics are also known as inferential statistics.

As a simple example, let's have a look at a documentation centre of a transport operator. They sit somewhere remote in a back room, earn little money and do nothing but prepare the documentation that accompanies every transport. It is a boring job, they are badly trained because they will not stay long anyway, and the number of mistakes is high. No wonder that there is a striking number of complaints from customers. Something has to be done in order to improve the quality of the documentation and the company has decided to give a small number of randomly picked staff special training whereas others shall receive this training only after it has proven to be successful. So we have two samples – one comprising staff who have only received the standard training and another one with staff who have participated in additional dedicated training. All other factors like the type of documents they handle are sufficiently identical and we can assume that there are no other factors that have an effect on the rate of mistakes.

We have two hypotheses. The null hypothesis H_0 states that the two samples – staff with and without additional training – come also with regard to the rate of mistakes from the same statistical population, which means that any difference in the error rate can be explained by chance and is caused by sampling. Logically, the corresponding alternative hypothesis H_A says that with additional training the rate of mistakes is lower. The decision which hypothesis we accept will be based on a test of significance.

It is essential to understand that the underlying logic follows an indirect line of arguments. We assume that H_0 is true and reject this null hypothesis only if it is very unlikely that it is true. In that case, we accept H_A instead. To make this decision, we define a percentage of most extreme cases of the sample distribution around the unknown true value ξ of the statistical population. These cases are very unlikely under the assumption of a *true* null hypothesis. A look at Figure 7.1 makes it obvious that some deviation of the measured value in the sample is rather likely because we work with a sample instead of the much larger statistical population. However, large deviations are less likely and in the case that the likelihood for the value that we have measured in our sample is smaller than the defined percentage of most extreme cases, we reject the null hypothesis and do not believe any longer that the difference between the number of mistakes made by both groups are just caused by the samples. Instead, we accept the alternative hypothesis that there is actually a 'significant' relation between additional training and the rate of mistakes.

What was just described as 'very unlikely' is called the level of significance, which is usually marked as α. Common values for α are 5 per cent, 1 per cent or 1 per mille but in fact, it is at the researcher's discretion to choose the critical range that decides on accepting or rejecting the null hypothesis. In case we reject H_0 in favour of H_A, the connection between the variables would be described as 'significant at the α-level'.

It depends on the research question if the test is one- or two-tailed. Most hypotheses are two-tailed, which means that the direction of deviations is not specified. Accordingly, the critical region (or region of rejection) is spread equally over both ends of the sample distribution whereas in the case of a one-tailed test, the critical region covers only one end of the distribution – as shown in Figure 7.1. It is essential that the decision regarding a one- or two-tailed test must be made based on the underlying theoretical model and *before* the data are inspected. In our example of a test of training effects one could rightfully go for a one-tailed test because one would not assume that the training results in more mistakes.

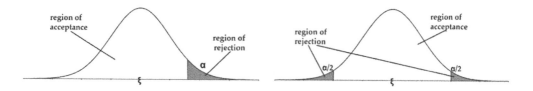

Figure 7.1 **Distribution of α per cent extreme cases in one- and two-tailed tests of significance around the true value ξ**

Under the assumption that H_0 is correct, we can now calculate if the likelihood of the observed difference of the rate of mistakes made by the staff representing the two samples falls into the region of acceptance. If this is the case, we maintain H_0, which means that there is no significant connection between the rate of mistakes and the additional training. However, if the value lies in the critical region, we reject H_0 in favour of the alternative hypothesis H_A and assume that there is a significant difference in the number of mistakes made by the two groups with and without additional training – telling the management that it is time to approve an extension of the training programme.

There are quite a number of tests of significance. They differ especially with regard to the level of measurement and the number of samples. Some focus on central tendency, others on the variance of the underlying sample distribution. Tests may also have a different statistical power, which describes the likelihood of correctly rejecting a false null hypothesis.[7] Furthermore, it plays a role if the samples are dependent or independent. In our example, we worked with two independent samples. One could also have chosen a different design and measure the average rate of mistakes in the same group before and after the training. In that case, we would have had two dependent samples, which would require a different test model. Table 7.2 (overleaf) provides an overview of important tests of significance.

Instead of looking into each and every test of significance, it is much more important to deal with some elementary issues because there are a number of pitfalls and misunderstandings around these statistical models. First of all, one must be aware that such tests are based on likelihood. To accept or to reject a null hypothesis is a decision along the research process. As every decision, it can be right or wrong. Indeed, it can well be that based on another sample from the same statistical population we arrive at a different conclusion.

It is the nature of a test of significance that in α per cent of all cases[8] it comes to a wrong decision even if H_0 would always be true, which means that we postulate some connection although it is not true. This is called the type I error or probability of error, which is α by definition. On the other hand, it can also happen that one maintains H_0 although H_A is true, which means that one does not recognize an existing connection between variables. This is called type II error and described as β. Table 7.3 (overleaf) summarizes the different decisions and potential mistakes.

---

7   In other terms: the probability not to make the type II error as described below.

8   Which is the chosen level of significance.

Table 7.2   Overview on common tests of significance

Samples	Level of Measurement		
	Nominal	**Ordinal**	**Interval**
1	**Chi-squared test** (comparison of observed and expected frequencies) **Binomial test** (dichotomous variables)	**Wald–Wolfowitz runs test** (randomness of a dichotomous data sequence)	**t-test** (for means) **Chi-squared test** (for variances) **Standard normal distribution** (e.g. for correlations)
2 Independent	**Chi-squared test** (for 2x2 tables) **Fisher's exact test** (hypergeometric distribution)	**Median-test** **Mann–Whitney U-test** (central tendency, no ties) **Kolmogorov–Smirnov test** (grouped data) **Wald–Wolfowitz runs test** (no ties) **Moses test** (dispersion, no ties)	**t-test** (for means) **F-test** (for variances)
2 Dependent	**McNemar's test**	**Sign test** (central tendency) **Wilcoxon matched pairs signed rank test** (central tendency, no ties)	**t-test**
Several Independent	**Chi-squared test**	**Kruskal–Wallis H-test** (central tendency, no ties)	**One-way analysis of variance**
Several Dependent	**Cochran's Q test**	**Friedman test** (central tendency)	**Multiple analysis of variance** **Bartlett's test** (for variances)

Table 7.3   Type I and type II error in statistical decision-making

	H_0 is True	**H_A is True**
Decision for H_0	correct decision $1-\alpha$	β Type II error
Decision for H_A	α Type I error	correct decision $1-\beta$

It is important to realize that α and β behave antagonistically but *not* complementarily. In other words, the smaller α the larger β but $\alpha \neq 1-\beta$. That means that for example rejecting the null hypothesis at a 5 per cent level of significance does *not* imply that the likelihood of the alternative hypothesis is $1-\alpha = 95$ per cent. It is also wrong to assume that under these conditions, one will make in 95 per cent of all cases a correct decision. After all, the likelihood that the data fall into the critical region is calculated under the assumption of a *true* null hypothesis. If, however, the null hypothesis is not true, the likelihood to maintain H_0 depends on how much the parameters differ under H_0 and H_A – or how much H_0 'differs from reality'.

It is an unfortunate but widespread practice to publish only significant results. Somehow, it is deemed more noteworthy having found a significant connection between variables than having come to the conclusion that there is none. This can easily result in artefacts. We have shown that it is the nature of the type I error that in a certain percentage of cases a wrong decision is made in favour of the alternative hypothesis although the null hypothesis is actually true. Such mistakes could be corrected naturally if non-significant results would also be published. The problem is, however, that non-significant results can also be caused by reasons such as too small samples or inappropriate test models. So always also publishing all non-significant results would not get us any further. The only appropriate answer to this dilemma is a substantiated discussion that considers the content as well as the methodical aspects of the results.

It is another bad habit to work with variable levels of significance. In many publications this is done by attaching little stars to the published data. One star stands for significance at 5 per cent level while 1 per cent and 1 per mille are decorated with additional stars. It looks like orders of merit as evidence of the level of significance and, nevertheless, these stars signify nothing but a lack of understanding of the logic of tests of significance.

As a matter of fact, tests of significance do not say anything about the strength of a connection between variables. This requires different statistical models, which are known as correlation.[9] Similar to correlations, tests of significance also cannot be interpreted in a causal manner. Furthermore, tests of significance are decision models that are based on probability. And that makes it imperative to define beforehand and without inspecting the data at which level of significance the null hypothesis shall be rejected in favour of the alternative hypothesis. Everything else would turn the logic of the decision-making process upside down. It is like a lottery – once the lucky numbers are known, it is no big deal to predict them and claim being a fortune teller.

One more thing. Significance should not be misinterpreted as relevance. The decision-making process of a test of significance depends on mathematical algorithms. These are helpful in the research process. But the discussion if significant differences between variables are actually relevant is still subject to theoretical reflection in the context of the research question. And this discussion must keep in mind the question of what a significant result can actually contribute to decision-making and future social action. It is this aspect of social action that turns significance into relevance. Without such relation to social action, even a significant result would be irrelevant.

---

9   See section 7.1 on descriptive statistics.

7.3 A Complex World

The world of services is more complex than a statistical model comprising only one or two variables can adequately reflect. It is usually a bundle of variables that determine customer satisfaction and service quality. One could break down such a complex structure of variables into a number of bivariate statistical models and test them individually but this would result in a disproportionate increase of the number of two-dimensional statistics, which will cause new problems and would hardly provide the hoped-for knowledge. Multivariate statistics can offer a more appropriate approach to complex research questions.

A multivariate approach to a complex theoretical construct like customer satisfaction comprising elements such as friendliness, competence, responsiveness, price, competition, customer group and others is obviously a more suitable model than a number of bivariate analyses because it reflects interrelations and interdependencies that bivariate models may not reveal. Multivariate statistical models are an attempt to reduce the number of variables and observations in a complex empirical structure without reducing the essential information of the data set.

It is obvious that the targets of simplicity of the structure on one hand and completeness and fidelity of the information on the other are to some extent contradicting and demand for compromises. So there are basically two approaches to the complex structure of multivariate models. Either one tries to derive a structure from the data or one defines a structure and analyzes if the data fit into this model. The first approach is part of descriptive statistics whereas the second one is more related to analytical statistics. Whatever model is chosen, it is solely a theoretical decision which statistical model is deemed appropriate.

Once hardly used because of their complex mathematical operations, multivariate statistical models have gained dramatic popularity in conjunction with the technical development of computers. Suddenly it became fashionable to garnish empirical research with complex statistics – regardless if the theoretical background and the quality of the empirical data justified it. Adding a multivariate analysis to an otherwise rather mediocre study was deemed something like an accolade of statistical excellence – that was rarely deserved.

The critical point of multivariate analyses is that most of the traditional models demand for normally distributed metric data – a requirement that social scientific data can hardly meet. But instead of focusing on the development of multivariate models for topological data, a lot of efforts was put into trying to prove that applying metric multivariate models to topological data would not have too much of a negative impact, which is a methodologically rather questionable undertaking. Less sensitive researchers simply ignored the problem. After all, it will always be possible to assign some interpretation to the 'results' that the computer produces. Just do not ask if it makes sense.

Over recent decades, the development of topological and discrete multivariate models that meet typical characteristics of social scientific data has made much progress. But what has quickly made its arrival in scientific research is still rather alien to practical or commercial marketing research, which is often characterized by a remarkable methodological unscrupulousness.

Among the models that are supposed to 'discover' structures in a data set, some reflect research questions that are common in the context of quality research. The most prominent multivariate model is probably the factor analysis that was once good form in every decent research project – regardless how meaningful it actually was. After all, factors trigger connotations with facts and finding facts in a data set is something of a discovery – Eureka!

Factor analysis targets at a reduction of a high number of empirical and possibly related variables to few independent theoretical variables – the so-called factors – explaining a social phenomenon. This matches the typical model of customer satisfaction, which comprises variables like peace of mind, prestige, credibility, responsiveness, courtesy, price and so on. It is obvious that with a growing number of variables, the likelihood for interdependences between these variables grows. So much complexity demands for a reduction to essential factors – reducing a data set of several variables to a much simpler structure of a small number of theoretical and mutually independent 'factors' as explanation of customer satisfaction. That is the basic concept of a factor analysis.

What sounds ideal for the analysis of service quality (and many other concepts) comes unfortunately with several pitfalls. The major obstacle is the requirement of metric and normally distributed data, which is rather unrealistic in social research. Hardened researchers may argue that factor analyses are mathematically rather robust. Nevertheless, it is hard to guess what actually happens if the requirements regarding the quality of the data are not met.

Furthermore, it is important to realize that the existence of factors as well as the number of factors is not a result of the analysis and a 'discovery' but its postulate. Asking for a certain number of independent factors, the mathematical model will deliver – regardless how meaningful the factors are. Also the meaning that is assigned to these hypothetical constructs is not a stunning discovery but based on those empirical variables that contribute most to the respective factor.

Considering that factor analysis targets at a reduction of complexity, the number of factors should be very limited. In any case, working with more than three independent factors would make little sense because four or more dimensions go beyond imagination. These concerns show that factor analysis has its natural limitations in social scientific research.

Factor analyses and cluster analyses deal with similar questions. The major difference is that factor analysis usually assumes a stringent model of independent (orthogonal)[10] factors in a space that is made up from correlations whereas cluster analysis compiles groups rather with regard to similarity concerning certain aspects or variables. In that respect, cluster analysis remains more semantic-descriptive. The target of a cluster analysis is to develop clusters of people or variables that are internally as homogeneous as possible and in comparison to other groups as heterogeneous as possible. For example, having measured the quality expectations of a complex group of customers, it could be a next step to identify homogeneous subgroups – so-called clusters – with mostly identical expectations. These groups could be defined as target groups for public relations measures. Also here it is not an automatism but a theoretical decision how the distance between sample elements is defined and how many clusters shall be identified.

Similarly, multidimensional scaling provides a descriptive approach to multivariate structures and can deal with metric as well as non-metric data depending on the definition of distance between items. It is an attempt to visualize objects in a multidimensional space whereby the dimensions represent their major characteristics and the related distance of the objects reflects their degree of similarity. This is of particular interest when analyzing service quality. For example, the perception of service offers as a function of various characteristics can be presented as a structure of similarities of these characteristics.

---

10   At this point, we ignore oblique factor rotations, which are a particular challenge when it comes to interpretation.

The models that have been described so far are descriptive and try to reduce the complex structure of empirical data to fewer theoretical variables or groups. It is the search for some structure underlying the untidy empirical world. Compared to that, the multivariate models in Table 7.4 follow a different approach. They are based on the assumption of a theoretical – in most cases linear – structure and test if the observed empirical structure matches the theoretical model. It is worthwhile having a closer look at some of these models. Again, the major focus is on the level of measurement.

Table 7.4   Overview on some statistical models for the analysis of multivariate structures

Level of Measurement		Independent Variables	
		Topological	Metric
Dependent Variable(s)	Topological	Log-linear models Logistic regression (Logit models)	Discriminant analysis
	Metric	Analysis of variance Analysis of covariance	Multiple correlation Multiple regression Canonical correlation

Note: Most of the models describe actually a bundle of similar approaches. In addition to the level of measurement, there are further requirements depending on the specific model.

Multiple regression is a model for metric and normally distributed variables that describes the dependent variable as a usually linear function of several independent variables. This is a causal model whereby the regression coefficients represent the influence of independent variables on the dependent variable. Taking for example the price of a service as a dependent variable, one could include various independent variables in the regression model and measure what their individual contribution to the price is. The example is, however, limping as one will quickly recognize that meaningful independent variables that one would introduce into such a model hardly meet the requirement of metric data. Once again we are struggling with the level of measurement.

Discriminant analysis deals with the difference between two or more groups with regard to certain characteristics. In this model, the independent variables must be metric and normally distributed whereas the dependent variable, which is the affiliation to a specific group, is nominal. The question is if the groups are significantly different with regard to the independent variables and how much these variables contribute to the discrimination of the groups. For example, having different service offers with different customer groups, the discriminant analysis could answer the question which variables eventually determine their affiliation with a specific group.

The multivariate analysis of variance is an approach for several topological independent variables and one or more metric dependent variables. It tries to explain the variance of a dependent variable by means of several independent variables and their interactions. So it is not only dealing with the (additive) effect of the various independent variables but also with their joint effect. This is important because it is possible that two variables each have a relatively minor impact but jointly they contribute substantially to the total variability of the dependent variable.[11] The basic question is if the variance *between* samples is larger than *within* the samples, which allows the decision if the samples distinguish significantly. For example, if a training programme for service staff has been conducted and one has two groups – one with and another one without training – one could test the effectiveness of the training programme by checking if there is a significant difference in the customer service performance of these two groups.

Once again, the required level of measurement can easily cause some concern when dealing with social scientific data. But there is an alternative. Log-linear and logit models are an approach analogous to variance analysis but require only nominal data. In this case, data of higher quality like ordinal data will be reduced to nominal level so some information may be lost. Log-linear models are a test of significance of hypotheses about the dependence structure in multidimensional contingency tables. Their name refers to the natural logarithm of the expected cell frequencies in the contingency tables, which are part of the underlying formula.

Whereas log-linear models deal with non-directional relations, which means that no distinction is made between dependent and independent variables, logit models[12] are a special case assuming a dependent variable. So being interested in the relationship between customer satisfaction and competence, friendliness and accessibility, one would have a four-dimensional contingency table whereby all variables have been dichotomized[13] and customer satisfaction is treated as a dependent variable. In this case, a logit model would provide an appropriate analysis. It makes obvious that as much as the nominal data level meets the requirement of social research, information is lost once the data meet a higher level of measurement.

The objective of log-linear models is to find the least complex model that can describe the observed data appropriately. The most complex saturated model would comprise all main effects and their interactions, which makes clear that with a growing number of variables, the complexity of the model will increase disproportionally because of the interactions between the variables. However, excluding those effects or interactions from the model that contribute little to the explanation of the model could still result in an adequate description of the empirical observations. So the target is to find a parsimonious non-saturated model that is sufficient to explain the data.

It is a theoretical decision which effects and interactions are introduced into the log-linear model. Nevertheless, there may be cases where no a priori hypothesis is available. For such cases, most computer programs offer the possibility of calculating all log-linear models and examining which model fits best. But of course, such a hypothesis-generating approach would require that the selected 'best' model undergoes another test based on a sample that is independent from the first one.

As much as log-linear models meet the requirements of social research, they also have some limitations. It is a basic requirement that all observations are independent. As a rule of thumb, the sample size should be at least five times the number of cells, which means that complex models demand for large samples. Furthermore, the expected cell frequencies in the contingency tables should be greater than one and the vast majority should not be less than five. And it should also be considered that with a growing number

---

11   This effect is called superadditivity.

12   Sometimes the term logistic regression is also used.

13   Broken down into two categories.

of variables, the models become very complex, which can make an interpretation of the results rather difficult. So as much as log-linear models are in many cases more appropriate than the classical metric models, they are not a panacea.

Indeed, statistics offers a vast field of mathematical models for many types of research questions and software packages make it easy to calculate even the most complex statistical models. The very point is, however, that all this only makes sense if the mathematical operations have some empirical meaning. The ultimate decision of which model is deemed appropriate depends solely on the research question and the available data. That makes it crucial to realize that shortcomings of the theoretical concept or the empirical data cannot be compensated by any statistical model regardless of how elaborated it is. Statistics makes data analysis easier and more systematic but it cannot substitute for lacking meaning.

8 *Presenting Results*

Coming cheerful to the boardroom with a fully animated presentation showing the trailblazing results of the latest study of the company's service performance can easily result in a cultural shock. Our researcher has packed his state-of-the-art show with the latest statistical models. Terms like factor analysis, log-linear models, cluster analysis, multi-level, multi-method and whatever else comes along with some awe-factor cross his lips easily. It is a firework of statistical excellence. And then he looks into the faces around the big boardroom table. No applause. Nobody is batting an eyelid. Instead, awkward silence. At last, a visibly irritated response: well, that sounds interesting. Perhaps you can send us a short summary by mail so that we can discuss it further. But please, not more than a page.

After such a debacle, the board members will probably look for some niche in the organization where this statistical highflier can be parked without causing any damage to the company. And our researcher will put an eternal curse on the board members who are too ignorant to follow his empirical virtuosity. Casting pearls before swine, he will mutter. It will take some time until all participants have recovered from this traumatic experience.

As a matter of fact, in most companies it will be rather futile to impart elaborated statistical concepts. The same applies to readers of consumer magazines or other test reports. And this is fully understandable. After all, the world is complex enough. Recipients of the results of empirical and statistical studies are not looking for more complexity but for its reduction. They look for simplicity. A reduction of complexity. That's what statistics is all about. Unfortunately, things are not that easy.

The world of the researcher is different from the world of the recipients of research results. Where researchers struggle to impart the details of their state-of-the-art research design, customers as well as managers of service providers want a straightforward answer to their ultimate question about quality. Don't bother me with details. Quality labels from more or less reputable consumer and other testing organizations that are used for advertising purposes are all that many consumers want to know. Such labels have the power to change markets. Also managers like it simple. Percentage figures or a simple curve that points into the right direction, a colourful histogram or a three-dimensional pie are easy to grasp. And if there is any doubt, the personal impression of the boss will decide on what is the truth. Only when research results point obviously into the wrong direction and do not meet expectations may the interest in details grow, and either blame is put on the design of the study or it is indeed high time to look into the processes behind the service performance.

This demand for simplicity makes it difficult to impart research results and to present them appropriately. Nevertheless, research must find its way out of the ivory tower of the researcher in order to become relevant for social action. Where research does not simply have an alibi function but is undertaken with the interest of better understanding business processes and consumer behaviour, research results have the power to create awareness and change behaviour – internally as well as externally. Management decisions may be affected and purchase patterns may change. The responsibility for an appropriate communication of research results lies first of all with the researcher. It depends on the background and expectations of the target group how results can be presented but, in any case, a presentation of research results must reflect their context and the context in which they can claim validity. This chapter will deal with some basic issues of this important aspect of research relevance.

8.1 Hard to Digest

Practical research takes place somewhere between scientific requirements, practical constraints and the necessity to make the results comprehensible for recipients who are usually not familiar with the methodology and methods of empirical research. The last point is particularly tricky because all recipients will bring along some bitty knowledge that they apply to the research situation. But instead of contributing to a better understanding, it causes confusion. With some everyday knowledge as background, it appears to be easy to assign meaning to statistical data. You see, people will say with a triumphant look in their eyes and, suddenly, figures develop a momentum of their own and turn into a power game of the sovereignty of interpretation. While in natural sciences onlookers would listen in awe, in social research everybody feels called upon to comment with trivialities. That can make imparting research results rather tricky.

Research is not an end in itself. Depending on the problem that marked the start of a study, it serves a purpose. It may target at improving service performance, finding weaknesses in processes, comparing competitors, informing the public about the quality of different services or something else. In any case, research only becomes relevant when its results are made understandable to those who will eventually make the necessary decisions that have to follow the findings. This can be the management that has to make changes to processes or consumers who get a better understanding of the market and may consider changes to their buying patterns. Such decisions demand information that related research can provide. But its relevance for social action depends on a successful communication of the research results. The responsibility for this important final step in the research process is with the researcher. He is not usually the decision maker but assumes the role of an adviser – and faces the crucial question of which information shall be provided and how it shall be presented in order to make it comprehensible and effective.

It is regrettable but to some extent understandable that managers as well as consumers usually have little interest in methodological questions and advanced research and statistics. They demand facts and do not really care about epistemological considerations. It is part of ritual management behaviour to call for simplicity in a complex world. Results shall be straightforward and to the point, please. Executive summaries are requested that deliver bare results – and ignore the context that determines their validity. Such information is meaningless. But it is an expression of the desire for a one-dimensional world that overcomes the complexity of decisions.

Researchers, on the other hand, have spent a lot of time on their study and tend to develop a fond relation to their data and do not like to see them evaporate. They become fascinated by details and easily forget that the purpose of statistics is the *reduction* of complexity. Their presentation charts moan under the heavy load of detailed tables that excite nobody but the speaker. After a few charts at most, the audience hangs on to other thoughts. So how much information is really required?

It is a crucial question and the answer does not lie somewhere between many and few data but, as usual, at a different level. It is all about relevance. Which information is actually relevant for an adequate understanding in the context of the research question? And this does not only refer to the bare results but must also comprise the underlying methodology, which is an inherent part of research results. What is the research question? What theoretical approach has been chosen and why? What are the underlying assumptions? What is the statistical population? How large is the sample and how was it drawn? How were the data collected? What are the characteristics of this approach in comparison to others? How can the statistical data be interpreted? In other words: for what population can the results be generalized and how reliable and valid are they? And: what practical meaning do the results have? This is essential information that prevents research results from being transferred into a context where they cannot claim validity. Wrong decisions would be the likely consequence.

One should not argue that nobody is interested in so much background information. Apart from its essential relevance, the actual interest will depend on how this information is presented. It can be short and concise – adding life to otherwise boring figures. A good presentation can make such information captivating and initiate the necessary discourse that challenges the results and creates common sense. Even if managers are not interested in advanced statistics, for sure they have an interest in relevant, reliable and valid information before they make decisions. After all, they have spent money on research. That is a commitment for the researcher to present research results in a way that they become relevant. And it is a commitment for the management to comprehend the results in a way that contributes to making the best decisions for the business.

Admittedly, it is difficult to explain statistical models such as, for example, a test of significance or log-linear model to an audience that is a stranger to statistics. Indeed, there is no need to explain the mathematical algorithms behind these models. But a brief verbal summary of the underlying question and concept as well as its prerequisites is a must. What does the statistical model state – and what does it not? This provides the recipients of research results with an understanding of how to interpret results and allows those who bring along some statistical knowledge to gauge the expertise of the researcher. Hearing for example that the researcher has 'factor analyzed' his data and 'discovered' three factors that determine service quality, one can assume that his explanations are at least rather sloppy but, more likely, they are an indicator of lacking statistical understanding. No, a factor analysis does not discover factors. Whatever factors are determined, they are a postulate of the model. Sometimes, the wording reveals how much substance is behind.

One does not have to enter the world of multivariate analyses to stumble over peculiarities of practical research. It is one of the rather doubtful merits of programs like PowerPoint or Keynote that all presentations look pretty much alike. One could describe it as some kind of epistemological synchronization. Instead of considering what is the most appropriate way to impart research results, creating presentations has largely been reduced to the question of if columns, doughnuts or pies look best. Two-dimensional graphics or perhaps better three-dimensional? And don't forget the custom animation. After all, it is not so important what you say. A successful presentation is all about *how* you transfer your message.

This would hardly be worth mentioning as long as the content is meaningful. But reality often looks different. PowerPoint does not ask if certain graphical presentations make any sense. It is absolutely indulgent to all kind of statistical nonsense. It does not ask if a statistical model is adequate in view of the research question as well as the available data. PowerPoint does not hesitate to draw lines between nominal or ordinal data. Suddenly one can see dramatic developments where empirical substantiation is lacking. A simple arrow between two variables turns a correlation into a causal relation. Or the range of a scale is reduced to a fraction of the total, which adds some drama to otherwise hardly noteworthy variations. Even if data values are added, the visual impression will be stronger than the figures. There are many ways to consciously or subconsciously bias research results and turn facts into artefacts. One could argue that this is not new. It was also not unusual in the days before PowerPoint largely automated and standardized presentations. But what once required some effort is now independent of endeavours and consideration.

No doubt, statistical data are sometimes hard to digest. But it is part of their interpretation to fill them with life and meaning. As described earlier, statistics is nothing but a means to circumnavigate the intellectual hurdles that prevent us from drawing immediate conclusions from a bunch of observations. That's why we translate the empirical observations into numerical relations, which opens the door to the world of statistics. This has been described as measurement. Of course, subsequent mathematical–statistical operations are only meaningful if their relation to the empirical world is meaningful. The process of measurement does not detach the data from the empirical world. It depends on the measurement as to which statistical models and related arithmetic operations are meaningful. Eventually, we have to transfer statistical parameters to the empirical world. The information that the average is 3.5 or the standard deviation is 1.8 is meaningless as long as it is not translated back into the empirical world where they can become relevant. This interpretation of statistical results is an essential step that must consider which conclusions are actually valid.

In this context, a researcher assumes high responsibility. He must not only provide reliable, valid and relevant – in a word, meaningful – research results, he must also provide the framework that defines the limits of their validity. It is possible. After all, practical research is not an end in itself. It creates awareness, can change behaviour and impacts on management decisions and consumer behaviour. That's why it is so essential to make hard-to-digest statistics more digestible.

8.2 Reactions

While many quality studies are internal and not supposed to be published beyond a small community, the situation is different when consumer organizations do comparative testing of service performance. Provided such studies meet essential scientific requirements, they can be great guidance not only for consumers but also for service providers. As anxiously as service providers await the results of such tests, they provide some kind of consultancy that would otherwise cost thousands of dollars and many competition data may not even be accessible. Furthermore, such tests are carried out from a neutral perspective. They are neither affected by the supposed expectations of the bosses nor by the possible interest of a consultant who already has a follow-up project in mind or just follows his standard concept that he sells every client as a unique solution.

Leading consumer organizations are committed to scientific standards – not only because of their constitution that will demand for something like best practice but also as self-protection against legal cases and claims for damages. These organizations are well aware how much their reputation and survival depends on their proven records of expertise, neutrality and scientific competence. They cannot hide in the intellectual seclusion of an ivory tower but have to publish their research results and consider the expectations of their readers as well as the relevance and effects of the results. Research of established consumer organizations can be extremely effective and has a strong impact on consumer behaviour as well as product development. This power derives to a large extent from their ability to turn methodologically sound research into catchy results.

It was a breakthrough idea when Germany's leading consumer organization, Stiftung Warentest, introduced quality labels in 1968. So far, only a general impression of the quality of products and services had been provided in their publications. Now, things were straight to the point: very good, good, satisfactory, less satisfactory, not satisfactory. It is a classic labelling approach. A norm is defined and deviations from this norm result in stigmatization. A 'less satisfactory' or even 'not satisfactory' service has little future. Obviously, reducing the complex characteristics of products and services to a one-dimensional quality label met the demand for simplicity. Consumers jumped on this idea and, suddenly, the sluggish sales of the consumer magazine *test* developed the long-awaited momentum.

This proves how important it is for practical research to make the results catchy – to the point, appealing, easy to digest and remember. However, so much simplification will only work as long as the results prove reliable, valid and relevant for actual consumer behaviour. To some extent, catchy results on one hand and high scientific standards on the other are a contradiction. Stiftung Warentest tries to overcome this conflict by adding a description of essential elements of the research design to the publication. Furthermore, detailed results are presented as tables showing the various service providers as well as variables that were measured and their weighting, which results in the final assessment. This gives readers the opportunity to compare individual data or to adjust the weighting of quality criteria and recalculate test results according to their individual requirements and expectations. There may not be many readers who make use of this possibility and one can assume that it is mostly the service providers who do such in-depth analysis, but nevertheless, it is an essential element of scientific honesty.

So much openness has contributed to the reputation of consumer organizations and has made their quality assessments a powerful tool that has eventually also been discovered by service providers for their purposes. In fact, being on top of a comparative test of service quality is a strong selling point whereas providers of less satisfactory services have to expect to be shunned by critical consumers. It may even be a stigma to be just 'good' as long as there are other services that are 'very good'. The winner takes it all.

The power of quality judgements of established consumer organizations is far-reaching and makes it very difficult to challenge negative verdicts. Unless obvious mistakes have been made, one can only recommend not to initiate legal action because this would have the sole effect that the negative judgement gains even more publicity and would eventually be manifested in public opinion. Even winning such cases can easily turn into a Pyrrhic victory. Something will always stick. It is usually the better way to handle such publications proactively as a tool for further improvement. One cannot deny the power of the test results of well-known consumer organizations. But one can turn it into a positive approach towards better service performance.

Although comparative studies of the quality of services are very much an accustomed domain of consumer organizations, many writers, consultants and self-styled testers have also discovered this market niche and publish test results. They neither follow the same approach nor do they necessarily arrive at the same results. That is no surprise and not only an effect of a sometimes rather doubtful methodology that feels more committed to the freedom of the press than scientific principles. It is also caused by different approaches that consider specific target groups. There is no objection. Neither consumer organizations nor other testers can claim that they have found the ultimate truth. Provided basic scientific standards are met, they simply deal with different aspects of the potential reality. The trouble is though that these standards are in many cases ignored. So the very point is transparency of the framework or research design that defines the validity and relevance of the results. So much information allows a critical discourse and the recipients can judge the adequacy of the research approach.

The demand for transparency applies of course also to advertisements that make use of test results. Leading consumer organizations know why they have established strict rules for the use of their test results for advertising purposes. This shall ensure their integrity and protect the consumer from misleading advertising. Stiftung Warentest (2012) clearly defines the conditions for advertising that makes use of the results of their comparative tests. For example, test results must refer to the original test to give readers a chance to understand their context. They must not be generalized but only be used for those services that were actually tested. Furthermore, a test result must not be used for advertising purposes without a respective reference when competing services came out with better results. Accordingly, good results for certain aspects of quality must not be highlighted without naming the overall result. And of course, the results must not be used any longer when they are outdated. It is all about transparency and honesty.

What consumer organizations have clearly defined for all kinds of advertising with test results applies in analogy to research that is done for internal purposes. It sounds almost trivial when demanding that results are presented in a way that is not misleading because, otherwise, they will trigger inadequate reactions and decisions. However, looking at practical research, it is rather a necessary reminder than a trivial statement.

9 *In a Nutshell*

Success and sustainability in the service sector demand quality. But quality is not an objective characteristic. Instead, it is defined by customers and competitors. The service offered by competitors provides the environment in which customer expectations and customer satisfaction on one hand and the balance sheet of the service provider on the other are the ultimate yardsticks of quality. Both should highly correlate. Good service can pay off.

The Internet has made service offers transparent – not so much with regard to service quality but, most of all, with regard to the price. As a result, in many segments of the service industry the fight for market share has turned into a battle of the prices that leaves little room for service quality because reduced prices demand for austerity measures. As long as customers accept a declining service quality because they focus only on price, this concept may be successful. But it is a short-lived strategy because it has a natural end. Sooner or later the point will be reached where the delivered service quality is simply no longer acceptable and customers stay away. No doubt, price is an important factor but in the long run, it cannot substitute service quality.

After all, service is a people business. It is performed by people and judged by people. Service is social action and social interaction. Measuring service performance means measuring social behaviour. The methods and methodology of empirical social research provide access to a better understanding of the complexity of quality. Practical research for better service quality is required.

This book is an appeal for quality research that meets quality criteria itself. It is food for thought and a committed argument against a widespread but rather meaningless dealing with measurement, data and statistics. And it is a call for a reconsideration of the underlying epistemological approach to quality and its methodological implications. This demands for a break with an unfortunately customary but nevertheless inadequate procedural understanding of the research process that focuses on methods instead of contents. It is a dedicated plea for adding quality and meaning to otherwise meaningless research.

Readers who expected to find in this book a handy ready-made method for quality research could be disappointed. It turned out that alleged magical formulas are rather questionable approaches when confronted with basic methodological requirements. On the other hand, having read the book up to here, it should have become clear why there are no panaceas available – even if some bestselling management books claim to have found the Holy Grail of epistemology that promises eternal service quality.

The proven methods of empirical research still provide the most appropriate approach to service quality and related topics. This should not discourage the development of new models for the measurement of quality. Leaving the well-trodden paths and trying out new avenues requires some creativity together with an understanding of social research as a model that reflects a certain perspective of potential reality instead of a method or tool that provides access to the ultimate truth. One should just keep in mind that it is rather unlikely that something as complex as the quality of services can be covered with one simple measurement that has it all.

Of course, one could simply point at the bottom line of the balance sheet as the ultimate yardstick and argue that this is the best indicator for quality. Unfortunately, this only allows for a retroactive perspective. Moreover, it comprises more factors than just the service performance and provides little help when searching for the root cause of a specific development. It is a measurement that comes too late and has limited predictive value.

As a matter of fact, complex social situations demand for complex studies. That makes it all the more surprising that practical research approaches are often remarkably plain. It is not always clear if this says more about the researcher or about the subject of his study. One should consider that quality studies do not only gather feedback from customers but also contribute to the perception and image of the company that is behind the research. This goes beyond the basically positive message that the company is interested in the opinions and feedback of their customers. A questionnaire that hardly deserves this name, badly managed focus groups and similar methodical shortcomings can easily have a detrimental effect and leave nothing but a negative impression behind. Sometimes it may be more conclusive to understand the reasons behind a low response rate than looking at the actual responses from the participants in a study.

It should have become clear that what has been said in this book about research in the field of service quality must not be misunderstood in a way that one would just have to do it correctly in order to arrive at the right results. Empirical research is not about doing it right or wrong, it is about adequacy and relevance in the context of the research question. High time to bid farewell to the idea of an ultimate truth.

This understanding of research calls for an open and critical discourse of its methodology and the underlying conscious and subconscious decisions of the research process. The awareness of these decisions and their implications is a prerequisite for a better understanding of the research topic, the adequacy of the approach as well as the validity and relevance of the research results. This requires a thorough reflection of the research process and its underlying meaning. Brushing off these essential considerations as 'academic' means opening the door to artefacts – fallacies that cannot claim validity but are the result of an inadequate research process.

Nevertheless, practical research is often dominated by a questionable pragmatism – don't think, just do it. But exactly this is an approach to service quality that is as meaningless as it is expensive because it reduces research to an alibi role. It becomes even worse when research serves as what British statesman Winston Churchill (1874–1965) once called political statistics: 'The first lesson that you must learn is that, when I call for statistics about the rate of infant mortality, what I want is proof that fewer babies died when I was Prime Minister than when anyone else was Prime Minister. That is a political statistic.' If this is the intention, one should indeed not worry about any epistemological or methodological questions and just bend figures according to the political requirements. But this will not move a business forward. This is politics, not research and statistics.

Often, the wording that is used when presenting research results already reveals what methodological understanding is actually behind it. Where results are presented as ultimate truth, one would be better to put them aside. When promised transparency of the research process hardly goes beyond terms such as prestigious, respected or trusted, whereas the actual methodology remains largely a secret, one should be suspicious. Where the number of respondents replaces a clear statement about representativeness, it is good to be cautious. Social scientific data that come with several digits behind the decimal point should make the alarm bells ring. Correlations that are interpreted causally, inferential generalizations of descriptive statistics, tests that work with changing levels of significance, applying metric statistical models to qualitative data – there are many warning signals that demand a closer look at research results. If they are just published as a funny story in a magazine one could brush them off and just blame the journalists for writing nonsensical articles. But when it comes to management decisions or consumer behaviour, the warning lights should blink nervously.

Assuming that a study has more than an alibi function, one has to understand research as a process of decisions and actions from the definition of the research question and development of hypotheses via the operationalization of the theoretical concept, the development of research models and the collection of information, the systematic processing of data and their analysis by means of statistical models through to the interpretation of the results and their presentation in the context of all these steps and related decisions. It is not about right or wrong but about adequacy and relevance in view of the research question. And, of course, this does not only apply to studies dealing with service quality but to all social research.

Coming from an understanding of an intersubjective constitution of reality, it is no surprise that this book very often uses terms such as adequacy and relevance. It has been highlighted repeatedly that there is no such thing as an objective reality. Instead, empirical research reconstructs a specific aspect of potential reality. This segment of reality looks different depending on the method of social research and related decisions. Interviews, observations, content analyses and so on reflect different facets of reality. The very question is if the chosen approach is adequate in the context of the research question. And this is subject to a discourse that cannot be replaced by a management verdict.

The discussion of adequacy is closely related to the relevance of a study. It is the essential question for the actual effect of a study. Research results that have no predictive value, do not say much about social action and have no impact on management or consumer decisions are hardly worth the effort. Quality research is done for a purpose – to find weaknesses in processes, improve quality and profitability, predict developments, help to make decisions and eventually change behaviour.

Adequacy as well as relevance are not statistical parameters but criteria that are subject to a discourse that is only possible if the research design is understandable and reproducible and the research process is transparent. Without this information, research results turn into a matter of faith – believing the results or not. But this has nothing to do with research. It is exactly this discussion process that can unleash the power of empirical research and lead to a much better understanding of service quality.

In this context, it is prerequisite to do away with some basic misunderstandings of empirical research that are expressed in dichotomies such as measurement versus observation, hard versus soft data, objective versus subjective or quantitative versus qualitative methods. These are all terms that express the subconscious belief that there is something like an ultimate reality that can be measured provided one has the right tools and methods ready. But instead of guiding the way to supposed reality they easily mislead.

We have seen that supposedly hard data can be rather soft when they are used as indicators of social behaviour. Of course, one can meticulously count how many complaint letters are received and after how many rings a phone is picked up at last. But this information only becomes relevant when it is used as an indicator of service quality. It is not a natural thing that the number of rings until a phone is answered indicates service quality. It is rather a decision in the research process and one can discuss how adequate and relevant this decision is. What does that indicator actually mean? Does picking up the phone faster mean better service? Does twice the number of rings until pickup reduce the service quality by half? Is it a service failure when a call is missed because the customer service is just busy dealing with another customer's issue? Does it fully explain service quality or is it just one of many facets?

Apparently, what looks like hard data turns out to be rather soft when discussing the methodology. Telephone rings as a quantitative variable are in fact quite subjective when used as an indicator for latent variables – and only in that role can they claim relevance when talking about service quality. The decision to work with the supposedly 'objective' number of rings until customer service answers a call is obviously a chiefly subjective and not at all compelling decision. There are many other variables that also contribute to service quality. This raises the question of how adequate and relevant this indicator can be in the context of service quality. Internally, it may be a highly relevant indicator because the management defined it as a KPI. At the same time, customers may not really care as long as it stays within a 'reasonable' range, however that is defined. They may be much more interested in the quality that they experience after the phone was picked up sooner or later. But exactly this aspect is likely to fall victim to a misleading understanding of measurement as something delivering objective, quantitative and hard data that are supposedly superior to data from observations, which are considered qualitative, subjective and soft.

It is an expression of the centuries-old empiricist desire to record the given reality as objective, accurate and complete as possible in order to find underlying laws and theories. Over the centuries one can find quotes reflecting this misleading epistemological understanding that persists still today, especially in so-called practical studies. As outstanding as the contribution of physicist and astronomer Galileo Galilei (1564–1642) to the development of science was, his concept of measurement was very much determined by classical physics when he demanded: 'Measure what is measurable, and make measurable what is not so.' From Galilei's perspective, measurement had nothing to do with social sciences; it was the domain of mathematics: 'What has philosophy got to do with measuring anything? It's the mathematicians you have to trust, and they measure the skies like we measure a field.' That's how genuine faith in an ultimate truth sounds. One will just have to find it: 'All truths are easy to understand once they are discovered; the point is to discover them.'

Almost three centuries after Galilei, German philosopher and political economist Karl Marx (1818–1883) paid tribute to mathematics as an epistemological authority. From his perspective, 'a science is only fully developed when it has reached a point where it can make use of mathematics' (Lafargue 1980).[1] From today's perspective, one could describe it as a somehow naive epistemological understanding that followed the tradition

---

1   'Eine Wissenschaft ist erst dann als voll entwickelt anzusehen, wenn sie dahin gelangt ist, sich der Mathematik bedienen zu können.'

of Galilei. Nevertheless, looking at research studies, the hunt for the ultimate reality is still on. The belief that one would just have to apply the 'right tools' in order to find the truth appears to be ineradicable. In fact, Marx's view of science has failed – as much as other parts of his theory.

Compared to such empiricist worldview, physicist Albert Einstein (1879–1955) had a very different understanding of the relation between mathematics and reality when he highlighted that 'as far as the laws of mathematics refer to reality, they are not certain; and as far as they are certain, they do not refer to reality' (Einstein 2010: 133).[2] This is the crucial point when talking about measurement in empirical research. It describes perfectly the difference between an understanding of research as method versus model. Research methods are not mathematical algorithms that are right or wrong but are better characterized as models reflecting a certain aspect of the potential reality that should be adequate and relevant in the context of a specific research interest.

In practical research, this aspect of the dependency of the results on the research approach is easily overlooked. The problem of inadequate research is that there is always some interpretation that can be assigned even to meaningless figures. Worst case, the figures will be made suitable. Only a critical discourse may reveal that the supposed facts are nothing but artefacts. This adds to the dilemma that the methods of empirical research look so similar to everyday perception and are, nevertheless, so different. As Albert Einstein worded it: 'The whole of science is nothing more than a refinement of every day thinking' (Einstein 1936). It is this very refinement that makes the difference. Turning ordinary questions into a scientific questionnaire, distinguishing the reading of complaint letters from a content analysis, differentiating between observations in daily life and observations as a method of data collection in empirical research, and so on. What look so similar at first glance are actually rather different processes. Unfortunately, in view of so much alleged similarity amateur researchers feel time and again compelled to search for the ultimate truth – resulting in the production of artefacts instead of facts.

One has to understand and internalize that research does not become less practical or less expressive when considering the essential methodological issues that are highlighted in this book. They do not turn practical research into something that practitioners sometimes like to run down as 'academic' and out-of-touch with the 'real' world. Instead, it adds meaning to an otherwise rather meaningless research process.

Service excellence deserves research excellence.

---

2   'Insofern sich die Sätze der Mathematik auf die Wirklichkeit beziehen, sind sie nicht sicher, und insofern sie sicher sind, beziehen sie sich nicht auf die Wirklichkeit.'

Bibliography

Achenwall, G. 1748. *Vorbereitung zur Staatswissenschaft der heutigen fürnehmsten Europäischen Reiche und Staaten* [Preparations for the Political Science of the Most Distinguished European Kingdoms and States]. Göttingen: Vandenhoeck. Available at: http://gdz.sub.uni-goettingen.de/dms/load/img/?PPN =PPN637704622&IDDOC=614356 [accessed: 26-03-2013].

Berelson, B. 1952. *Content Analysis in Communication Research.* Glencoe, Ill.: Free Press.

Berger, P.L. and Luckmann, T. 1966. *The Social Construction of Reality. A Treatise in the Sociology of Knowledge.* Garden City, N.Y.: Anchor.

Bryson, M.C. 1976. The Literary Digest Poll: Making of a Statistical Myth. *The American Statistician* 30(4), 184–185.

Central Intelligence Agency 2012: *The World Factbook 2012* [Online]. Washington, DC. Available at: www.cia.gov/library/publications/download/download-2012/index.html [accessed: 05-03-2013].

Clark, C.G. 1940. *The Conditions of Economic Progress.* London: Macmillan.

Davie, S. 2010. Ranking University Rankings. *The Straits Times*, Prime, A2. Singapore 5 June. Available at: http://newshub.nus.edu.sg/news/1006/PDF/RANKING-st-5jun-pA2.pdf [accessed: 05-03-2013].

Donoghue, F. 2008. *The Last Professors. The Corporate University and the Fate of the Humanities.* New York: Fordham University Press.

Einstein, A. 1936. Physics and Reality. *Journal of the Franklin Institute* 221(3), 349–382. Translated by Jean Piccard.

Einstein, A. 2010. *Mein Weltbild* [My World View]. Edited by Carl Seelig. Berlin: Ullstein 2010 (first published 1934).

Engels, F. 1925. *Dialectics of Nature.* First published Moscow, Leningrad. Available at: www.marxists.org/ archive/marx/works/download/EngelsDialectics_of_Nature_part.pdf [accessed: 05-03-2013].

Fisher, A.G.B. 1935. *The Clash of Progress and Security.* London: Macmillan.

Flanagan, J.C. 1954. The Critical Incident Technique. *Psychological Bulletin* 51(4), 327–358. Available at: www.apa.org/pubs/databases/psycinfo/cit-article.pdf [accessed: 05-03-2013].

Flesch, R. 1948. A New Readability Yardstick. *Journal of Applied Psychology* 32(3), 221–233.

Fourastié, J. 1963. *Le grand espoir du XXe siècle. Progrès technique, progrès économique, progrès social* [The Great Hope of the 20th Century. Technical, Economical, Social Progress]. 2nd Edition. Paris: Gallimard.

Ganz, W. 2005. *Research in the Services Sector.* Stuttgart: Fraunhofer Institut für Arbeitswirtschaft und Organisation. Available at: http://ec.europa.eu/research/social-sciences/pdf/conf-kte-walter-ganz_ en.pdf [accessed: 05-03-2013].

Goffman, E. 1959. *The Presentation of Self in Everyday Life.* New York: Anchor.

Gremler, D.D. 2004. The Critical Incident Technique in Service Research. *Journal of Service Research* 7(1), 85–89.

Hofstätter, P.R. 1963. *Einführung in die Sozialpsychologie* [Introduction into Social Psychology]. Stuttgart: Kröner.

ISO 2012. *The ISO Survey of Certification 2011.* Survey data are available at: www.iso.org/iso/home/ standards/certification/iso-survey.htm [accessed 05-03-2011].

Keiningham, T.L., Cooil, B., Andreassen, T.W. and Akzoy, L. 2007. A Longitudinal Examination of Net Promoter and Firm Revenue Growth. *Journal of Marketing* 71(July), 39–51. Available at: http://www.marketingpower.com/resourcelibrary/publications/journalofmarketing/2007/71/3/jmkg.71.3.039.pdf [accessed 05-03-2013].

Kriz, J. 1988. *Facts and Artefacts in Social Science. An Epistemological and Methodical Analysis of Empirical Social Science Research Techniques*. Hamburg/New York: McGraw-Hill Research.

Kriz, J. and Lisch, R. 1988: *Methoden-Lexikon für Mediziner, Psychologen, Soziologen* [Encyclopedia of Methods for Medical Doctors, Psychologists, Sociologists]. München, Weinheim: Psychologie Verlags Union.

Lafargue, P. 1890. Karl Marx, Persönliche Erinnerungen [Personal Memoirs]. *Die Neue Zeit* 9(1), 10–17, 37–42. Available at: www2.cddc.vt.edu/marxists/deutsch/archiv/lafargue/1890/09/marx.htm [accessed: 05-03-2013].

Lages, L.F. and Fernandes, J.C. 2005. The SERPVAL Scale: A Multi-Item Instrument for Measuring Service Personal Values. *Journal of Business Research* 58(11), 1562–1572. Available at: http://docentes.fe.unl.pt/~lflages/papers/Serpval_JBR.pdf [accessed: 06-03-2013].

Likert, R. 1932. A Technique for the Measurement of Attitudes. *Archives of Psychology* 140(June), 5–55.

Lisch, R. 1979. Assoziationsstrukturenanalyse. Ein Vorschlag zur Weiterentwicklung der Inhaltsanalyse [Association Structure Analysis. A Proposal for the Further Development of Content Analysis]. *Publizistik* 24(1), 65–83.

Lisch, R. 1984. *Spielend gewinnen? Chancen im Vergleich* [Winning Hands Down? A Comparison of Chances]. 2nd revised edition. Berlin: Stiftung Warentest.

Lisch, R. 2012. *Ancient Wisdom for Modern Management – Machiavelli at 500*. Farnham: Gower.

Lisch, R. and Kriz, J. 1978. *Grundlagen und Modelle der Inhaltsanalyse. Bestandsaufnahme und Kritik* [Basics and Models of Content Analysis. A Critical Review]. Reinbek bei Hamburg: Rowohlt.

Lockhart, C. and Giles-Sims, J. 2010. *Aging Across the United States: Matching Needs to States' Differing Opportunities and Services*. University Park, Pa.: The Pennsylvania State University Press.

Luhmann, N. 2002. *Die Religion der Gesellschaft* [The Religion of Society]. Edited by A. Kesterling. Frankfurt: Suhrkamp.

Machiavelli, N. 1532 (written 1513). *The Prince*. Translated by W.K. Marriott. Available at: http://www.gutenberg.org/ebooks/1232 [accessed: 06-03-2013].

Merton, R.K. 1949. *Social Theory and Social Structure*. New York: Free Press.

OECD 2013. *National Accounts at a Glance*. OECD Publishing. DOI: 10.1787/na_glance-2013-en.

Osgood, C.E. 1959. The Representational Model and Relevant Research Methods. *Trends in Content Analysis*, edited by I. de Sola Pool. Urbana, Ill.: University of Illinois Press, 33–88.

Osgood, C.E., Saporta, S. and Nunnally, J.C. 1956. Evaluative Assertion Analysis. *Litera* 3, 47–102.

Osgood, C.E., Suci, G.J. and Tannenbaum, P.H. 1957. *The Measurement of Meaning*. Urbana, Ill.: University of Illinois Press.

Parasuraman, A., Berry, L.L. and Zeithaml, V.A. 1991. Refinement and Reassessment of the SERVQUAL Scale. *Journal of Retailing* 67(4), 420–450. Available at: http://areas.kenan-flagler.unc.edu/Marketing/FacultyStaff/zeithaml/Selected%20Publications/Refinement%20and%20Reassessment%20of%20the%20SERVQUAL%20Scale.pdf [accessed: 06-03-2013].

Parasuraman, A., Zeithaml, V.A. and Berry, L.L. 1988. SERVQUAL: A Multiple-Item Scale for Measuring Consumer Perceptions of Service Quality. *Journal of Retailing* 64(1), 12–40. Available at: http://areas.kenan-flagler.unc.edu/Marketing/FacultyStaff/zeithaml/Selected%20Publications/SERVQUAL-%20A%20Multiple-Item%20Scale%20for%20Measuring%20Consumer%20Perceptions%20of%20Service%20Quality.pdf [accessed: 06-03-2013].

Petty, W. 1690. *Political Arithmetick or A Discourse Concerning, The Extent and Value of Lands, People, Buildings: Husbandry, Manufacture, Commerce, Fishery, Artizans, Seamen, Soldiers; Publick Revenues, Interest, Taxes, Superlucration, Registries, Banks, Valuation of Men, Increasing of Seamen, of Militia's, Harbours, Situation, Shipping, Power at Sea, etc. As the Same Relates to Every Country in General, but More Particularly to the Territories of His Majesty of Great Britain, and his Neighbours of Holland, Zealand, and France.* London. Available at: http://books.google.com.sg/books?id=ARnwAAAAMA AJ&pg=PP7&dq=Petty+Political+Arithmetick+or+a+Discourse+Concerning [accessed: 05-03-2013].

Reichheld, F. 2006. *Questions about NPS – and Some Answers.* Net Promoter® Blogs July 27. Available at: http://netpromoter.typepad.com/fred_reichheld/2006/07/questions_about.html [accessed: 05-03-2013].

Reichheld, F.F. 2003. The One Number You Need to Grow. *Harvard Business Review* 81(December), 46–54. Available at: http://www.thedatashop.co.uk/docs/NetPromoterScore_HBR.pdf [accessed: 06-03-2013].

Roos, I. 2002. Methods of Investigating Critical Incidents. A Comparative Review. *Journal of Service Research* 4(3), 193–204. Available at: http://www.ihroos.fi/rapporter/SPAT%20compared%20ot% 20other%20critical-incident%20methods.PDF [accessed: 06-03-2013].

Satmetrix 2009. *The Power behind a Single Number. Net Promoter: The New Standard for Measuring Customer Loyalty.* White Paper. Available at: www.satmetrix.com/resources/research/net-promoter-the-power-behind-a-single-number/ [accessed: 05-03-2013].

Schumpeter, J. 1942. *Capitalism, Socialism and Democracy.* First published New York/London: Harper.

Snider, J.G. and Osgood, C.E. 1969. *Semantic Differential Technique.* Chicago, Ill.: Aldine.

Stiftung Warentest 1989. SOS – Schiffe Ohne Sicherheit [SOS – Ships without safety]. *test* 24(11), 79–88.

Stiftung Warentest 1990. Sicher nach Skandinavien und England [Safely towards England and Scandinavia]. *test* 25(5), 73–78.

Stiftung Warentest 2012. *Bedingungen der Stiftung Warentest zur 'Werbung mit Untersuchungsergebnissen'* [Conditions of Stiftung Warentest for the Use of Test Results for Advertising Purposes; Online]. Available at: www.test.de/unternehmen/werbung/nutzungs bedingungen/ [accessed 05-03-2012].

Sun Tzu. *The Art of War.* Translated from Chinese by Lionel Giles. First published 1910. Available at: http://www.gutenberg.org/files/17405/17405-h/17405-h.htm [accessed: 06-03-2013].

Taylor, W.L. 1956. Recent Developments in the Use of 'Cloze Procedure'. *Journalism Quarterly* 33, 42–49, 99.

Taylor, W.L. 1957. 'Cloze' Readability Scores as Indices of Individual Differences in Comprehension and Aptitude. *Journal of Applied Psychology* 41(1), 19–26.

Thomas, W.I. and Thomas, D.S. 1928. *The Child in America: Behaviour Problems and Programs.* New York: Knopf.

Thomson, W. 1889–1891. *Popular Lectures and Addresses.* 3 volumes. London: Macmillan and Co.

Tönnies, F. 1922. *Gemeinschaft und Gesellschaft* [Community and Society]. 4th and 5th Edition. Berlin: Karl Curtius. First published 1887.

Vershofen, W. 1940. *Handbuch der Verbrauchsforschung.* Erster Band [Handbook of Consumer Research. Volume I]. Berlin: Heymanns.

Weber, M. 1922. *Wirtschaft und Gesellschaft* [Economy and Society]. Tübingen: J.C.B Mohr (Paul Siebeck).

Welt Online 2012. *Hitparade – Mysteriöses Ranking der attraktivsten Stewardessen* [Hit Parade – Mysterious Ranking of the Most Attractive Stewardesses; online]. 12 July. Available at: www.welt.de/108265428 [accessed: 05-03-2013].

Weymann, A. 1973. Bedeutungsfeldanalyse. Versuch eines neuen Verfahrens der Inhaltsanalyse am Beispiel Didaktik der Erwachsenenbildung [Semantic Field Analysis. An Approach to a New Content Analytic Method Illustrated by Didactics of Adult Education]. *Kölner Zeitschrift für Soziologie und Sozialpsychologie* 25(4), 761–776.

Weymann, A. 2012. Review of Lockhart C., Giles-Sims, J. 2010. *American Journal of Sociology* (AJS), 117(4), 1286–1288.

Weymann, A. 2013. Wolfgang Glatzer. Pioneer of Social Indicators Research. *Applied Research in Quality of Life (ARQOL)*, 8(1), 117–120.

Weymann, A. 2014 (in press). *States, Markets, and Education. The Rise and Limits of the Education State.* Basingstoke and New York: Palgrave Macmillan.

Wingens, M. and Weymann, A. 1988. Utilization of Social Sciences in Public Discourse – Labeling Problems. *Knowledge in Society*, 1(3), 80–97.

Wittgenstein, L. 1922. *Tractatus Logico-Philosophicus*. First published London: Kegan Paul. Translated by F.P. Ramsey and C.K. Ogden. Available at: http://people.umass.edu/klement/tlp/tlp.pdf [accessed: 05-03-2013].

Index